Greenhill Books

ALEXANDER

VOLUME II

Also by Theodore Ayrault Dodge

HANNIBAL
A History of the Art of War among the
Carthaginians and Romans down to
the Battle of Pydna, 168 BC, with a
detailed account of the Second
Punic War
Volume I: 350 pages. ISBN 1-85367-147-9
Volume II: 348 pages. ISBN 1-85367-152-5

With 227 charts, maps, plans of battles and
tactical manoeuvres, cuts of armour,
weapons and uniforms.

ALEXANDER

A HISTORY OF THE ORIGIN AND GROWTH OF THE ART OF WAR FROM THE EARLIEST TIMES TO THE BATTLE OF IPSUS, 301 BC, WITH A DETAILED ACCOUNT OF THE CAMPAIGNS OF THE GREAT MACEDONIAN

By *Theodore Ayrault Dodge*

WITH 237 CHARTS, MAPS, PLANS OF BATTLES AND TACTICAL MANOEUVRES, CUTS OF ARMOUR, UNIFORMS, SIEGE DEVICES AND PORTRAITS

VOLUME II

Greenhill Books, London

This edition of *Alexander* first published 1993 by
Greenhill Books, Lionel Leventhal Limited
Park House, 1 Russell Gardens, London NW11 9NN

British Library Cataloguing in Publication Data
A catalogue record for this book is available
from the British Library

ISBN 1-85367-153-3

*Library of Congress
Cataloguing-in-Publication Data available*

Publishing History
Alexander was first published in 1890 (Houghton Mifflin
Company) and is reproduced now exactly as the original
edition, complete and unabridged, in two volumes.

Printed and bound in India

TABLE OF CONTENTS.

LIST OF ILLUSTRATIONS.

ALEXANDER.

XXVI.

ON TO BABYLON. SPRING TO SEPTEMBER, B. C. 331.

ALEXANDER now marched to Tyre and thence to Thapsacus, where he crossed the Euphrates. The Persians expected him to move straight on Babylon and had devastated the district in his path. But Alexander turned northerly and marching to the Tigris crossed this river, likewise unopposed. Darius's evident plan was to let him reach the very bowels of the land and then crush him on the level plain by numbers. Moving down the left bank, Alexander ran across the Persians drawn up on the plains of Gaugamela. He camped and gave his men four days' rest. Parmenio advised a night attack, but Alexander refused to "steal a victory." Darius had forces estimated between a quarter million and one million one hundred thousand. Alexander had forty-seven thousand men. Alexander left his impedimenta in a stockaded camp in the rear, so as to go into action unfettered, and addressed words of noble encouragement to his men, who were at the highest pitch of enthusiasm.

So soon as spring opened, Alexander, having bridged the Nile, crossed with his army and marched to Tyre, where he found his fleet already riding at anchor. Passing through Samaria, he deemed it necessary to chastise the inhabitants for having assassinated his deputy Andromachus, whom he replaced by Memnon. In Tyre he again celebrated rites and games at the temple of Hercules, with great splendor and pomp. Here the Athenians once more sent an embassy asking that their fellow citizens, captured at the Granicus, be released, to which request, in view of the better tone of the Athenian political atmosphere, Alexander, according to Curtius, now acceded with gracious generosity. It is said that Demosthenes, on this occasion, sent a letter to Alexander craving pardon for his virulent opposition. Alexander also dispatched a fleet to the Peloponnesus to counteract the Spar-

tan influence still being exerted against him, with all the
national stanchness of that wonderful people.

The king placed trusted men in charge of the receipt of
custom. Cœranus was appointed to Phœnicia and Philoxenus to the Cis-Taurus region. Harpalus, just returned from
desertion, Alexander made treasurer of the army chest, he
not being rugged enough for field service. Harpalus had
been among the small crowd of Alexander's intimates who
were expatriated when he himself fell under his father's dis-
pleasure. Alexander never forgot his friends. Harpalus had
been in favor, but, guilty of some misdemeanor, had fled, just
before Issus. He was now recalled and put in charge of the
moneys. A remarkable judge of men, Alexander sometimes
went too far in relying on his intimates. It was once a friend,
always a friend with Alexander. Unqualified treachery alone
could warp his affection. Nearchus, later the admiral, was
made viceroy of Lycia as far as Mount Taurus; Asclepiodorus was appointed viceroy of Syria, vice Menon, removed
for negligence. Menander was given office in Lydia. Clearchus succeeded the latter in command of part of the Greek
auxiliaries; Frigyius was made chief of the Greek allied cavalry; Laomedon was appointed provost marshal, as he was
well acquainted with the Persian language.

Having made sundry other changes in the command of his
troops, he marched on Thapsacus, no doubt drawing in some
of the Asia Minor garrisons to reinforce his ranks. His
route was by way of the Orontes Valley to Antioch and thence
easterly; and from Phœnicia he reached the Euphrates by a
march of eleven days. From Myriandrus to Thapsacus the
ten thousand Greeks had marched in twelve. This was close
upon twenty miles a day. It was early summer. Thapsacus
had a much used ford and was the place formerly chosen by
Cyrus for crossing the Euphrates. Here Alexander's engi-

neers, whom he had sent out with a vanguard, had undertaken
to build two bridges of boats. They had not completed them
to the farther bank, for Mazæus with five thousand cavalry
and two thousand Greek mercenaries, under orders from
Darius, was guarding the river. But they had the work
substantially done. This force under Mazæus was the farthest outpost of the new army which Darius had raised to
defend his kingdom. On hearing of Alexander's arrival,
Mazæus at once decamped. He could do no good in disputing the passage, for Darius was already prepared to meet the
invader, and anxious for the encounter. The military theory under which the Persians seemed to be acting, was that
of allowing Alexander to come into the very heart of the
kingdom, where, presumably, if beaten, he could be more
utterly destroyed. And in this view Mazæus' orders were
confined to reconnoitring and reporting Alexander's movements. Delay was the last thing Darius wished. The bridges
were completed, and one other which Mazæus had broken
down was repaired.

Alexander laid the foundation of a city, Nicephonium, at
this spot, before he crossed into Mesopotamia, a work which
consumed some weeks. This constant founding of cities was
in pursuance of a clearly defined policy. It had three ob-
jects, — one, to provide an asylum for the wounded or invalided Macedonian soldiers who were no longer fitted for the
field; again, to form a chain of military posts on the line of
communications; and the third, to build up in the country
a knowledge of Hellenic arts and methods. In so founding a
city its outline was first drawn up by the engineers upon the
site selected, then the location for a citadel was chosen and
protected by a ditch and rampart, and gradually made strong;
then the inhabitants of the surrounding country were invited
to come in and settle under the protection of the garrison, and

were no doubt secured certain privileges. The population of Asia, then very considerable, soon produced a thriving city in each of these locations. The choice of sites was generally excellent and no doubt, as to-day, corner lots were sold at a premium. Moreover, the advantage, in a military sense, of having a series of garrisoned towns at no great intervals all along his line of operations was pronounced. For there was a constant movement to and fro along this line of couriers, reinforcements, material of war, and impedimenta of all kinds. We shall see how effective these posts were.

Having founded Nicephonium, Alexander crossed and marched into Mesopotamia, "having the Euphrates River and the mountains of Armenia on his left," says Arrian, — that is, his route was northerly as if towards Armida. He took this course, which was not an unusual one, on account of its being an easier region to march over and having greater abundance of forage and victuals. The country between him and Babylon on the direct road down the Euphrates, which was the one pursued by the Ten Thousand, had been wasted by the Persians to impede his advance by that route on the capital; they having calculated that he would attempt to march the same way. Moreover the heat was much more excessive along the plains of the Euphrates than on the uplands of the Tigris. The route down the Euphrates was, Xenophon tells us, naturally an exceedingly poor one for an army to pass over, being arid and without a sufficient supply of breadstuffs. It may be suggested that Darius ordered the devastation to bring Alexander towards the position he had selected for the *coup de grace*. There is no doubt that the Great King was eager for battle, and was pleased when the Macedonians headed in his direction. He had this time no fear for the result.

Alexander had intended to march to the point now called

Eski Mosul, near ancient Nineveh; but having heard from captured Persian scouts that Darius lay on the Tigris with a large army, he feared that he intended to dispute his crossing. He did not deem it wise to try to force the passage of so great a river in the teeth of Darius' enormous army, though indeed the army of Darius was his objective; but preferring an open battlefield for the final conflict, he altered his direction to a point above, where, when he reached the Tigris, he would be apt to find no opposition. The army had none the less great difficulty in crossing the river on account of the swiftness of its current, the ford being up to the armpits of the men. Indeed, the name of the river in Persian signifies "arrow." It flows to-day quite six miles an hour. It may be worth while to state that the limit of depth for cavalry is generally assumed to be less than four feet, and for infantry less than three. A line of horse was stationed above, to break the current; and one below to catch those who might be carried away. Alexander crossed on foot, first of all, carrying his arms above his head, to encourage the infantry. Some of the men joined hands, and not a soul was lost. This is in some respects one of the most interesting cases of fording a difficult river by a large army in history. The place of crossing was most probably near Bezabde, — which better fits Arrian's relation, — though some modern authorities put it near Eski Mosul. The point need not detain us.

While resting here after crossing, there occurred a total eclipse of the moon (September 20), usually an ominous portent; but Aristander, the soothsayer (probably under instructions from Alexander, who well knew how to sway the superstitions of his men), construed the startling event as a favorable omen. It was not the sun, Apollo, the deity of the Greeks, but the moon, Astarte, the goddess worshiped by so many nations under Persian rule, which was obscured. Alex-

ander's tact always rose superior to his superstition. No
doubt this eclipse produced a profound impression also upon
him ; but his uppermost thought was always his scheme of
conquest, and nothing which could affect his only means of
carrying this on — his army — ever failed to engross his whole
intelligence. There is nothing more marked in the character
of Alexander than the way he browbeat his own often intol-
erant superstition by the exercise of his superior intelligence.

Having crossed the Tigris, the army moved down the left
bank of the stream with the Gordyæan Mountains (the Car-
ducian Mountains of Xenophon) on his left, and on the
fourth day ran across the immediate outposts of Darius'
army, — a force of one thousand cavalry. Darius had wasted
the land, and there was scarcity of breadstuffs.

Extensive as Alexander's conquests had been, Darius had
in reality lost but a small part of his immense kingdom.
Asia Minor, Syria, Egypt were as nothing compared to the
vast territory from the sources of the Euphrates to the Indus
and Jaxartes, with its brave and loyal peoples. But the Great
King had done practically nothing for two years except to
recruit another army. This he had accomplished by a general draft of the entire population of his empire. He had
neither attempted to prevent Alexander from overrunning his
distant provinces, nor interfered with his sieges, nor blockaded the mountain passes he must cross, nor — most near-
sighted of all — sought to aid his own fleet in the Ægean.
Not only had Darius failed to defend the mountain passes,
but he had allowed Alexander to cross the last two broad and
difficult rivers unopposed. He might easily have made the
country a desert, and have thus rendered all but impossible
Alexander's advance. The result of his system, or lack of it,
was that the Macedonians had marched through a country
rich in supplies, had accumulated vast treasures, and had

arrived in Assyria in the best of condition and *morale*. Instead of the numberless chances he had neglected of crushing the Macedonians, he was reduced to a single chance. A lost battle now meant a kingdom lost for good.

No doubt all these points had been fully discussed by the Persian strategists, who in their way were able and intelligent, though wont to be divided in counsel; but still confident that on a plain their enormous numbers, especially in horse, must beyond a peradventure crush Alexander's small army out of existence, they deemed it their best policy to allow him to reach Mesopotamia, and there give him, far from any possibility of retreat, the final blow. And they had preferred to let him cross the Tigris as well as the Euphrates, for on their theory, the farther from home, the more dangerous his situation. Moreover, behind the Tigris, should Alexander be defeated, he would be thrown back on the mountains of Armenia, or on Mesopotamia, where he could be easily followed up and destroyed; while, should Darius again suffer a reverse, his road was open to Babylon.

Alexander had now been on the throne five years. He had made himself master of Greece. He had conducted a successful campaign against the Danube barbarians; had chastised the Illyrians; had taught Greece, by the fate of Thebes, what his anger could do. He had conquered Asia Minor; had crossed the mightiest mountain ranges and rivers; had defeated Darius in a great pitched battle, and destroyed his army, root and branch; he had carried through to a successful issue the greatest siege of antiquity; had overrun Syria, Phœnicia and Egypt, and had captured an hundred fortified cities, and built others. He had driven the Persians from the Ægean, and reduced to control the entire coast-line of the Mediterranean; he had advanced into the heart of the Persian empire, and had placed behind him its two great river bulwarks. He had marched over six thousand miles, despite the delays of sieges and the difficulty of establishing new governments in every section he traversed. And all this, no doubt, with as large trains and as much in the way of impedimenta as a modern army boasts. Yet he had but begun his work. The final struggle for the mastery had yet to come.

Darius appeared to have lost the character for strength which he was thought at one time to possess. An excellent ruler in peace, he was his own worst enemy in war. He was to all appearances paralyzed by the loss of his family, since Issus, as we remember, in Alexander's hands. These acted, as it were, as hostages for Darius' good behavior. It is not unlikely that Alexander's treatment of them, so noble from one aspect, was dictated by a motive to keep their value as hostages up to the very highest point, both as regarded Darius and his own army as well. In case of a serious reverse, these royal persons might prove of incalculable value. There was more than one reason why Alexander should keep Darius' family with his army instead of sending them to some city in the rear. Their own safety was nowhere so secure as in the midst of the Macedonian soldiery. This the royal captives knew full well, and showed in the coming battle. Turned adrift, where could they go when Darius himself was all but a fugitive? Moreover, by keeping them near him and giving them royal state, Alexander was increasing his own importance and standing in the eyes of all ancient friends and subjects of the Persian king; and multiplied his power of dictating terms a hundred-fold. At some period antedating the battle of Arbela, Queen Statira, the wife of Darius, sickened and died. It is said by some historians to have been in child-birth. It may have been later than such a cause would place the sad event, and was perhaps from the toils of the way, perhaps from humiliation and homesickness. Alexander is reported to have done everything which was possible to show his respect for the deceased queen, and to have exhibited genuine good feeling. All this is presumably true. He had enough enemies to record the facts if they were not as stated.

Darius had now assembled a much larger army than had been on foot in Cilicia, and had armed it with swords and longer spears, thinking thus to meet the Macedonian sarissa. But he had not probably been able to alter its drill and discipline to correspond. This required time and experience not at his command, though he is said to have been assiduous in practicing the men in their new manœuvres. That he should have committed the imprudence of not defending the passage of the Euphrates and the Tigris can be partly accounted for on the supposition that he still hoped for a peaceful accommodation, by which he might recover his family. It may have been for the purpose of further negotiation to this end, that, instead of risking his battle in Mesopotamia, where the ground was quite as favorable to his numbers, and whither he had marched from Bab-

Advance to Gaugamela.

ylon, he turned eastward from this province and himself crossed the Tigris. Having done this, he stayed his march at Arbela, where he established his magazines, harems, and treasury, subsequently moving his army forward across the Lycus (modern Great Zab) to Gaugamela, on the Bumodus, seventy miles westerly from Arbela.

Darius appears to have here again renewed his offer of half his kingdom, his daughter's hand, and thirty thousand talents of gold to Alexander for peace and the surrender of his family. He is said to have been deeply touched, not only by Alexander's respectful treatment of his wife, — so unusual in a conqueror, — but quite as much by Alexander's generosity to the queen during her fatal sickness, and to his mother and his children. On learning these facts, he is represented as having implored the deity, that if he could no longer sit upon the Persian throne, the crown might rest on the head of the Macedonian monarch, his bitterest foe, his greatest benefactor. Alexander submitted the proposal of Darius to the Council as a matter of usual routine; but himself eventually decided that Darius was endeavoring to corrupt his friends, and sent away the ambassadors with contumely.

When Alexander's scouts had reported a Persian force in his front, he had at once put the army in order of battle, and continued his advance; but further scouts ascertaining the force to be only a small body of perhaps one thousand cavalry, he took an ilē of horse-guards, the royal squadron and Pæonian dragoons, and himself led the van forward. The army followed in two columns, with cavalry on the flanks and the baggage in the rear, every man on the *qui vive* for what might soon be coming. The Persian outpost decamped; a few were slain, some captured. From these latter the king learned the composition of Darius' army. There were assembled all the nationalities under the Persian sceptre. In numbers the army is stated by different authorities at from two hundred thousand infantry and forty-five thousand horse to a million infantry and one hundred thousand horse. There were two hundred scythed chariots which had scythes on the axles and yokes and a spear on the pole, and fifteen elephants brought by the Indian contingent, and now for the first time introduced into warfare against Europeans. The troops were commanded as follows : Bessus, viceroy of Bactria, commanded the Bactrians, Indians, and Sogdianians ; Mavaces commanded the Sacians, who were mostly horse-bowmen ; Barsaëntes, satrap of Arachotia, led the Arachotians and Mountain Indians ; Satibarzanes, satrap of Aria, led a large body of Arians ; Phrataphernes led the Parthian, Hyrcanian, and Tarpurian contingents, all horsemen ; Atropates led the Medes, Cadusians, Albanians, and Sacessinians ; Orontobates, Ariobarzanes, and Otanes led the divisions raised near the Red Sea ; Oxathres commanded the Uxians and Susianians ; Boupares commanded the Babylonians, Carians, and Sitacenians ; Orontes and Mithraustes commanded the Armenians ; Ariaces led the Cappadocians ; Mazæus led the Cœle-Syrians and Mesopotamians.

The places in line of some of these troops are not given by any of the authorities ; and there is as considerable variation in chiefs and nations as in numbers. As usual, unless manifestly wrong, Arrian has been followed. The discrepancies are readily to be explained by the assumption that, when deployed in line of battle, the commands of many of the important chiefs were enlarged.

Darius' position was well chosen. It was on a large plain, near Gaugamela, and the ground had been carefully leveled, all obstacles had been removed, and the brush cut down, to allow the free evolutions of the chariots and horse.

Alexander gave his army four days' rest. We can imagine the Macedonian soldiers repairing and sharpening their weapons and polishing their shields and armor with unusual care.

The camp, which was but seven miles from Darius' army, was fortified with a ditch and stockade; the utmost circumspection on all hands was ordered. Here Alexander intended to leave all his heavy baggage and hospitals, so as to be able to go into battle with his troops bearing nothing but their arms. From all indications he judged that Darius proposed to choose his own ground on this occasion, and not allow his impatience to lure him to a battlefield where he could not employ his masses.

After the four days' rest and preparation, Alexander broke up about the second watch, and made his march towards the enemy under cover of darkness (September 29–30), hoping to reach and attack the Persians by daybreak. But he was delayed on the way. The Arbela plain is full of huge conical mounds to-day, the burial places of ancient cities; perhaps many existed then. A ridge of rolling ground lay between the armies, so that Alexander came within four miles of the Persian host before he caught sight, as he finally did through the morning mists, of their huge masses darkening the plain. Darius had them already drawn up in battle array, " in enormous squares of prodigious depth " of cavalry and infantry mixed.   From the top of the last of the hills Mazæus and his cavalry had just retired, and Alexander, who halted his phalanx on this high ground, reconnoitred the situation from a distance, and called together his Companions and officers of rank for the usual council of war. Many of the younger ones advised at once to attack, for the troops were in high spirits and eager for battle; but Parmenio and the older officers advised by all means to delay until the ground could be examined, so as to discover if pit-falls and such like obstructions had not been dug in front of the enemy's army; and until the enemy's tactical arrangements could be learned. Though Alexander's councils of war, unlike the proverbial ones, were not slow to fight, under his casting vote, this advice prevailed. A new camp and stockade were here made on the hill-slope near modern Börtela. The army lay on their arms in order of battle, while Alexander with some light infantry and Companion horse busied himself in thoroughly reconnoitring the ground.

On his return from this important duty, he again called together his Companions and officers, and addressed them. We can readily imagine, if we do not know, his soul-stirring words. Arrian but gives us the summary of them, most likely from the relation of Ptolemy, son of Lagus, one of his most interested auditors. He knew, said the king, that he could rely on their so often proved valor, but it was essential for them to infuse their ardor into every man of the command. In the approaching battle they were to fight for the whole of Asia, as well as for existence. Discipline must be maintained with an exactness never before demanded. Instead of chanting the pæan as usual, the men were to advance in perfect silence and order, so as not only to hear the trumpet calls the better, but so that their battle-cry, when given at the word of command, should strike an unwonted terror in the breasts of the enemy. Orders must be quickly transmitted and absolutely obeyed. Each man must remember that on his own individual courage depended largely victory or defeat. The council responded to his stirring words by a demand to be at once led against the enemy, that they might prove their obedience and valor. But Alexander bade them rest and refresh themselves by food, so as to go into action strong and vigorous the next day.

Late that evening Parmenio visited Alexander in his tent, and urged a night attack, as the Persians would be more liable to panic and confusion in the dark. They had the habit of unsaddling their horses and hobbling them, and of taking off their own armor, so that they would be helpless and more easily overcome.   But Alexander replied, partly for effect, — for there happened to be others listening to the conversation, — that it was more worthy to conquer without artifice, and not to steal a victory.   He fully understood, moreover, the dangers which beset the attacking party at night, in the midst of a hostile population full of the enemy's spies; and knew not only that unless he defeated Darius in open battle he could not morally conquer Asia, for Darius would be able again to explain away his defeat, but also that if he were not certainly victorious, retreat would be all but impossible in the night, from a foe who perfectly knew the *terrain* of which the Macedonians were ignorant, — except merely the path they had just pursued.   He rejected the proposal.

Alexander.

(From Cameo in Zacharia Sagrado Collection.)

XXVII.

ARBELA. OCTOBER 1, B. C. 331.

DARIUS anticipated a night attack and continued his troops under arms all
night. Having stood thus all through the previous day, they became tired and
unstrung. Early in the morning the Macedonians deployed into line, Alexander and the Companions on the right, Parmenio and the Thessalians on the left.
The Persians had leveled the plain for their cavalry and chariots. They far
outflanked Alexander, who, to meet this threat, made two flying columns of
reserve, one behind each wing, with orders to wheel outward and stand against
any outflanking force, or to the rear, or to reinforce the phalanx, as needed.
The battle opened by Alexander's taking ground to the right to avoid entan-
glements in his front. Darius launched his chariots against him and hurried
Bessus with a cavalry force to fall upon his right flank. The chariots proved
useless; Bessus was checked by Alexander's right flying column. Alexander
sharply advanced against the Persian left centre. Here was a gap made by the
Persian first line edging to the left, to follow Alexander when he edged to the
right. Perceiving this, the king formed a wedge and drove it sharply at this
gap and at Darius, whose station was near by. Meanwhile Alexander's taking
ground to the right had rent a gap in his own line, as Parmenio could not follow him, because Mazæus had smartly attacked his left. The Thessalians held
head against Mazæus, but a column of Persian cavalry rode down through the
gap and penetrated to the camp at the rear. Again the army was saved by the
wisely disposed left flying wing, which attacked this Persian column. Parmenio feeling sore pressed sent to Alexander for aid. The king had just driven
his wedge into the Persian line, and again Darius, as at Issus, terrified by the
dangers which beset his person, and unmindful of his duty as a king, had taken
to flight. This gave rise to a headlong flight in the whole centre and left.
Alexander was about to pursue when he heard of the danger to his left. Turning rapidly from pursuit, he headed the Companions and galloped back to
strike the cavalry which had ridden through his lines. He met them just as
they were coming back with the left flying column at their heels. Here occurred
the stoutest fighting of the day. The Companions outdid themselves. The
Persian column was annihilated. Bessus had been driven off; Mazæus had
been defeated; the Persian centre and left were broken; the right now followed them in flight. The battle for the kingdom of Persia was won. Alex-

ander pursued sharply, reaching Arbela, seventy miles distant, next day. The Persian loss was from forty to ninety thousand men, the Macedonian killed were five hundred. As at Issus, the Persian army was dispersed. Darius took with him but nine thousand men and fled to the interior.

THE Persian army at early dawn had watched the small array which had ventured within the wrath of the Great King, gathering on the heights west of the Gaugamela plain. They had anticipated a speedy attack and had come into battle order. But Alexander had spent the day in preparation and reconnoitring. Having no stockade, and fearing an attack after night-fall, Darius gave orders for the troops to remain under arms all night. (September 30–October 1.) This made a long twenty-four hours that the Persians had so stood. Their *morale*, already weakened by Issus, was probably far from heightened by this fatigue; and still less by the dread thus instilled of the Macedonian prowess. Darius rode his lines at night to show the royal countenance and to inspirit his men.

A document containing the arrangement of the Persian army was captured among the archives after the battle. This showed not only the formation of Darius' army, but also made mention of the above facts. No doubt it was a species of order of the day. The marshaling of the Persians was as follows : In the left wing from the left stood the Bactrian cavalry under Bessus with the Daans and Arachotians; the Persians, horse and foot; the Susians and Cadusians. In the right wing from the right were arrayed under Mazæus the Cœle - Syrians and Mesopotamians; the Medes; the Parthians and Sacians; the Tarpurians and Hyrcanians; the Albanians and Sacessinians. All these were in three lines and in large squares or in deep masses. In the centre was King Darius, surrounded by his "kinsmen" soldiers or body guards, fifteen thousand strong; the Persian guards with spears butted with golden apples, the Indians, Carians and Mardian archers. The Uxians, Babylonians and Red Sea men, and the Sitacenians were behind the centre in a deep column as reserve to the body surrounding the Great King. The Scythian cavalry was in front on the left, and near it one hundred scythed chariots. In front of Darius stood the fifteen elephants, and beside them other fifty scythed chariots. In front of the right were drawn up the Armenian and Cappadocian cavalry, and still other fifty scythed chariots. The Greek mercenaries, on whose skill and courage Darius relied to meet Alexander's phalanx, but whose fidelity at the same time he needlessly suspected, were stationed in two divisions, one on each side of the king and his body-guards. Bessus commanded the left wing; Mazæus the right.

Darius had likewise encouraged his army by a stirring address. He bade them not be disheartened by the partial defeat at the Granicus or by the defeat at Issus, where the mountains and the sea so shut them in that the Macedonian fighting force was as large as their own. He bade them do battle for their families and hearthstones. " It has become a contest for existence, and what is dearer still, the liberty of your wives and children, who must fall like mine into the hands of the enemy, unless your bodies become a rampart to save them from captivity." He conjured them by the splendor of the sun, the fire on their altars, and the immortal memory of Cyrus, to preserve the Empire and its glory.

The Macedonians filed out of their camp on the hills at early morn, after a hearty sleep and breakfast (October 1). They moved forward in order of battle which was marshaled thus: The right was held by the cavalry Companions, the royal squadron leading under Clitus, accompanied by Alexander in person. Then to the left, the squadrons of Glaucias, Aristo, Sopolis, Heraclides, Demetrius, Meleager, Hege-

370

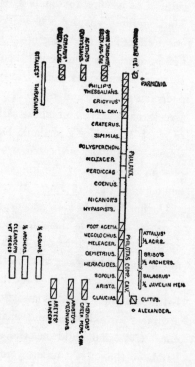

Position of Troops before the opening of the Battle of Arbela.

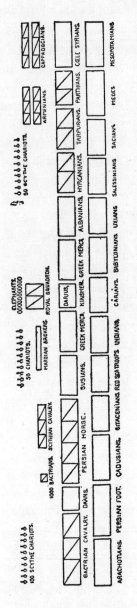

lochus. The whole body of cavalry Companions was as usual under supreme command of Philotas, son of Parmenio. Then came the Macedonian phalanx, according to Curtius in two lines, meaning probably hoplites and peltasts; first the agema of hypaspists, then the other hypaspists under Nicanor, son of Parmenio; then the phalangites under Cœnus, Perdiccas, Meleager, Polysperchon, Simmias (commanding Amyntas' brigade), Craterus. The latter was in command of the left wing of the infantry. Then came the allied Greek cavalry under Erigyius, and the Thessalian cavalry under Philip, which body at Issus had shown itself to be the peers of the Companions, and was therefore posted on the left, as the Companions were upon the right. Parmenio with the Pharsalian horse, the best ilē of the Thessalians, as body-guard, commanded the left wing, as was the rule.

The Persian army far overlapped the Macedonian flanks. This was unavoidable, if the king was not to jeopardize the solidity essential for attack. To provide against this danger, Alexander for the first time formed a second or reserve line, or rather a column in rear of each flank, so placed that it could face about or wheel to the right or left, and fight to the rear or on the flanks if needful to resist attack from these directions. It was a flying column behind each flank. He naturally feared that he might be surrounded by the immense number of the enemy, for to attempt this was the one usual manœuvre. This disposition has been called a grand hollow square, but it was more than that. The arrangement was such as to insure greater mobility than a square is capable of possessing. For the flying columns were so organized and disposed that they could face in any direction, and were prepared to meet attack from front, flank or rear. Indeed, the left flying column met an attack from within, and beat it off. "In fine," says Curtius, "he had so disposed his army that it fronted every way" — he should have said could front every way — "and was ready to engage on all sides, if attempted to be encompassed; thus the front was not better secured than the flanks, nor the flanks better provided than the rear."

In this second line, in his right wing, Alexander had disposed the cavalry at intervals, so that it could wheel into line at such an angle to the front line as to be able to take in flank any body which might advance on Alexander's right; and this force had orders, if need be, to close in like a sort of rear or reserve line so as to form a huge square; or if called for to reinforce the first line or phalanx for a front attack by filing in behind it. In the right flying wing were half the Agrianians under Attalus, and the Macedonian archers under Briso; next the veteran Macedonians under Cleander. In front of these were the light cavalry, and the Pæonians under Aretes and Aristo. In front of these again were the newly arrived Greek mercenary cavalry under Menidas, placed where they might win their spurs. And covering the agema and Companion cavalry were half the Agrianians and archers and Balacrus' javelin-men, the latter opposite the chariots in the centre of Darius' army. The special duty impressed on Menidas was to ride round and take the Persians in flank if they tried to surround this Macedonian wing.

On the left was a similar flying wing in which were the Thracians under Sitalces, the Greek auxiliary cavalry under Cœranus, the Odryssian cavalry under Agatho. In front of all these stood the cavalry of the Greek mercenaries under Andromachus. The exact description of this formation, excepting that of the main line, is difficult to decipher from Arrian, and impossible from the other ancient authorities. Diodorus calls it a semicircle. We know better what these reserve troops, or part of them did during the battle, and this suffices. The accompanying chart satisfies quite closely the statements of the several authorities, and suits Alexander's manœuvres as developed by Arrian from Ptolemy and Aristobulus with reasonable accuracy. It is moreover consistent with itself, and the successive manœuvres as shown by the charts accord with all the ancient authorities.

The baggage, prisoners and camp followers had been left in the stockade in charge of the Thracian infantry. Here also was the family of Darius. The heavier part of the train was in the first camp seven miles to the rear. Alexander's whole force numbered seven thousand cavalry and forty thousand infantry, plus some few Asiatics. The latter were useless. They were not engaged, nor do they appear in line.

Alexander had passed the night in unusually careful discussion of plans for the morrow's battle. He is represented by some historians as having been exceedingly apprehensive as to the situation, by Curtius as alternately haunted by fear and hope. This is not Alexander. It is more probable that the king did not become in any degree anxious. It was not characteristic of him. He belonged to the type of man a

large part of whose strength lies in a constant, almost audacious, hopefulness. This, however, never clouded Alexander's
intellect, which remained open to a full comprehension of all
factors on which he must act. It is just this exceptional
combination of character and intellect which goes to make up
the great captain, and no less suffices. It is related that, late
at night, after fully completing his battle plan, he fell into a
deep sleep, out of which he was awakened by Parmenio long
after dawn. He was so confident of victory that he could
sleep. This does not look like nervous anxiety. He arrayed
himself with care, and appeared in his most glittering armor
and with a face which presaged certain success to the army.
The ilēs and taxes had in due order filed out of the camp and
into line. The stockade which had been erected to protect
the camp was left intact to protect the non-combatants and
prisoners, and the army stood forth ready for battle. After
riding the line, the advance at slow step was ordered, and the
Macedonians strode forward, as proud a force as ever relied
on its courage and discipline to wrest victory from so vast a
foe, or perish sword in hand.

Nothing leads one to rely upon Arrian rather than Quintus
Curtius more than their respective descriptions of this battle.
Arrian's portrait of Alexander is uniform, and commends
itself to one's judgment; his description of the battle enables
the careful student to place and manœuvre the troops. There
may be some variance as to details, but the main facts are
there, clear and crisp. The relation of Curtius of all battles
and sieges is obscure, and inconsistent in most parts; while
his sketch of the king makes him alternately a demigod and a
milksop — never an Alexander.

Darius, though he proposed to fight upon his own prepared
ground, was ready to open the battle by a charge of chariots.
Anticipating this, and to receive such a charge, Alexander

had ordered the phalangites to be ready — as at Mount Hæmus — to open spaces for the chariots to pass through, and, as we have seen, had detailed javelin-throwers in their front to wound or frighten the horses as they came by. Alexander proposed to open by a charge of his cavalry *d'élite* on the left of the Persian centre, opposite which his own right stood arrayed. As he was about to advance, he learned by a deserter that caltrops had been scattered in certain parts of the field. He took some ground to the right to avoid these, probably by a right half wheel and an advance by ilēs in echelon. It was moreover natural for him to manœuvre in this direction lest the much longer Persian line should overwhelm his right flank.

It is not improbable that Alexander anticipated that this obliquing manœuvre might induce the Persian left to follow in a parallel line, and thus open a gap between the Persian left wing and centre, or at least unsteady the line. Whatever his intentions, his movement had this effect. For, perceiving this manœuvre, and fearing that Alexander might get his whole army beyond the leveled ground where alone the scythed chariots could operate to advantage or the cavalry act effectively, Darius impatiently launched the chariots against him, followed up by an advance of his centre, and at the same time ordered forward the leading squadrons of his cavalry, one thousand Bactrians and some of the Scythians, to envelop the Macedonian right and prevent any further obliquing. Alexander ordered out Menidas to oppose this charge. But the Scythians and Bactrians so largely outnumbered Menidas that they bore him back. Aristo with his Pæonians was then launched on the enemy, and drove him back some distance, till the rest of the Bactrians under Bessus, fourteen thousand in all, they and the Scythians wearing more and heavier armor than the Macedonians, reëstablished the Per-

sian diversion, and seriously threatened the Macedonian right.
A sharp and for some time indecisive cavalry battle was here
fought.   But finally, when Alexander put in an appearance,

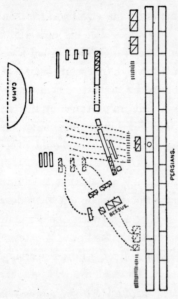

cheered and rallied the
troops, and Aretes, at the
king's order, charged in on
the left of the Bactrians and
Scythians with the splen-
did discipline for which his
corps was noted, he enabled
the Macedonians to score an
advantage; and the entire
body of cavalry continued
to charge upon the enemy
"squadron by squadron,"
with the peculiar tenacious-
ness which this tactical
manœuvre called forth, and
which Alexander's cavalry
always so markedly exhib-
ited.

Arbela (second phase).

Nothing is stated in the old histories as to what orders
were given to Parmenio on the left when Alexander began to
take ground to the right.   No doubt he was instructed to
follow the manœuvre.   But he was not able to do so with
equal speed; and his movement in support of Alexander was
roughly interrupted, as we shall see.   The ardor which Alexander had put into the work of his right wing, and the fact
that the left Macedonian wing was prevented from keeping
pace with him, again transferred what began as a parallel
order into a semblance of oblique order, left refused.   Inasmuch as Alexander always intended that the right, where he
commanded, should take precedence in attack, which was

indeed the usual thing among the Greeks, this fact, coupled with his natural aggressiveness offset by Parmenio's always more deliberate though courageous onset on the left, gave to this as to other battles, as has been already observed, the appearance and effect of an attack in oblique order, which came about partly by intention and partly by the operation of other causes.

While the cavalry forces on the right flank were gallantly stemming the tide of overwhelming numbers, the charge of chariots against the Macedonian phalanx, from which so much was expected on the one side and which was so much dreaded on the other, had been made, — and had failed, like the charges of elephants and so many other abnormal schemes of warfare have often done. For as the chariots galloped rapidly over the leveled surface towards the phalanx, the hoplites frightened the horses by clashing their spears upon their shields ; the Agrianians, archers and acontists received them with a formidable shower of arrows, stones and javelins ; they stopped some of the horses from simple fear ; they wounded others. Habituated to manœuvre with cavalry, they were quick of foot as we can scarce imagine ; they leaped at and seized the horses' reins ; they cut the traces ; they killed the drivers and warriors ; and while many forced their way to the rear through the purposely opened ranks of the Macedonian army, many others rushed on the protended sarissas, and fell or turned from the bristling array. Those who reached the rear were nearly all captured by the non-combatants, or broken up by the peltasts of the second line. The result was that the vaunted chariots accomplished little good commensurate with expectation or dread, and many charged back on the Persian lines, where they did vastly more damage than they had inflicted on the Macedonians, on account of the Persian greater depth. They had but unsteadied Alexander's line, and good discipline would repair this evil.

Chagrined by the failure of the charge of the chariots, Darius gave orders to set his entire centre phalanx in motion forward. This required some time. But the cavalry of the Persian first line, — Bactrians and Scythians, — in moving away from its post to join the columns which were threatening Alexander's right flank, had to a certain extent been followed by the infantry line, which had also edged to its left as Alexander had to his right. This had produced a marked gap in the Persian front, which the second line should have moved up to fill, but lacking orders, did not. Alexander, who had not only been leading his Companion cavalry, but also directing and personally rallying the dangerous and still doubtful combat on the right flank, when Aretes began to hold head against Bessus again turned to the front. His eye on the battlefield was like the hawk's for keenness; he instantly perceived the opening gap in the Persian line, and seized with quick apprehension this coveted chance. With a speed which no troops could then rival, — if, indeed, any have rivaled since, — he formed from that part of the Macedonian phalanx which was on the right — hypaspists, Cœnus and Perdiccas — a deep column or wedge; and heading it by his cavalry Companions in serried ranks, he wheeled round obliquely to his left towards this gap, and for the first time on this day raising that battle-cry by which the Macedonians never failed to shake the courage of their foes, he thrust this wedge at the double-quick, with the impetus of a battering-ram, into the Persian line, straight at the place occupied by Darius in person. Here, if anywhere, as at Issus, victory was to be snatched by boldness.

The Macedonian wedge struck the Persian line as a thunder-bolt rives an oak. Hand-to-hand the bravest hearts of

Macedon and Persia for a brief instant contended for the mastery; but nothing could resist the impetuosity of the Companions, who, headed by their gallant king, and instinct with the glories of the Granicus and of Issus, thrust at the faces of the foe and hewed their way through living masses; nothing could stand against the sarissa of the phalanx, which had never yet found its match. Darius was once more seized with alarm. Not waiting for support or for reinforcements, without personal effort to retrieve what might have been but a temporary disadvantage, but full of terror, especially when his own charioteer fell transfixed by a spear, he turned and fled. The splendid array of Oriental legions has lost its leader. Will no one fill his place and call into action the myriads of brave souls eagerly waiting to do the Great King service?

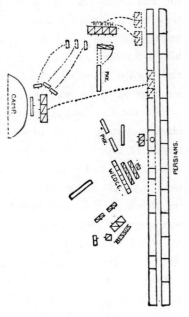

Arbela (third phase).

The cavalry of the Persian left had by this time also broken and was being driven back by Aretes upon the second line, which should but did not advance to its support, throwing it into quick confusion. The flight of the Great King put an end to any idea of resistance by the Persian centre and left. The vast mass began to melt to the rear, and but a few charges of the Macedonian right were needed to send them, as at Issus, ebbing in consternation from the battlefield.

While Alexander was heading his wedge for the Persian centre, and the cavalry of the right was charging home upon the Bactrians and Scythians of Bessus, the Macedonian left had been almost fatally compromised. Into the king's wedge had been thrust the brigades of Cœnus and Perdiccas, and the rest of the phalanx as far as the right of Simmias had tried to follow the movement to protect its flank. The latter brigade and that of Craterus, however, could not join in the king's forward movement, for Parmenio was hard pressed, and needed every man he could collect. The scythed chariots here may have won more success than on the right. It is not stated. But the cavalry on the Persian right was already moving out to attack the Macedonian left, and the troops in the Persian right centre were moving forward. These causes had operated to keep Parmenio from seconding the king. He had remained *in situ* to resist these threatening attacks. Thus Alexander's manœuvre, as masterly as it was pregnant with promised victory, had produced a gap in his own line which Parmenio, occupied with the serious onslaught of Mazæus, had been unable to fill.

Here was a grievous danger. There was no lack of able generals on the other side, and perceiving the chance, a part of the cavalry of the Persian right wing (said to be Parthians and Indians, together with some Persians, though these are not elsewhere mentioned as being in this part of the field) had left the line and headed straight for the gap, had ridden clean through the opening, had thrown the Macedonian left into the utmost confusion, and had actually reached the camp and baggage in the rear, before any means to arrest their swinging charge could be devised. The Thracian foot fought stubbornly at the gate of the stockaded camp, but many of the prisoners rose and attacked them in the rear. The enemy's cavalry released many others, who at once flew to their

assistance, and they all but rescued the family of Darius.
These, however, wisely refused to be carried off, feeling no
manner of personal safety in the wild turmoil outside the
camp.

The second line, which Alexander had posted in rear of
the left wing with orders to face to the rear if necessary, now
came into play. Sitalces, Cœranus, Agatho, Andromachus
were not the men to stand about idle. So soon as they saw
the danger, wheeling about their squadrons, they galloped to
the rescue, fell sharply on the rear of the enemy and drove
him off in wild confusion, killing and capturing men wholesale. What was left of these squadrons rode back the way
they had come. This special danger seemed to be averted.

But a more threatening danger was at hand. At the time
this irruption was at its height, Mazæus, commanding the
Persian right, with the Armenian and Cappadocian cavalry
of that wing, perceiving the effect of the charge through the
Macedonian centre, and thinking to clinch the matter here
and now, ployed his men into a heavy column and rode down
upon the Macedonian left flank with a concentrated energy
which threatened to overwhelm the entire force under Parmenio. Happily Alexander's Thessalians were here. As
proud of their record and as stanch as the Companions themselves, these splendid squadrons, anxious not to be left out
of the fray, wheeled to the left, received Mazæus half way
with a counter charge, and as at Issus, by dint of hard
knocks and clean-cut purpose, held the gallant Persian, despite his utmost efforts, from passing the limit they drew to
his advance.

The situation was curious. On the Macedonian right
Menidas, Aristo and Aretes were still struggling manfully to
save the army from the furious and constantly repeated assaults of Bessus. Alexander's wedge had just aimed its

mighty thrust at the heart of the Persian centre. The Thessalians were holding gallant head against Mazæus' overwhelming numbers. The Parthians, Indians and Persians were about to be taken in the rear by the reserves of the Macedonian left. An instant might change the current of the fray. The battle was anybody's, — were it not for Alexander.

Parmenio, unaware of Alexander's success on the right, felt, from the utter confusion in which the squadrons which had ridden through his lines, and Mazæus' thundering charge, had left his wing, that the case was desperate. He sent to Alexander urgently begging for reinforcements. This word reached the king at the moment he saw victory fairly wavering in the balance. He sent back answer to fight it out to the death. " Tell Parmenio," spake the king, " that if victorious, we shall regain all ; if defeated, we shall die blade in hand. Let him fight as becomes Philip and Alexander ! "

But victory sometimes marches fast. " Le sort d' une bataille est le résultat d' un instant, d' une pensée. On s' approche avec des combinaisons diverses, on se mêle, on se bat un certain temps ; le moment décisif se présente ; une étincelle morale prononce, et la plus petite réserve accomplit " (Napoleon). No sooner had the columns near Darius become aware of the flight of the Great King than they melted away once more, as they had done at Issus. There was no head, no purpose. The enormous columns of gallant men ready and eager for the fray if but some one would direct, were so many inert masses — dangerous to each other from their very numbers. A few more vigorous blows and the tide set back ; nothing could retard its ebb. The retreat of the centre quickly became rout ; Bessus perceiving the fatal effect of Alexander's charge, withdrew his cavalry ; the splendid wedge of the Macedonian right had won the victory, — the Persian centre and left were in full retreat.

But danger still lurked in the situation of the left. Reluctantly yielding up immediate pursuit, and leaving his infantry to hold what he had won, the king wheeled his Companion cavalry to the left, and galloped to the aid of his embarrassed lieutenant. Just as the Parthian, Indian and Persian cavalry, driven from the camp by the reserves of the left, were retiring through the lines, Alexander struck this body in full swing. Here occurred the most stubborn fighting of the day. The enemy's horse must cut its way out or perish; the Com-

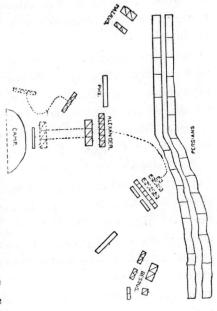

Arbela (fourth phase).

panions, furious at delayed pursuit, determined to give no quarter. It was hand to hand work. The fighting was close and quick and bitter. Some sixty Companions bit the dust within a few brief minutes; many, including Hephæstion, Cœnus and Menidas, were severely wounded. Few of the enemy cut their way through; nearly all remained upon the field. For, taken in the rear by the reserves as well as met in front by Alexander, they had no outlet but with sword in hand; and it was the Companions who barred the way.

The Thessalian cavalry had, during this interval, completed the defeat of Mazæus despite this officer's splendid struggle, and, aided by the fast spreading demoralization, had driven back the Persian right. Alexander's strong arm had not really been required. Seeing that Parmenio could now attend to this part of the field, Alexander once again turned to the pursuit of Darius, too long delayed. It is said that the fugitives made a cloud of dust so thick that only the sound of the whips urging on the horses were his guide in following up the enemy. Parmenio easily completed the destruction of the Persian right, which had not only been checked, but, on learning of the flight of their king, at once yielded up the struggle. Mazæus, with a body of troops, escaped around the left of the army, crossed the Tigris, and made for Babylon.

Alexander advanced across the Lycus, in which thousands had been drowned in trying to escape, and camped to give his men and horses a little rest. Parmenio seized the Persian camp at Gaugamela with all the elephants and camels. At midnight, the moon having risen, Alexander again set out in pursuit towards Arbela, hoping to capture Darius, the treasure and royal property, and reached the town, seventy miles distant, the next day. But Darius had kept well ahead. He could not be caught, though, as at Issus, Alexander took his spear and bow and chariot, and a large amount of gold.

In the battle and pursuit Alexander lost one thousand horses from wounds or from fatigue; and, according to Diodorus, whose figures here seem most reliable, five hundred in Macedonian killed. Taking the usual ratio of wounded, the loss of the Macedonians fell little short of twelve per cent. Of the Persians the slain are estimated by Curtius at forty thousand; by Diodorus at ninety thousand. "There were said to have been three hundred thousand slain," relates Arrian, this time manifestly quoting an error.

Arrian's Anabasis generally contains internal evidence of accuracy. From what he says you can plan out what Alexander did. But in quoting losses he is sometimes less correct.

He may allow himself to exaggerate here as a harmless species of flattery to his hero, whom at other times he is not wont to overpraise. But the loss was enormous. The rule in all old battles is the same. The victors lose little; the vanquished are cut to pieces. The elephants and chariots were all captured. Whatever the relative losses may have been, it is certain that the Persian army was dispersed, as it had been at Issus. Doubtless the various detachments made their way to their several homes, there being no head to keep them together. Darius collected some three thousand cavalry and six thousand foot, and made for the interior.

This battle is remarkable for the valor and skill of the commander of the victorious army, to whose constancy and intelligence the success was clearly due, as well as for the vacillation and cowardliness of the defeated monarch, despite some most excellent work by his subordinates. Never were dispositions better taken to resist the attacks of the enemy at all points; never on the field were openings more quickly seized; never threatening disaster more skillfully retrieved than here. However great the advance in battle tactics as the ages roll on, the world will never see more splendid tactics than the day of Arbela affords us. Even had Darius stood his ground, his lines would scarcely have resisted Alexander's able combinations. Mere inert masses would have availed nothing. The Persians still relied on multitudes. Alexander was introducing new tactics. As Frederick taught the modern world how to march, and Napoleon showed that not masses but masses properly directed were of avail, so Alexander first of all men taught that a battle was not to be won by weight of masses, but by striking at the right place and right time. Macdonald's column at Wagram was scarcely comparable to Alexander's wedge at Arbela. For this was the first of its kind.

Parmenio may, by comparison with his chief, be found wanting; and some historians have laid much at his door, even going so far as to charge him with sluggishness from envy of the king's success. This seems overdrawn. Parmenio was none the less a good soldier, in view of his age a remarkable one. Mazæus' attack was made in grand style and was not easy to beat off, and it was Alexander's very success which opened the gap for the Indian, Persian and Parthian column to ride down through the centre of the Macedonian host. No wonder Parmenio felt that his case was desperate, ignorant as he was of the king's advantage. The wonder lies in Alexander's rescuing victory from so desperate a strait.

Only the Persian cavalry was engaged *au fond*. But this force behaved with valor, and in seizing the opportunity of the gap in Alexander's left to ride through the Macedonian army, showed clearly that it was led by able men. The nearby Persian infantry was routed by Alexander's wedge so soon as it struck the line, and Darius' flight completed the disaster for the remainder. The value of discipline cannot be better shown than by the fact that the gap in the Persian line produced demoralization which proved irretrievably fatal; the gap in the Macedonian line but a temporary disturbance by no means affecting the temper of the troops. The Macedonians were quickly rallied, and were at once again ready for work; the Persian army went to pieces.

XXVIII.

BABYLON, SUSA. THE UXIANS. OCTOBER TO DECEMBER, B. C. 331.

ALEXANDER marched on Babylon, fearing a second Tyre. With walls three hundred feet high, it could well have delayed him as long as did the queen city of Phœnicia. But Mazæus, who, after his gallant efforts at Gaugamela, had retreated on the capital, deemed it wise to surrender the city. He received his due reward. Here Alexander gave his men a long and well-earned rest, and distributed to them a handsome gratuity out of the treasures taken from the Great King, and here, too, Alexander made a number of army changes, fitting the organization to its new conditions. Babylon became a secondary base. Susa had also been surrendered, with its vast treasures, to an advance column, which Alexander had sent thither from Arbela. The next objective was Persepolis. To reach this home of the Persian monarchs, Alexander had to cross several rivers and an Alpine range; but, though it was now winter, he set out. The first opposition he encountered on the way was at the defile of the Uxians, who had for generations compelled a tribute for passage even from the Great King. This defile Alexander captured by a clever manœuvre, and reduced the Uxians to submission.

FROM Arbela the fugitive king fled through the mountains of Armenia towards Media, with the remnants of the Bactrian cavalry under Bessus, the "kinsmen," a few apple-bearers, and a handful of Greek mercenaries, all told some six thousand infantry and three thousand cavalry. Ariobarzanes, one of his generals, who had commanded part of the Red Sea troops, rescued from the turmoil a force stated at from twenty-five to forty thousand men, and retired to defend the Persian Gates. Anticipating that Alexander would march on Babylon and Susa, the great prizes of the campaign, Darius retired in a quite opposite direction towards Ecbatana, where it would have been difficult for an army to follow. He seemed to forget that it was possible for him still to make a successful defense of his kingdom at the entrance to Persis, which was covered by one of the most difficult mountain barriers in the world, and inhabited by a hardy population ready to do sterling service for the defense of their master. He fled as if his life were the only thing worth saving. His desertion left no head to the state. Ariobarzanes had probably no idea that Darius would abandon Persis. He saw that Babylon, in the open plain, was scarcely to be saved. Susa was equally accessible. But Persepolis was behind the mountains, and afforded abundant chances for defense.

Alexander was obliged quickly to leave Arbela, lest the stench of corpses should breed a pestilence. The army advanced on Babylon by the main road, and crossed the Tigris at Opis. With his usual care to leave no danger in his rear, and to make sure of his booty, Alexander neither followed Darius in his flight to the mountains, nor Ariobarzanes in his retreat to the Persian Gates. He preferred to take immediate possession of Babylon, before any one could organize for its defense. He naturally expected opposition here. He knew its history and had heard of its mighty walls. Perhaps the sieges of Halicarnassus, Tyre and Gaza were to be repeated. He could not tarry an instant.

The extent of the power of Persia can, to a small degree, be measured by its capital. It must be remembered that although Greece was the actual seat of the intellect and liberties of the world, Persia represented its material prosperity. Many of the now desert regions of the vast empire were, in Alexander's day, covered with smiling fields and a contented people; and the vast structures and illimitable luxuries of the Persian kings do not point alone to a selfish centralized power, and a yet more selfish and cruel system of serfdom, but also to rich as well as vast dominions from which these yet unapproached creations of kings could emanate.

Babylon, within its outer fortifications, was superficially about seven times as big as Paris within hers, being not far from fourteen miles square. Of this enormous territory of nearly two hundred square miles, but a small third was covered with buildings like a city. The rest was open country, as it were, where farms, tilled to the highest limit of productiveness, were capable of feeding the population almost indefinitely. The Euphrates cut the city into two parts, and on one side was the royal quarter, with its hanging gardens and palaces; on the other the work-a-day world. Fifty main streets, one hundred and fifty feet wide, and four boulevards divided up this territory. The walls of the city in its prime were two hundred cubits (three hundred feet) high and seventy feet wide, and were surmounted by towers. One hundred gates of brass offered access to the country beyond. Perhaps ancient Babylon in its glory was never approached by any other city. And though conquerors antedating Alexander had destroyed many of its features, these had, no doubt, been replaced so that it was still the most wonderful of cities, and to the plain Macedonian of double wonder.

Alexander had heard that Mazæus, who had fought so bravely on the Persian right at Gaugamela, had posesssion of the city. Nearing its walls he marched slowly and in battle array. But instead of being saluted with closed gates and ramparts manned, he saw to his surprise and delight the portals open, and the population with wreaths and presents, led by the Chaldæans and elders and Persian officials, emerge to do him honor and bid him welcome. Mazæus, the servant, surrendered to Alexander, the conqueror and new master, as was the Oriental custom, and the Macedonian king entered without a blow into the impregnable city of Semiramis.

The surrender was duly rewarded. Alexander appointed Mazæus viceroy. No doubt Mazæus counted on this result, for Alexander's reputed generosity had preceded him. Apollodorus was made commanding officer of the city, and Agatho chief of the garrison in the citadel. Asclepiodorus was appointed collector of customs. Mithrines, who had surrendered Sardis, Alexander made satrap of Armenia. Menes was made hyparch of Cilicia, Phœnicia and Syria, and given the duty of keeping the roads on the line of operations free from predatory bands, of which, since the dispersion of the Persian arms at Issus and Arbela, there were many and troublesome. It will be noticed how scrupulous Alexander always was, while leaving the civil authority in the old channels, to place the military control in the hands of his own soldiers. This, as we remember, was Cyrus' plan, and Alexander ably carried it out.

To his army Alexander gave a long rest, richly deserved. No doubt these rough Macedonians enjoyed to their full this gorgeous city of the East, with all its luxurious habits, palaces and temples. From the vast treasures captured here, according to Curtius and Diodorus, Alexander distributed gratuities to his men. He gave each Macedonian cavalryman six minæ or six hundred drachmas, a sum equal to one hundred and twenty dollars ; each Greek and light horseman five minæ or one hundred dollars ; each Macedonian infantryman forty dollars ; and the allied infantry and peltasts two months' extra pay. These sums at that day had many times greater purchasing value than now. Alexander sacrificed to Belus according to the Babylonian rites, adding games and races in the Macedonian manner. His ideas of merging races were being matured. Babylon now became a secondary base from which Alexander could proceed on his march of conquest, and where he could accumulate his stores and material of war.

Susa was the more central capital of the Persian Empire, and had been the winter residence. This city now became the next objective, and Alexander was wont to be restless, and anxious to be on the road, as long as there was work to be done or danger to be encountered. After the stay of a month in Babylon to make his footing secure, — he may have feared too long delay for its effect on his Macedonians, — he moved on Susa, which he reached in a march of twenty days, probably in November. The weather was auspicious. During the hot season the march could hardly have been made. The country then was rich and fertile, now it is a desert. But the geological conditions are still the same; the meteorological ones have not materially changed. On the way Alexander learned that Philoxenus, whom he had dispatched to Susa with a light advance-corps, immediately after the late battle, had received its surrender with all its treasures. These amounted to from fifty to eighty millions of our money, part ingots and part Darics. There was besides endless wealth in jewels, stuffs and other valuables, and the statues of Harmodius and Aristogiton, carried away by Xerxes, were found in the treasure house and restored to Athens. At Susa, too, Alexander offered sacrifices and celebrated games.

As an almost uniform rule, Alexander rewarded what was really treachery to Darius, though a common Oriental habit. Arbulites, the commander of the city, had welcomed Philoxenus. His son had come to meet Alexander with a procession of camels and elephants, laden with treasures as presents to the conqueror. Alexander made Arbulites, in consequence of this service, viceroy of the province; but Mazarus, a Companion, was associated with him as commander of the garrison in the citadel, and Archelaüs as general of the force of three thousand men left in the city. The treasure at Susa came in good stead. Alexander was enabled to send, through

Menes, to Antipater three thousand talents to carry on the war with the Spartans, a much needed remittance.

In Susa Alexander domiciled the family of Darius, and surrounded it with royal state.

Here were received considerable reinforcements, brought by Amyntas, son of Andromenes, from Macedonia. These are stated by Curtius to have been fifteen thousand men, including fifty pages. Alexander found it desirable to make some changes in his army organization. We are told that the mora or battalion (two syntagmas) up to this time had been five hundred strong. Alexander increased it to one thousand. The chiliarch or colonel, one of the most important of officers, because commanding the unit of service, given above as a taxis of one thousand and twenty-four men, was ordered to be chosen by certain judges appointed by Alexander, who were obliged to give their reasons for their selection, so that every soldier might see that the best man had been promoted. The king, like all others, had his favorites; but beyond favoritism was the desire to keep an army on which he could rely. The earliest promotions numbered Adarchias for gallantry in retrieving a failing assault at Halicarnassus, Antigenes, Philotas, Amyntas, Antigonus, Lyncestes, Theodotus, Hellanicus, each to the command of a new mora. This statement does not accord with what we have given of Philip's organization, but it shows that Alexander, under his new conditions, was compelled to make changes, to assimilate the new material entering the army. It is not impossible that the old historians have, in reporting the changes made, used misleading phrases, or employed Greek rather than Macedonian terms. But the matter is not of the essence. Alexander's changes were all of a similar and excellent kind. All distinctions in the foreign cavalry were abolished. He doubled up his cavalry organization by dividing each ilē or squadron into two companies, and placed reliable Companions in command, supplementing the small offices with the old pages, who had already learned something of war. This gave him a larger *cadre* which he could fill by drafts from the Oriental nations. Up to this time the Macedonians had always broken camp to the sound of the trumpet. Alexander now introduced a system of signals, partly by torches at night and smoke by day, given from a masthead erected near his headquarters. He thus evaded giving the enemy notice of his intentions, and made them clearer to his men. Prior to Arbela, the Macedonians and Greeks always marched to battle chanting the pæan. At that battle Alexander, it will be remembered, gave orders that the troops should not raise the battle-cry until instructed to do so, when it would have all the more effect. This was noted and acted on in after days. The reinforcements which Alexander received consisted of men, all of whom knew their trade, and could at once fall into the ranks. But they had to learn discipline. Alexander could teach them that better than any one alive. It is always hard to impose new rules on old and successful soldiers. Alexander wisely chose a time when reinforcements were arriving, and new elements were being introduced into the army to inaugurate his changes.

Xenophon, speaking of certain officers, says: "Proxenes of Bœotia was made to command honest people; he had not that which is essential to inspire adventurers with respect or fear. Clearchus, on the other hand, always hard and cruel, could obtain from his soldiers only that sort of sentiment which children have for a schoolmaster." This is a crisp distinction, which every man in service has noticed. Alexander was of a different stamp. In his treatment of his army or of conquered peoples he was alike happy. "I have not come to Asia," said he, "to destroy nations; I have come here that those who are subdued by my arms shall have naught to complain of my victories." And he accomplished what he set out to do by the singular ability to control all classes of men, and to fuse discordant elements into a homogeneous mass.

Alexander now set out from Susa. His next objective was Persepolis, the capital of Persis, the place of origin of the Persian conquerors. The possession of Persepolis would mean to the superstitious population the possession of the kingdom. It was important, not only to reach the treasures

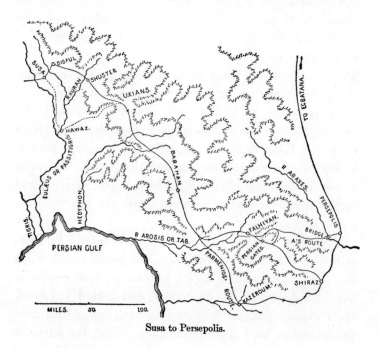

Susa to Persepolis.

in the cities of Persis, but to reach them before Darius had time to get together another army for their protection. For Alexander was as yet unaware of Darius' plans and purpose. He merely knew that he had fled from Arbela. Between him

and Persepolis lay a rugged Alpine country, traversed by but
a single practicable road, and with defiles easily held by a
handful. But the Greeks were always good mountain fighters. They were mountaineers by birth, and had had training
in mountain warfare from their earliest campaigns. It is
doubtful if any modern nation has ever come near to equal-
ing the mountain tactics of Xenophon or Alexander. Mountains had no terrors for the Macedonian army.

It is perhaps difficult to give an adequate idea of the tremendous difficulties to be surmounted in this march from
Susa to Persepolis, which some of the ancient historians dismiss with a sentence. There is to-day a plentiful lack of information about this rarely visited region. From the lowlands where stood Susa, to the uplands of Persepolis five
thousand feet higher, Alexander had to cross a mountain
range as well as several large and rapid rivers. The Coprates
and Kuran or the Passitigris, the Heduphon, the Arosis, the
Araxes were among these, not to mention scores of good-sized
affluents. The ancient names of some of these rivers are
uncertain, but they stood in his path then as now. The mountain chain which separates Susiana from Persis was so high
and rugged as to make the march much like a passage of the
Alps. Perhaps no mountains with which we are familiar can
convey the idea of these snow-clad heights except the Alps,
no passes show the difficulties of the road he had to follow so
well. This is no figure of speech. It was winter, and while
on the plains a winter campaign might be preferable to one
under the midsummer sun, in these mountains even summer
scarcely mitigated the severities of the march.

It has been claimed by excellent authority that this mountain barrier is the worst which any army has ever crossed.
This is probably inexact. The passage of the Parapamisus
must have been more difficult. And no similar feat will ever

equal Hannibal's passage of the Alps. But it was none the less a wonderful undertaking. The mountain chain rises in eight or nine successive terraces and water-sheds, to an altitude of fourteen thousand feet. It is a labyrinth of rocks, precipices, torrents, valleys, passes. Through this snow-clad range ran the one usual road. The first serious obstacle to be encountered, not to speak of the enormous difficulties of the route, was the defile of the Uxii, the next that known as the Persian Gates. These latter could be avoided by a more southerly route, along the plain from modern Babahan by way of Kaizeroum to Shiraz, though, indeed, this also is described as " a bad rock-bound road up and down."

Among the most remarkable qualities of Alexander as a general was his ability to get hold of geography, topography, climate, and the other factors of the problem of each country he was about to invade. No doubt he had all the means of knowledge at hand, in the presence of numerous professional and scientific men, Greek and Persian, who crowded about his headquarters; but the knowledge he acquired was nevertheless wonderful. That he never forged ahead until he knew all that was to be ascertained about his route is abundantly demonstrated by the results of his marches.

On his way towards Persepolis, Alexander must first reduce the land of the mountain Uxians. He started early in December. He is said by some geographers to have made a détour to avoid the Coprates (Dizful), and to have crossed the Passitigris above modern Ahwaz. Others put his route *via* modern Dizful and Shuster. The fact is not material. The tribes of the plains, which had always been subject to the king of Persia, had at once tendered their submission on learning of the capture of Susa; but the mountaineers, who had not only held out against Persian conquests, but had actually compelled the payment of tribute by the Great King for a passage through their defiles, headed by Madates, sent word to Alexander that he could not march over their mountains into Persis, without paying the same tribute which the late monarch had been wont to pay.

These mountains are to-day equally full of brigands, as intractable now as then. Alexander received their ambassadors with courtesy, and sent them back with word to be at

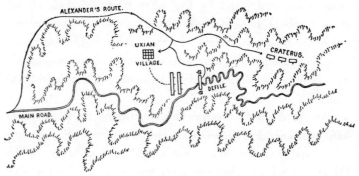

Uxian Campaign.

the entrance of their passes on a given day, when he would come with toll in his hand, and they should receive their just due. The Uxians naturally expected Alexander by the usual road, and he did in fact dispatch the bulk of the army that way. But having ascertained that there was another but very difficult road, he took his royal body-guards, the hypaspists, and eight thousand other troops, and marched at night with great toil, and led by native Susian guides, over mountain roads, to a position near by the Uxian villages.

The Uxians had built walls across the defile which they proposed to hold. The king dispatched Craterus by a circuit to occupy high ground to which the barbarians would be apt to retire if he could drive them from the wall. At daylight the next morning the king fell suddenly and unexpectedly upon these barbarians, destroyed their villages, and captured much booty. And having demoralized them, so that they were unprepared to act, he anticipated them by a forced march to the defile they had proposed to defend, reaching the place well ahead of any considerable body of the Uxians. When the Uxian warriors put in their appearance they found the defile occupied, and the Macedonians drawn up in order and ready to advance upon them. Utterly nonplussed by Alexander's celerity, and by the surrounding of their chosen position, the Uxians did not pretend to sustain themselves, but fled. Many were slain; many in their flight were thrust over the precipices; many sought refuge in the mountains, and were captured or killed by Craterus. Their defeat was total.

This is Arrian's account, who mentions no particularly hard fighting; but Quintus Curtius and some other authorities state that the Macedonians laid regular siege to the Uxian stronghold, while the light troops took it in the rear. There was such stanch defense that the siege threatened to be a failure. On one occasion, in fact, the shower of arrows and darts was so heavy that the troops were on the point of falling back, and had formed a tortoise, under the protection of which they were seeking to force even the king to fall to the rear. For a moment Alexander was helpless to control his men. He was reduced to shaming them into their usual vigor by recalling their past deeds. Stung by his vigorous reproaches, the phalangites recovered their courage. The ladders and engines were got into position, and Craterus now appearing in the rear of the barbarians, the works were eventually carried. Only the bald details of this interesting manœuvre are narrated by the old historians.

Alexander founded his course on the well-known habit of many barbarians to fight and prepare for action only by day.

They had by no means anticipated that Alexander would come upon them, over all but impassable mountain roads, by night. This very thing Alexander seized and acted on, — as he was wont to do; and by putting into execution the unexpected, he won with a handful in a few hours, and with slight loss, what all Persia had not been able to win in many generations and with unlimited forces. Alexander's capacity for doing the apt thing was always equaled by his utter contempt of difficulty, and both together gave to his efforts such uniform success.

The Uxians at once sued for peace. Alexander proposed to extirpate this tribe, but Sisygambis, the queen-mother, pleaded for them, and, after some hesitation, Alexander granted her prayer, and gave them permission to retain their territory by delivering as tribute one hundred horses, five hundred beeves, and thirty thousand sheep a year, — they being shepherds, and never having money or other treasure. The Uxian territory was added to the Susian satrapy.

Alexander.

(From a broken Cameo in the Louvre, thought to be by Pyrgoteles.)

XXIX.

THE PERSIAN GATES. DECEMBER, B. C. 331, TO MARCH, B. C. 330.

From the Uxian mountains Alexander sent Parmenio with the train and heavy troops towards Persis, by the road south of the range; with the lighter and picked troops he advanced through the mountains, where at the Persian Gates Ariobarzanes and forty thousand men now held the defile. Reaching the position, Alexander essayed to force it, hoping for the same success he had met with at the Cilician Gates. But he found the task impossible, and was driven back with much loss. He was at a standstill. The pass could not be carried. Yet he must not leave this force behind him in his advance on Persepolis; it could create a dangerous diversion in his rear. Luckily, among his prisoners, Alexander found a Lycian slave who had been shepherd here for many years. This man pointed out to Alexander paths by which he could turn the defile. Leaving Craterus behind to hold the attention of the Persians, Alexander set out along these paths with a picked force. His exertions were incredible, but they were rewarded with success; on the second night he reached Ariobarzanes' rear, and attacked him at daylight. Craterus joined in, and between them the position was carried. Alexander then moved towards the Araxes, which he had sent forward to bridge, and reached Persepolis in season to prevent the despoiling of its treasury. But in revenge for the burning of Athens, Alexander gave the city up to pillage, and set fire to the palace. Here he gave his men a four months' rest, but he himself spent the time in reducing the mountain tribes of Persis, and especially the Mardians to the south.

From the Uxian mountains Alexander advanced in two columns. He sent Parmenio by the road along the foot-hills to the south, with the baggage and siege train, the Thessalian cavalry, the Greek allies and mercenaries, and the heavier part of the phalanx, while he himself, with the lighter part, the Companion cavalry, the lancers and horse-bowmen, the Agrianians and archers, pushed on by forced marches over the nearer but more difficult mountain road. Having marched one hundred and thirteen miles, probably reckoned from near modern Babahan, which is at the outlet of the Uxian mountains, on the fifth day he reached the vicinity of the Persian or Susian Gates, also called the Susiad Rocks, or Pylæ Persicæ or Susæ. Alexander hoped to surprise the pass as he had once done the Cilician Gates; but the satrap of Persis, Ariobarzanes, had occupied, and had built a wall across this defile, which is now called Kal-eh-Sefid, and begins to narrow four miles east of modern Falhiyan, and held it with a force of forty thousand foot and seven hundred horse, all Persians and good, reliable troops. Kal-eh-Sefid means " white fortress," and is " a mountain of one piece of rock, inaccessible on all sides, and battlemented at the top like a castle." It is the key and entrance to the plateau of Iran, and all travelers agree as to the difficulty of its approach.

Alexander might have reached Persepolis by the longer but easier road over which he sent Parmenio, which skirted the range along the southern foot-hills, but he could not leave so dangerous a force in his rear. Ariobarzanes had an army in number equal to the total of his own, and might at once have marched on Susa so soon as he saw Persepolis wrested from his grasp. And while Susa was left abundantly garrisoned, and could probably take care of itself, the moral effect of such a diversion would have nullified much of Alexander's work already done. It was no part of Alexander's plan to pass by any well-posted armed force, unless he could completely neutralize it. The distance from Babahan to Shiraz, *via* Kal-eh-Sefid is reckoned by La Gravière at one hundred and seventy-three miles; *via* Kaizeroum at two hundred and thirty-eight miles.

Having gone into camp, Alexander reconnoitred the position, and next day made a determined effort to take the walls by direct assault. The description in Arrian reads somewhat as if the king had stumbled into a species of ambuscade. Even Alexander was not beyond committing an occasional blunder. He had before him no common antagonist, nor indeed an ordinary line of defense. The rapidity of his

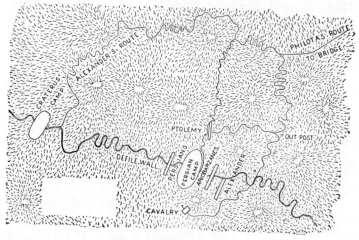

Operations at Persian Gates.

marches, which had so often snatched the prize of victory from the grasp of his unsuspecting enemies, was here of no avail. Ariobarzanes had fully anticipated him, and lay prepared at every point to dispute his passage, in the best chosen position, fortified by nature and by art as no obstacle Alexander had yet encountered had been. He allowed the Macedonians to march up the defile, which some modern travelers liken to the St. Gothard, without making the least demonstration. Barely three men could march abreast through this contracted path. When the head of column had reached the narrowest and most dangerous part, before it had got near the wall, while the Macedonians were marching between two perpendicular walls, suddenly they were startled by a bitter shower of sling-stones and arrows, by the shouts of the enemy and by heavy rocks being cast down upon them, in such a manner as to crush whole files of men. Against the ordinary missiles they could use their shields, but nothing could resist the immense boulders which the enemy rolled upon them — an enemy unseen and out of reach. It is asserted that Ariobarzanes had collected a number of missile-throwing engines at the wall ready for use if an assaulting party should reach so far.

Not to be easily discouraged, the Macedonians tried their best to scale these walls of granite. They helped each other up; they formed a tortoise; they pulled themselves up by the bushes; they clung to the rocks like flies. The men who later scaled the rock of Chorienes were among them. They essayed every avenue of approach; took advantage of every crevice. But all was of no avail. Alexander was compelled to sound the retreat, a rare thing with him. After the loss of many men — the casualties are not given, though Diodorus says a great number were killed and wounded — he returned to the camp at the mouth of the defile, some four miles from the wall — for the moment foiled. Napoleon, stopped by the Fort of Bard, comes strongly to mind, when we see Alexander for the moment reduced to helplessness at the foot of these unassailable defenses. But the Fort of Bard was a trifle compared to this. Here were defenses held by forty thousand men.

Alexander had captured some prisoners. From these at first he learned nothing; but finally a shepherd, who had been a slave, and for many years had fed flocks in these mountains, told him that by certain other, but unknown and difficult foot-paths, he could reach the farther end of the defile, or in other words, the rear of the position of Ariobarzanes. Alexander was always prolific of his gifts for services rendered. This guide was a native Lycian who had been sold into slavery, and while pasturing herds here had learned the lay of the land. Alexander well knew that a camel laden with gold was of no value compared to the life of one of his men; of less than want of immediate success; that rewards were of more effect here than many batteries of catapults. He promised this Lycian untold wealth if he led him aright, and gave him assurance of summary death if he betrayed him. In the event Alexander gave him thirty-three thousand dollars, — an enormous sum in those days. In his gifts Alexander always acted on the superb theory; " It is not what Parmenio should receive, but what Alexander should give " was his motive.

Alexander always undertook the most difficult work in person. Perhaps this was personally the most hazardous enterprise he ever carried through. He left Craterus with his own and Meleager's brigades, and some archers and cavalry in the camp in front of the wall, charging him to keep up the appearance of being still present in force by lighting many camp-fires at night, and by keeping up by day a series of minor demonstrations, so as to attract the enemy's attention and keep him on the alert, and finally to attack briskly when he should hear Alexander's trumpets call the charge from the farther side. Taking with himself his best troops, the shield-bearing guards, the taxes of Perdiccas, Amyntas and Cœnus, the lightest-armed archers, the Agrianians, the royal squadrons of Companions and four other cavalry ilēs — sure footed-horses they must have had indeed to scramble along these mountain cattle-paths over the December snows — he set out at night with three days' rations carried by the men. A distance of nearly a dozen miles was made with great speed considering the road. It was stormy, and the toil must have been great. But Alexander's physical endurance was abnormal, and he always managed to get wonderful feats of marching out of his men. He had made half the distance. The balance could probably have been made during the remainder of the long winter night, had not his path been cut by a deep and apparently impassable ravine which he had to wait till daylight to find a means of crossing. He then ascertained that it was readily got around.

He was now on the north slope of the range. Before him lay stretched out the plain, across which beyond the Araxes was Persepolis; behind him the range he must cross to reach Ariobarzanes' rear. He was in perilous case. His own army was cut up into small detachments, by the circumstances of the march and check; the barbarians were all in one body. Nothing but good fortune and a complete surprise of the enemy could save him from annihilation. The least failure, or what elsewhere would be but a small disaster, must prove utter ruin. But in this direction lay his only chance. Nothing except retreat or this was left. He might have held the mouth of the defile against Ariobarzanes with a small force; have returned down the mountain; have followed Parmenio, and thus taken the Persians in a trap. Or he could march on this side the range, direct to Persepolis, but only by bridging the Araxes. Time was precious. If Ariobarzanes should guess his intention, and either manœuvre was perhaps a matter of several days, he might speedily retire to Persepolis, which he could reach by the main road long before Alexander. And the thing the king most wanted was to reach this city before its treasury could be rifled, or its walls put into a state of defense. Moreover, either of these plans would necessitate the leaving the bodies of the men slain in front of the defile to lie without burial, a thing Alexander was loath to do.

With his usual grit he embraced the danger. He had marched all night in single file where there were no roads, over treacherous snow. The men strode on, hushed into silence by the unusual excitement and the great exertion. From where he stood led a path to Ariobarzanes' camp. He must avoid this road, for along it lay not only certain detection, but failure of his plan, for he would strike the enemy from a direction enabling him to escape.

It was now morning. From the point he had reached, with his usual foresight, a part of the detachment under Amyntas, Philotas, Cœnus, was sent forward, along the northern foothills, to the Araxes, with instructions to bridge the river. As this was a swift torrent with high and rocky banks, to bridge it rapidly argues no small engineering abilities at Alexander's command. The bridge was constructed from materials taken from adjoining villages demolished for the purpose. The king with the rest of his party waited again till night should cover his march, and then set forth, marching with rapidity, but circumspection. The exertion called for was extraordinary, but cheerfully borne. He reached the vicinity of the rear of the barbarians before daylight of this second night. His vanguard soon ran upon their outposts in the passes, and by very clever devices he successively surprised and captured two and dispersed a third. He reached the rear of the main camp unperceived. For the pickets had not only been cut off ; they had been so demoralized that they had fled into the mountains rather than towards the camp.

Ariobarzanes' camp was as usual long and narrow, and Alexander first reached a position near the left flank of it. The weather had as stated been stormy. Ariobarzanes' outposts had observed by day Craterus' detachment still in place, and had counted its watchfires by night. The Persians kept quietly to their camp, satisfied that the bold conqueror had at last met his match. They were expecting nothing less than attack, when suddenly the blare of many trumpets roused

them from their fancied security. So sudden was Alexander's
appearance on the scene, that Ariobarzanes had barely time
to range his army in two lines in front of his camp. Alexander drew up in parallel order, but reinforced his left with all
his cavalry, sending it around Ariobarzanes' right to turn it,
and, if possible, take possession of his camp, while Ariobarzanes was busy with Alexander's assault on his own front.
He had already sent Ptolemy with three thousand infantry
forward from his right, to the road above mentioned as leading to the Persian camp, to a position where he could make a
sudden onslaught on the camp while Ariobarzanes was being
kept engaged in front and on his right. There were thus
three attacks on Ariobarzanes' rear. However questionable
such a division of forces might be to-day, it was here not only
justifiable, but demanded by the circumstances. Alexander's
main force, or Ptolemy, could either of them hold head against
anything Ariobarzanes could probably bring forward, and
Alexander calculated especially on the demoralization these
several attacks would breed.

It was just dawn when Alexander's cavalry fell upon the
camp from the left, while Craterus, who had been holding his
men in readiness and happy indeed to hear the sound of the
king's bugles, assaulted the fortifications in the defile in its
front. The diversion of Alexander's cavalry enabled Ptolemy
to seize the camp by a *coup de main* with his three thousand
infantry. Craterus, the enemy in his front being weakened
by fear and by the sudden call of Ariobarzanes for more troops,
scaled the wall, drove the defenders back, and took the Persians at the camp in reverse. These operations were nearly
simultaneous — a rare and happy conjunction — and they were
followed by complete success. Thus attacked on all sides, and
utterly unprepared (for Ariobarzanes, even if he knew them,
had believed the mountain roads to be impassable), the enemy

was cut to pieces at close quarters; many in their escape
threw themselves headlong down the precipices. "A great
many fell on both sides," says Curtius. Ariobarzanes forced
his way through to the rear with a small body-guard, or, as
Curtius states, forty horse and five thousand foot, but found
himself cut off from Persepolis by Philotas, who had crossed
at the bridge.

Not waiting a moment for rest, lest the treasury of Persepolis should be plundered, as he had heard was the intention
in case of reverse, and leaving Craterus to follow, Alexander
marched with his Companions to the bridge, the completion
of which was due to his brilliant forethought, forty miles in
one night, over the snow, crossed the Araxes, and by hurrying ahead with these wonderful squadrons anticipated Ariobarzanes, who had escaped along the usual turnpike by way
of Shiraz, and reached Persepolis before any damage had been
done. For Tiridates had joined Philotas in preventing Ariobarzanes from pillage, hoping to earn Alexander's good will.
Ariobarzanes was slain in his efforts to resist. For this service Tiridates was made viceroy of Susa.

Here and at Passargadæ Alexander found over one hundred
and fifty million dollars of our money, plus other treasures in
fabulous amount. Nothing like it has been known except to
the Spaniards in America. The bulk of the treasure he deposited for the nonce at Susa. This wealth was later sent to
Ecbatana, whither it was said to have been conveyed by ten
thousand two-mule carts and five thousand camels.

As he approached Persis there came to meet him eight
hundred (Curtius says four thousand) mutilated Greek captives, — mutilation has always been common in the East as a
penal infliction, — who greatly excited his ire and sympathy.
These men he pensioned off by giving them lands with slaves
to cultivate them, in a colony by themselves. To each one he

presented a sum equal to six hundred dollars' weight in gold, ten complete changes of raiment, two yoke of oxen and fifty sheep.

Alexander was now in the home of Persia. Here in the valley of Passargadæ, Cyrus had overthrown the Median power, and in memory of his victory had established his court, erected his palaces, built his mausoleum. This was the place to which all vassals and dependents of the Great King looked as the home of the monarchy, as the Mecca of the kingdom. Cyrus and his successors had made this valley a wonder of beauty as it was by nature healthful. Palaces, temples, the king's gate of the "Forty Pillars," the rocky hillsides cut into terraces, huge sculptured oxen and horses at the entrances of the temples; the noblest and most colossal architecture on the grandest plan and most enormous scale adorned the entire valley of the Araxes and the Medus.

Alexander had penetrated to the very heart of the empire of the arch-enemy of Greece. The Persian king had burned and desecrated Athens. The hegemōn of Hellas could now inflict the same hardship on Persepolis. The two nations would be quits. Against his usual habit, which was to preserve and not to destroy what he conquered with so much toil and danger, and it may be alleged equally against policy, Alexander — perhaps unable to resist the demands of his Macedonians — not only gave the city up to plunder, but caused to be burned the magnificent palace of the Persian kings.

This act is stated by Diodorus, Curtius and Plutarch to have been the result of a drunken orgy, and done at the instigation of the Athenian courtesan Laïs, the mistress of Ptolemy. But the account of Arrian, coupled with what is said about the massacre by Plutarch, establishes the act as one of deliberate purpose committed in retaliation for the destruction of Athens and its sacred temples by the Persians. Parmenio strongly advised against the act for many excellent reasons. Not unlikely the burning of the palace may have occurred at the same time as the feast spoken of by Diodorus, Curtius and Plutarch. Such periods of revelry always and naturally succeeded the hard work of Alexander's successful campaigns. It is not agreed how much plundering and pillaging there was. As in all such cases the desolation was no doubt extensive and cruel beyond our modern conception, though it is said that the king gave orders to spare women and their jewels.

It is no doubt true that Alexander was beginning to show more markedly that intemperance which was his inheritance, personal and national. The Macedonians were always hard drinkers; his father — probably all his ancestors were such. This is not adduced to excuse or palliate the vice; it barely explains it. From this time on, the habit became more pronounced, and was more than once followed by lamentable consequences. But this must be borne in mind. Alexander at work was always Alexander. It was only when off duty, so to speak, and these periods were rare indeed, that temptation proved too strong. To insinuate, as has been done, that this monarch was a drunkard, in the usual acceptation of the term, is worse than absurd. It is puerile.

With reference to the pillage of Persepolis, it must be remembered that in Alexander's era war was not so near to being a mathematical calculation as it is to-day, when regiments and squadrons are mere masses of given value, but that the soldiers were assumed to need an occasional taste of blood. Unless there was a certain ferocity to the soldier of that age, he lacked in part the qualities most essential in battle. *Virtus* to-day means a very different thing from the *virtus* of Alexander's phalangites, who were wont not infre-

quently to demand in their acts, if not in words, the chance
to satiate their thirst for blood and other horrors.

The army had reached Persepolis late in the year, and
here Alexander quartered his troops four months in order to
escape the rigors and losses of a winter march in the mountainous regions of Persia. In this he exhibited his usual wisdom and the care he always lavished on his men. But he
himself, heedless of the pleasures of the gay capital, and
leaving Parmenio and Craterus in command, started in three
weeks, and made various excursions against the neighboring
tribes, so as to reduce the provinces of Persis to complete subjugation once for all.

The Mardians in the mountains to the south, between
Shiraz and the Persian Gulf, had, much like the Uxians, been
almost independ-
ent. These Mar-
dians were hun-
ters only, who had
never sowed a
seed. They dwelt
in caves. The men
and women did
equal work, and
both fought in bat-
tle. The women
were said to be the
fiercer. It was es-
sential to subdue
these tribes, in or-

Mardian Campaign.

der to secure the roads from Persis to the sea, which by and
by Alexander proposed to use.

To conduct a campaign at this midwinter season, in the
snow-clad hills held by these tribes, was very difficult and

exhausting; but with his usual sharp and skillful measures Alexander in thirty days subdued them. No man ever had such a record for fighting mountaineers.

Curtius states that the land of the Mardians was snow-covered and full of difficult and precipitous localities. The weather was misty, rainy and chilling. There were no roads, and the men felt that they had reached the end of the world, and that daylight would soon cease altogether. On one occasion, when the troops murmured at the toils of the way, the king dismounted and marched on foot, and his example was followed by all the horsemen. This act at once quelled the dissatisfaction. Difficulties of all kinds had to be overcome. A frozen slope which lay athwart the path was surmounted by cutting steps in the ice. Roads had to be hewn through the woods. But finally the Mardians were reached, and by mingled severity and generosity subdued; or, if not subdued, thoroughly quieted. The king had advanced to a point near Carmania, and its satrap, Aspastes, made haste to offer his submission. Alexander confirmed him in authority under himself, and then returned to Persis. Phrasaortes, son of Rheomithres, who nobly fell at Issus, was made satrap of Persis, and it is said that a force of three thousand men was left in garrison in the capital.

Alexander had now in four years (March, 334, to March, 330) conquered his way to the heart of the Persian empire, and reduced to possession all the territory between himself and Greece. He had accomplished the converse of the task which Xerxes had set himself a century and a half before; in lieu of incorporating Greece as a mere province into the great Persian empire, Alexander had stamped the intelligence of Greece upon the Eastern world. That more of this Western civilization did not last is largely due to Alexander's short life, which ended with his conquests, leaving him no years in which to consolidate his work and impress it with an element of permanency.

Additional treasure was found in Passargadæ, the original city founded by Cyrus, where also was his grave. Persepolis had later taken the place of Passargadæ in importance. There were two cities of the name. The Passargadæ in which Cyrus' remains were buried is now thought to be the one north of Persis, instead of east.

Alexander.

(From a Statue in the Capitoline Museum.)

XXX.

DARIUS. MARCH TO JULY, B. C. 330.

ALEXANDER followed Darius to Ecbatana, but the Great King retired to the Caspian Gates. At Ecbatana Alexander established his treasury, and deposited here some four hundred million dollars. This city was a central strategic point of great value, and Parmenio was left in command with a strong garrison. Darius still had money, weapons, officers, troops. He could at the Caspian Gates easily bar to Alexander the entrance to the eastern quarter of his kingdom. But there was treason in his camp. From Ecbatana Alexander headed his column and pushed on to Rhagæ, at the rate of twenty miles a day. Here he ascertained that Bessus and others had seized Darius, and held him prisoner, purposing to enjoy their several satrapies as kings. Taking the cavalry, and mounting a few phalangites, he pushed on ahead with but two days' provisions. Marching three nights and two days, with a rest of but a few hours, he came to a village where Bessus had camped the day before. He had exhausted men and horses. From here, selecting five hundred officers and men, — the best and strongest apart from rank, — he marched across a desert tract of fifty miles during the afternoon and night, and at daybreak came upon the enemy. Only sixty men had been able to keep up with him when he reached and charged in upon their thousands. But the very fact that he was Alexander saved him. The enemy dispersed. He had marched four hundred miles in eleven days. Alexander came too late. Darius had been murdered by the conspirators, and these had fled, each to his own satrapy.

DARIUS had fled to Ecbatana, in Media, five hundred miles from Persepolis, and remained there awaiting events. The exact position of this ancient city, where the kings of Persia were wont to spend part of the summer months (the spring was passed at Susa, and the rest of the year at Babylon), is disputed. It has been identified as Hamadan, and also as some fifty miles to the west of this place. Questions of topography constantly present the same difficulty. Its situation was at all events at the foot of Mount Orontes, six thousand feet above the sea level, in a lovely plain, where for eight months the climate was delightful. It had seven walls, each inner one higher than the next outside it, and each of a different color, the last two being covered with silver and gold plates. The citadel was a treasury, and the palace a marvel of beauty.

In Media Darius proposed to watch events, perhaps to fight again in case Alexander followed him up; perhaps to retire into Parthia and Hyrcania, or even as far as Bactria, laying waste the land, to prevent pursuit. He seemed intent only on personal safety. He had sent his baggage train, the women, and what treasures he had still preserved, to the Caspian Gates, a defile through the Elburz or Caspian Mountains, while he for months remained at Ecbatana, awaiting what Alexander might do. He had taken no military steps to meet his antagonist, but he had not been idle in other directions. By the present of three hundred talents he had induced the Lacedæmonians and Athenians to join in an attack on Macedonia.

Alexander now had all the treasure he needed to carry on the war to the confines of the known world, as well as to protect himself at home. He proposed to follow up Darius, wherever he might turn.

The Great King still had a kernel of strength about him, and possessed the ability to do much to defend the eastern quarter of his kingdom. Nabarzanes, general of the royal horse-guards, Atropates the Mede, Autophradates of Tarpuria, Phrataphernes, who controlled the satrapies of Hyrcania and Parthia, Satibarzanes of Aria, Barsaëntes, the ruler of Arachosia and Drangiana, Bessus, viceroy of Bactria and Darius' cousin, his brother Oxathres, and, most worthy of all, Artabazus, "the first nobleman of Persia," commander of the Greek mercenaries, with his sons, still surrounded him.

There were brave souls and wise heads enough were they but
controlled.   Here, too, he was joined by Ariobarzanes, from
the Persian Gates, who gave him what news there was, as to
what Alexander had been doing.   Nor was there any lack of
troops or weapons.   Curtius gives him thirty-seven thousand
men.   Nearly as well-appointed an army could still be collected at Ecbatana as Darius had yet commanded.   And the
Caspian Gates furnished a position which could be defended
against almost any force.   Here, perchance, he might finally
make peace with the Macedonians, and at least recover his
family and retain quiet enjoyment of his eastern possessions,
by yielding up the legal title to what he had already irretrievably lost.   Greece might still give such a turn to affairs as
to compel Alexander to make some such trade.   Or the Macedonian might tire of conquest.   Perhaps the unfortunate career of the Great King would yet flow into a more prosperous
channel.

Alexander left Persepolis, by a northerly route, about the
close of winter, 330 B. C.   The month in which he set out
is not certain.   He left the train to fol-
low, and marched, in hope and anticipation of battle, along the foothills
of the great moun-
tain barrier.   Alex-
ander was travers-
ing a country in
those days popu-
lous and peaceful.
To-day the land is

Persepolis to Ecbatana.

savage compared to its then condition.   But the geological

status was the same, and in places the population, which always more or less partakes of a geological flavor, was as wild as now. Heat and cold were then as fierce as now. The wet season lasts from November to February; the rest of the year is dry and parched. The people live in earth-covered huts, where they remain during the heat of the day.

In twelve days Alexander reached Media. Here he learned that the Lacedæmonians had been defeated and King Agis slain by Antipater, in the bloody battle of Megalopolis, and that the Cadusians and Scythians had therefore refused their aid to Darius. But he knew the Persian king to be still surrounded by many of his bravest nobles, and by an army by no means to be despised, one indeed which, ably led, might do better work than the numberless hordes of Arbela. So long as Darius lived, he must remain the centre-point for all the enemies of Alexander to rally on. And beside the Caspian Gates, there were plenty of positions readily susceptible of defense.

On his way from Persepolis to Ecbatana Alexander subdued the Parætacæ, a tribe living on the eastern water-shed of the mountains between Persis and Media, back to back with the Uxians. We have no details of the campaign. Like all his mountain work, bare mention is made of it. He left as viceroy Oxathres, son of Abulites, satrap of Susa, and hurried forward in pursuit of Darius.

Ecbatana was a central strategic point which Alexander was naturally glad to seize upon. It was situated upon the more direct line of commerce with Macedon, distant about three hundred and fifty miles from Babylon, by the valley of the Gyndes, and an equal distance from Susa, by the valley of the Choaspes. Alexander had hoped that Darius would stand, and had been marching with circumspection though rapidly; but three days from Ecbatana he was met by Bisthanes, son of King Ochus, who had left Darius to seek shelter with Alexander, and learned that the Great King was once more retiring to the east, with but three thousand cavalry and six thousand infantry. The Cadusians and Scythians had not joined him, afraid of the paling of his star, and desertions from his ranks were multiplying.

At Ecbatana Alexander discharged the Thessalian and Greek allied cavalry, whose term of enlistment was up, paying them in full, and presenting them with two thousand talents besides. In the distribution of bounty the best horsemen received a sum in gold equal in weight to eleven hundred dollars of our money; the least footman about four hundred dollars; and the others their due share. He made proper arrangements (Menes being charged with the details) for their transportation back by sea. The Thessalians appear to have owned their horses, and to have sold them before leaving the army. But many voluntarily reënlisted and remained. The bounty to these men, probably including the pay for the new term, was some thirty-three hundred dollars each. Out of these statements we are unable to construct any definite basis of compensation.

Alexander was now to operate in a different country, and against different enemies. He could no longer expect to combat in large masses, but needed lighter and more active troops. The Thessalian heavy cavalry was therefore more readily to be spared as a body than when he anticipated battles in the open field. Moreover, of the heavy armed only his Companion cavalry would be willing to stand the hardships of mountain and desert he now expected to encounter. Clitus, who had been left behind at Susa, sick, was to follow, and on the way pick up invalids who had become reëstablished, and rejoin Alexander in Parthia, bringing with him some six thousand men from Ecbatana. Alexander also, says Curtius, received reinforcements here of six thousand Greek mercenaries, under Plato of Athens. That this small body of men could march from the Hellespont through conquered Persia to Media shows how entirely the country had accepted its new yoke.

To Ecbatana Alexander now brought his treasures gathered in the camps and cities captured from Darius. The sum total of the precious metal brought hither by Alexander is variously stated at from two hundred to four hundred and fifty millions of dollars. It was guarded on the road by Parmenio, and was placed in vaults in charge of Harpalus. Six thousand Macedonians, some cavalry and light troops garrisoned Ecbatana.

From Ecbatana Alexander ordered Parmenio forward to Hyrcania, through Cadusia, with the Greek mercenaries, the reënlisted Thessalians, and all the cavalry except what was with the king, in order to bring that region into subjection. But later on Parmenio was ordered back to Ecbatana in command. He had grown gray in the service, and unfitted for severe exertions.

Though the army had just completed its march from Persepolis to Ecbatana, its labors were not interrupted. Alexander must keep upon his way. He at once called on the phalanx to follow him over the dry and arid plains of Parthia, under the July sun, and scale the mountains of Hyrcania. Never was army so hard worked.

In the Caspian regions the rainfall is excessive, and the country is hot and damp, feverish and most unhealthy. On the upper table-lands it is fiercely cold in winter, and very hot in summer, but being a dry, clear heat, not as unbearable as in India. Spring and autumn are the pleasant seasons. The mountains are snow-clad, ten to twenty thousand feet high, and on these intense cold prevails at all times. From Bushahr, on the Persian Gulf, to Teheran and the Caspian, you go through parching heat, sand and barrenness in the south, a temperate climate, pastures and cultivation in the centre, and severe cold, with bare and ice-covered mountains in the north. Even the best part of the country, which is lauded by the Persians for its climate, can be extremely hot, and is subject to drought and scarcity. The soil is good when irrigated, but two thirds of the table-land remains sterile from lack of water. The country may be well described as a desert, with numberless oases ; there are forests in the north and on the mountain slopes, but the table-lands are bare.

Having completed his work in Ecbatana, Alexander headed a column formed of the Companion cavalry, the light-armed and Greek mercenary cavalry of Erigyius, the phalanx except what was left in the garrison at Ecbatana, the archers and Agrianians, and set out on a forced march to overtake Darius. He proceeded with such speed that it exhausted many men and horses, but these were left behind, and in eleven days he reached Rhagæ, probably near the present Teheran, having averaged about twenty miles a day. This rate of speed under a midsummer sun in this country with heavy infantry is remarkably good.

He was now within one of his marches of the Caspian Gates. But Darius had already passed this defile towards Hyrcania on his way probably to Bactria. He had again neglected to bar the onward march of the Macedonians at this most available spot. So many deserters had straggled behind the Persian army that it had become more easy to ascertain its movements. Most of these made their way to their homes ; others surrendered to Alexander. All but despairing of catching up with Darius by mere pursuit, and his army being much exhausted, says Arrian, but not unlikely because he was far from certain of the direction taken by the

Persian king, as well as because his rapid march had depleted the commissariat, Alexander here gave his troops five days' rest. He made Oxodates, a man whom Darius had imprisoned for life in Susa, viceroy of Media in place of Atropates. In his case Alexander thought his treatment by Darius would vouch for his fidelity. He then marched to the Caspian Gates, thirty miles from Rhagæ, in one day, passed through the defile, a march of three hours' distance, and learning that the country

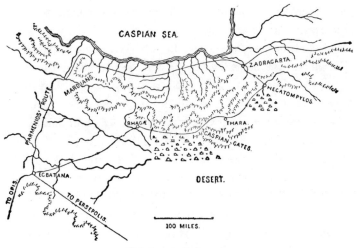

Ecbatana to Zadracarta.

beyond was nothing but a desert, he sent Cœnus out to forage, in order to collect rations for a further advance.

Darius began to fear that even flight could not rid him of his terrible pursuer. The farther he fled, the more his army dwindled from desertion. Might it not be wiser to turn and face the Macedonians, who were exhausted with the pursuit? He called a council of his nobles, it is said, and advised one more resort to arms. But his companions had not only lost courage and their faith in Darius, — there was treason in the camp. There occurred a stormy scene, in which his abdication was demanded, and Darius found that the ancient majesty no longer hedged the Great King's person. The dissension was, however, smoothed over. His nobles for the moment curbed themselves, and craved their lord's forgiveness. But the end of their fealty was near.

While pausing at the Caspian Gates, Alexander suddenly learned from Bagistanes, a Babylonian, and Antibelus, son of Mazæus, who came to him from Darius' camp, seeking amnesty, that a conspiracy headed by Bessus, Barsaëntes, and Nabarzanes had seized the person of Darius. In vain Artabazus and his sons, who controlled the Greek mercenaries — Patron was the immediate commander — had urged the king to place himself in their hands; for Artabazus had foreseen this treachery. The fidelity of mercenary troops is often remarkable. All Greek mercenaries had uniformly remained faithful to Darius. Like the Swiss guards of Louis XVI., these hired troops would have died to the last man in defending their master in his misfortune. But Darius, though suspicious of his nobles, and willing enough to put himself in Artabazus' hands, weakly delayed his action until the three conspirators seized him. This they did one night, bound him, as the fable goes, with golden chains, and placed him in a covered chariot, or, as Curtius says, in a cart covered with sordid skins, so that he might not be recognized. Upon his seizure, Darius' army melted away like snow under the midday sun; many chiefs dispersed with their troops to their respective homes; many more went over to Alexander with prayers for mercy. Artabazus and the Greek mercenaries retired north into the Tarpurian mountains.

This news spurred on Alexander to still greater speed. He formed a *corps d'élite* of the cavalry Companions, the horse-archers and lancers, and some phalangites selected for courage and endurance. These he mounted on the best horses, and started at once, following the flying conspirators as well as might be — not even waiting for Cœnus to bring in his rations. He had but two days' provisions for his own party. He left Craterus to come on behind at a lesser speed. He marched all night and till noon next day, rested till evening, and marched again till daybreak, when he reached the camp at Thara, from which Bagistanes had deserted. Here Alexander found Darius' interpreter, Melon, left behind sick, and from him first got the actual facts. These were to the effect that Bessus had the command of the flying army, and that Artabazus and the Greek mercenaries had remained faithful to Darius as long as they could, but that the king had preferred his native legions, and by these been finally betrayed. Bessus had been put in command by the Bactrian cavalry and the rest of the troops, for he was related to Darius, and this was moreover his vice-regal province. He knew the king's importance to Alexander, and his plan was to surrender Darius, if he should be overtaken, in exchange for quiet ruling over his own dominions as sovereign; if not, to seek to gain the sovereignty of Persia for himself. And in this the other conspirators had concurred on receiving the usual fair promises from Bessus.

Alexander pushed on with incredible speed. He marched all the succeeding night and until noon, and reached a village (perhaps modern Bakschabad) where the enemy had encamped the day before. It was with great exertion and much loss in men and horses that he had thus got within one day's march of Bessus. Here he heard that Bessus was doing his marching by night, and on careful inquiry the people showed him how, by taking a short cut across a desert tract, he could probably catch up with the Bactrian army, which had kept to the main road. Infantry could not cross this

waterless waste, nor indeed keep pace with Alexander's ever-
increasing speed.   Everything was exhausted except the
king's tremendous purpose.   This was inexorable.   Alexander selected five hundred of the best horses, mounted on
them five hundred of his best officers and men chosen irre-
spective of rank, but solely for their grit and bodily strength,
and armed as they were, despite the terrible heat, set out on
the indicated way.   Nicanor with the hypaspists and Attalus
with the Agrianians, who had come so far, were to follow on
the route taken by Bessus, with the utmost speed and in
light order; the rest of the column to keep on in the usual
manner but by forced marches.   Alexander started in the
afternoon, and with his abnormal energy put forty-seven miles
(four hundred stades) behind him during the night, and
before daybreak came upon the barbarians by surprise.   He
had marched one hundred and seventy-five miles in four days;
four hundred in eleven.

The king had hurried ahead of his small body of men
with such speed that he reached the enemy with but sixty
companions.   It was in the gray of the morning.   He waited
for nothing, but at the head of this mere handful he made
a sudden charge upon the thousands of the enemy, and as
they were in loose order, and many of them unarmed, happily dispersed them, killing the very few who turned to resist.
The mere sight of Alexander had paralyzed their arms.   But
all his exertions had proved of no avail, for, probably by
a preconcerted understanding, Nabarzanes and Barsaëntes,
those conspirators who had Darius in their immediate charge,
seeing that they could no longer prevent his capture, and as
he could be of no further use to them, purposing that he
should be of none to Alexander, transfixed him with their
spears and took to flight.   The place of this murder is supposed to have been near modern Damghan.   When Alex-

ander reached the carriage in which Darius had been conveyed, he found but a corpse, and upon this he threw his
purple mantle as a token of respect. This was probably in
July.

Alexander must have been grievously disappointed, after
his herculean efforts, at not taking Darius alive. By so doing, he would have made a much more easy conquest of the
eastern provinces, and it would have satisfied his inordinate
and naturally fast-growing vanity to have near his person in
some capacity — as Cyrus kept Crœsus — this last of the
Great Kings. Probably his remorseless pursuit of Bessus
from now on proceeded largely from his feeling of disappointment, though it was to punish him for the crime of regicide
that he ostensibly dealt. Alexander had no doubt succeeded
beyond expectation and beyond what he had a right to expect.
Yet he had deserved what he had got. His indefatigable pursuit was due to his own unrestrained, relentless will. It was
almost superhuman in its energy. Had he not himself borne
the heaviest load, it might well be laid up against him as
despotic and reckless cruelty to his men. As it was, he himself, as always, bore heat and thirst, hunger and toil, danger
and exhaustion best of all, and most cheerfully.

It was on this terrible march across the desert that some of
his men brought to the king some water in a helmet. When
about to drink, Alexander looked around, and saw the tired,
famished look of his companions. "Why should I drink,"
said he, "when you have nothing?" and returned the water
untasted. "Lead us where thou wilt," responded they, with
shouts of hearty affection; "we are no longer mortal, so long
as thou art king."

Perhaps it was better for Alexander that Darius was dead.
Alive, he might have been a constant rallying-point for mal-
contents. Now, Alexander had none of the blame, and might

reap the benefit, if any, of his violent death. By pitilessly
following up the murderers, he could appeal to the feelings
of the Persians. No other had a perfect right to the Persian
throne ; Alexander had possession of it ; and, except that he
lacked the legal title, was the most promising monarch Persia
had seen since Cyrus.

Alexander sent the body of Darius to Persepolis, — some
say to his mother Sisygambis, who was at Susa, — and gave it
most royal burial with all the pomp and circumstance usual
with Persian kings. He continued to treat his family with
the utmost distinction, for he felt honest commiseration for
the misfortunes of his brother king.

Darius, last of the Achæmenidæ, was of a character to
make a good king, but a poor soldier. He was personally
brave. Diodorus tells us that, under King Ochus, Darius
fought a Caducian champion in single combat, and killed him,
thus earning the name of " Bravest of the Persians." But
he lacked moral endurance and equipoise. He had brought
his fate on himself. His reign had been unfortunate. Coming to the throne in B. C. 336, he was soon involved in war
with Greece and Macedon, and his royal career opened almost
with the defeat at the Granicus. Darius was about fifty when
he died, — a fugitive among traitors, a king in chains.

Alexander appointed Amminaspes, a Parthian, who had
surrendered with Mazaces in Egypt, viceroy over the Parthians and Hyrcanians, and associated with him Tlepolemus,
a Companion, as general.

XXXI.

BESSUS. JULY TO FALL, B. C. 330.

THE murderers of Darius had retired, each to his own satrapy, to recruit, proposing to rendezvous in Bactria, there choose a king, and join in sustaining him. Bessus felt confident of being elected. Before following Bessus, Alexander crossed the Caspian range, and reduced the land of the Mardians and Hyrcanians. At the same time he captured the relics of Darius' Greek mercenaries. On the shores of the Caspian he determined, in the future, to create a fleet. Parmenio, from Ecbatana, had advanced along the north slope of the range to attack the Caspian tribes from the west, as Alexander did from the east. This territory subdued, and Sparta having been neutralized by its defeat at Megalopolis, Alexander could safely advance towards the Caucasus. He set out for Bactria. Having gone more than half way, he heard that Satibarzanes, left as satrap in Susia, had revolted. Alexander turned on him, and inflicted summary chastisement. This revolt showed the king that he must not cross the Caucasus until he had reduced all the territory north of the Gedrosian desert, and west of the Arachosian Mountains, to complete subjection, particularly as some of Darius' old officers held satrapies in these regions. He therefore headed south towards Drangiana instead of north towards Bactria, adding nearly one thousand miles to his task. Revenge on Bessus must wait.

IT had been understood by the conspirators who murdered Darius, that they should first disperse each to his satrapy, there raise forces, and finally join Bessus in Bactria, when they would elect a new Great King, and by their arms sustain him. No doubt Bessus, who was Darius' cousin and the most prominent among them, had good reason to feel that he would be the fortunate man. But no sooner separated than each of these conspirators began to distrust the others, and forget the common cause. Phrataphernes remained in Hyrcania, where Nabarzanes afterwards joined him. Satibarzanes fled to Aria, and Barsaëntes to Drangiana. This lack of unity was a happy circumstance for Alexander.

The army was exhausted, the divisions all strung out along the late line of march, at considerable intervals, in what, under other circumstances, might have been a highly dangerous condition. Indeed, had not Darius been in abject flight, the late pursuit would have been a foolhardy one. Alexander was absolutely incapacitated from continuing an immediate pursuit of the traitors. Indeed, he did not at the moment know their whereabouts. He concentrated and rested his army near Hecatompylus, north of which city the foothills of the Parachoathras or Caspian (modern Labuta or Elburz) mountains begin to rise. Thence he decided to invade Hyrcania. He not only desired to obtain a foothold on the Caspian Sea, but could not leave the restless tribes in and beyond the mountains upon his flank and rear as he advanced.

For the first time he here had some difficulty in inducing his men willingly to join in his project. They were tired of wandering, physically exhausted, and thought that by the death of Darius their work should be at an end, and that the homeward path should now be trod, or at least the road to Babylon. But the persuasiveness of Alexander was never overtaxed. By dint of appealing to their loyalty and affections, and by lavish promises for the future, well sustained by his generosity in the past, he overcame their scruples. Curtius says that the men were constantly in the habit of murmuring. To a certain extent this is true, and the more they did so, the higher it throws Alexander's ability into relief in the fact that he, as constantly, persuaded them to follow him and got from them such splendid efforts. His present object was not only to conquer Hyrcania, but also to find the Greek mercenaries, who had served under Darius, and punish them for fighting for pay against their compatriots. Moreover, he suspected that some of the Great King's fleeing nobles would have taken refuge in Hyrcania, and they, with the Greek troops as a nucleus, were too inflammable a matter to be passed by.

North of him lay the Caspian range, which divides Parthia from Hyrcania. On the south slope of the range dwelt the Tarpurians. The range was cut by comparatively few, but long and difficult, notches, and stood as a huge outpost to the Caspian Sea, with peaks of from twelve to twenty thousand feet above the level of the ocean. On the Caspian side, the multitude of mountain streams and the narrow stretch of land, often less than twenty miles in width, made the country all but one huge marsh. The forests were thick and easily defended; the vegetation was rank; it was parched in summer, overflowed in winter; the climate was that of the Pontine Marshes. In places, there were rich plains dotted with villages. But the roads were deep in mud, and a recent traveler found, in a journey of three hundred miles, no less than twenty rivers so large as to be rarely fordable. The Macedonians were remarkable soldiers. They passed from desert sands to mountain snows with equal unconcern, and their work on either was equally well done. Still more remarkable the leader, whose irrepressible energy and broad intelligence had made them what they were!

Leaving Bessus for further operations, — as of necessity he must, — Alexander advanced through the range in three columns, whose rendezvous was to be at Zadracarta, the capital of Hyrcania. He himself undertook the most difficult task along the route farthest to the west, with the largest column and the lightest troops. Craterus took a route farther to the east of him, and had his own and Amyntas' taxes, some six hundred archers and an equal force of cavalry. He was to attack the Tarpurians. Erigyius took the easier public thoroughfare to Zadracarta, with the Greek mercenaries and the rest of the cavalry, the baggage and the vast train of camp followers.

Alexander's advance had to be made with the utmost circumspection, for the barbarians beset every one of the many and intricate passes, and were ready to fall upon any unprotected part of this column; but what Alexander had early learned from Xenophon about doing this species of work, had since been supplemented by a goodly amount of individual experience. Having with his column crossed the first range of mountains, he learned that some of Darius' old officers were not far off. He pushed forward with the hypaspists, the lightest of the phalangites and some archers, over very hard roads, and in the midst of threatened attacks and

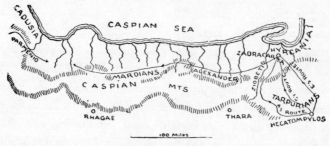

Caspian Campaign.

ambuscades. He was compelled to leave rear-guards at many points, to protect the passage of his column. Pity, indeed, that the details of his march have been lost! Reaching the river Ziobetis, which cannot now be identified, he camped four days, during which time many of these men came in and surrendered. Among them were Nabarzanes and Phrataphernes. The latter and his sons did subsequent excellent service for Alexander. Of Nabarzanes no further mention is made. He was probably relegated to obscurity. By the exercise of skill and care, Alexander drew in his rear-guards, and completed his passage of the mountains without material loss, though the Agrianians had a sharp rear-guard fight at the very close of the operations. He then advanced to Zadra-carta, the capital, where his other columns rejoined him. Craterus had subdued the country of the Tarpurians as he traversed it, partly by force, partly by capitulation. Erigyius had found little or no opposition. Here, too, came Artabazus with three of his nine sons, among them Ariobarzanes, whom we remember at the Persian Gates, and Autophradates, viceroy of Tarpuria, and handed in their allegiance. To Autophradates Alexander gave back his viceregal office.

No conqueror ever understood how to attach ancient enemies to his own cause better than Alexander. His treatment of the faithful old satraps and servants of Darius always made them his own stanch adherents. He understood that fidelity to Darius meant future fidelity to himself. This by no means clashed with his often rewarding what was actually treachery to Darius in those who surrendered strong places or treasures to him. Alexander had no hard and fast rules. He took men as he found them, and punished and rewarded according to the conditions governing the acts of each. He rarely made mistakes. Those occasions when we find him at fault merely serve to remind us that he was human.

Artabazus, whom Alexander had known in Pella as a refugee, with his brother-in-law Memnon, the Rhodian, and the sons of Artabazus, were rewarded by being kept on duty near Alexander's person. The Greek mercenaries, who were the survivors of those who fought at Issus and Arbela, begged for terms, but Alexander would accept nothing short of unconditional surrender, threatening them with summary vengeance if they did not at once come in. They were fifteen hundred in number, and when they gave themselves up were, after due censure for their misconduct, pardoned and drafted into his own service. The Lacedæmonian ambassadors to Darius, who were with them, he confined.

Alexander had clearly recognized the importance of Hyrcania as the future home of a Caspian fleet, and, as above
narrated, had ordered Parmenio to march from northern
Media by way of Cadusia, along the coast through Hyrcania,
and by that route join the army, so as further to reduce the
country to subjection and open a road north of the Caspian
range.

Alexander then turned back westerly from Zadracarta and
marched towards Parmenio and against the Mardians, a poor
but very warlike tribe, who were apt to interfere with this
scheme of a Caspian fleet, unless thoroughly subdued. He
took the shield-bearing guards, the archers, the Agrianians,
the brigades of Cœnus and Amyntas, half the Companion
cavalry, and a newly created body of horse darters ; leaving
the bulk of the army in camp at Zadracarta. Despite the
difficult nature of the country, which, as above described, was
without roads, heavily wooded, and affording no supplies (its
very poverty, and the fact that Alexander had already passed
beyond their territory, inducing the Mardians to believe
themselves free from attack), the king overran their land.

His route lay probably between the mountain range and
the marshy forest-covered coast-land, along the foothills.
The Caspian used to be higher in elevation than it now is.
How much this may have altered the topography of the coast
cannot be said, but its then descriptions are much like those
of modern travelers. Many of the Mardians fled back into
the mountain recesses of the interior. But even here they
were not safe. Alexander followed them up in the most systematic manner, sending detachments right and left, and
allowing them no manner of rest. Parmenio, at the farther
end of the Mardian land, gave the tribes no chance of exit.
They were caught between two armies of good mountain
fighters, and were thoroughly subdued. It is not stated

whether the king and Parmenio at any time joined hands on this campaign. Alexander found of much use in these operations, the above named troop of horse darters. They were equipped like the Parthian cavalry, and for a mountainous terrain were all but unapproachable in efficiency. The king was not above learning even from his enemies, and adopted a number of the Oriental methods, especially in the light cavalry.

Mardia was added to the satrapy of Autophradates, who had lately been continued in office as satrap of Tarpuria. Having thus made secure the whole mountain chain, Alexander returned to Zadracarta, where he celebrated games and held feasts for two weeks. Parmenio was sent back to Ecbatana in command.

As Alexander had learned when in Media, the anti-Macedonian turmoils of Greece had been settled for some time by the defeat of Agis, king of Sparta, and his death in the bloody battle of Megalopolis. The losses in this battle have already been referred to, and these, as well as modern losses, have often been compared to the moderate list of killed in Alexander's battles. These losses have been already discussed and their relation to modern casualties shown. But it must not be forgotten that losses in action are but one of the measures of a soldier's tenacity and value, and the measure of but one of the qualities of a captain. It is methods and results which guage a general, not the capacity to kill or stand killing. The most splendid triumphs of history are not the hecatombs. Would Arbela have been tactically any more superb a battle, if Alexander had lost thrice the number killed? Rather the reverse is true. To accomplish great results with the least expenditure of life is one of the very highest tests of ability. Nor is this incompatible with the courage to sacrifice troops to the last man, for an object worthy of the sacrifice and under conditions demanding it. It is altogether probable that Alexander would have won the battle of Megalopolis with but a fraction of the loss sustained by Antipater; it is all but certain that only Alexander would have won Arbela. That Alexander did not always encounter picked troops, by no means reduces his rank. He showed the same great qualities when he did encounter them. He matriculated in war by destroying the Theban Sacred Band, which no troops in Greece had been able to stand against. He never encountered Spartans, but he beat the Thebans who had vanquished these; and the very Persians whom, at Platæa, Pausanias had declined to meet till he was forced into battle, were Alexander's constant opponents in Asia. Nor must it be forgotten that the Parthians whom Alexander was at this time encountering were the same who defeated and destroyed Crassus' seven Roman legions. Shall we say that Grant's Virginia campaign was more splendid than Vicksburg because in the one he lost 60,000 men and in the other only 8,000? Comparisons such as these are of absolutely no value, for the reputation of a great captain rests on an entirely different basis. But such comparisons have been made and it is well to dissect them. Alexander never gave way in battle; he fought until he won. That his wonderful impetus and skill combined enabled him to win quickly and without the severe losses of other battles, is the very highest praise. Nobody can deduce from Alexander's history any conclusion except that he would, against the best troops ably led, have won any battle within the range of human skill and the endurance of soldiers to win.

Alexander had constantly run great risk by the machinations of Sparta. But he had been content to trust to good fortune, the ability of Antipater, and what treasure he could send him to prosecute the war. He was never for an instant deterred by any danger in his rear from pushing his schemes of Asiatic conquest. He always provided against such danger, as far as in him lay, and then moved on ahead. Many have called this blind recklessness, but it is rather close calculation and a spirit of bold hopefulness. Certainly no one ever became a great captain without the courage to face just such risks, and the ability to gauge their degree. But Alexander was now reassured by the defeat of Sparta, and relying on his communications being amply protected by the numerous garrisons along his victorious line of operations, he felt that he could press into the interior with less risk. He would have done so in any event; but no doubt he advanced with a feeling of greater satisfaction at the lessened cares behind him. Fortunate for him that there was in his rear no one who was able to cope with him, — in other words, that he was Alexander.

Alexander's route to Susia lay along the northern slopes of the Parachoathras. The population of these regions was considerable, and when the season was auspicious, the roads, except in the mountains themselves, were no doubt excellent. We can scarcely otherwise explain the ease and expedition with which the extensive baggage trains were moved at the exceptional rate of speed of the Macedonian army. An enormous amount of baggage had accumulated. The men had been allowed to load up the heavy train with all manner of loot; women had accompanied the army, probably in considerable numbers; useless luxuries of all kinds had grown to a bulk beyond reason. All this had by no means interfered with the capacity of the troops to march ahead in light order and live upon the country; but it had made the trains cumbrous to a degree. In his projected advance into an almost unknown territory, all this must be changed. Alexander gave the example. He burned his own baggage to satisfy the men of the necessity of doing the like, and the trains were summarily brought down to the old Macedonian standard.

It is said to have been here that the king first assumed Oriental attire, probably in part only. We shall see what this change of costume led to. It is not to be supposed that, as captain, Alexander ever wore anything but his Macedonian armor and cloak. His white plumes had too often led the van to be now discarded for the luxurious habiliments of the Median monarch. It was as sovereign alone that he was induced to adopt the manners and costume of the East.

Alexander had recently learned from some Persians who had come over to him, that Bessus had assumed the rank of king of Asia, adopted the royal robes and tiara, and had changed his name or title to Artaxerxes. Many of the Persians had escaped into Bactria, and the Bactrian divisions were with him. This last act roused Alexander to the utmost degree. He determined that the murderer of Darius should keep not even his own kingdom, and made ready to march against Bessus without further delay. For this purpose he put an end to the festivities at Zadracarta, in which he had perhaps been overindulging, and prepared for the march.

The king took under his personal command about twenty thousand foot and three thousand horse — consisting of hypaspists, phalanx, Macedonian cavalry, Agrianians and archers. With this force he set out by way of Aria for Bactriana, his immediate objective. Satibarzanes had tendered his submission in Susia (modern Tus); and though he was one of Darius' murderers, Alexander saw fit to continue him in charge of his satrapy, associating with him Anaxippus, a Companion, and sixty horse acontists, which he was ordered so to station as to prevent depredations by the Macedonian army in its march through Aria, as well as show a semblance of authority. This Alexander thought would suffice to neutralize

Satibarzanes for the moment, and save causes of complaint. Alexander hoped to reach Bactria before Bessus could be joined by any of his associates. For Bessus expected the aid of the Scythians, as well as had already many of the old

Route from the Caspian to the Caucasus.

adherents of Darius. At Susia, Nicanor, son of Parmenio, commander of the shield-bearing guards, died, much to the grief of the whole army. Alexander was unable to delay his advance; but he left Philotas behind with twenty-six hundred men to conduct the funeral rites with becoming splendor.

The plateau of Iran, as it stands to-day, has been described as "sterile plains, separated by equally sterile mountains," where the temperature ranges from 0° to 120° Fahrenheit. We know that the population was greater in Alexander's day than now, and no doubt the country afforded vastly more to a marching army. But heat and cold must still be borne, though rations may be plenty, and the sun burned as fiercely then as now.

When the column had made a considerable part of the march towards Bactriana, Alexander learned that Satibarzanes, through whose satrapy he had just passed, had massacred the guard under Anaxippus which had been left with him, as well as that officer, had declared for Bessus, whom he proposed to join, and had established himself in Artacoana (at or near modern Herat), where many confederates were joining him. Here was a grave danger. Alexander could not leave such treachery behind him, for Barsaëntes from Drangiana was very apt to cast in his lot with Satibarzanes. Much of his cavalry from Ecbatana, viz.: the Greek mercenaries, the reënlisted Thessalians, and the men of Andromachus, had now joined him under Philip, son of Menelaus. The king at once stopped midway in his march towards Bactria (he was pursuing a route thither much easier than the one he later trod), left Craterus in command of the bulk of the army, and taking the Companion cavalry, horse lancers, archers, Agrianians, and the taxes of Amyntas and Cœnus, he headed for the scene of hostilities. By one of his splendid forced marches of seventy-five miles (six hundred stades) in two days, he fell upon Artacoana like a hurricane. Satibarzanes managed to escape with a few Arian horsemen, but Alexander slew three thousand of his officers and men, and sold many others into slavery. He then proclaimed the Persian Arsames viceroy, and called in the command of Craterus.

From Artacoana northward there were several excellent gaps by which the army could cross the Caucasus into Bactriana. At this point the mountains do not reach the rugged altitude of the Parapamisus. But Alexander was imperatively called southward, instead, into Zarangeia or Drangiana (so named from Lake Zarangæ or the Arian lake) where Barsaëntes, another of the murderers, was satrap. This way he accordingly headed. Conscious of his guilt and treachery, and not waiting for the vengeance he had invoked but dreaded none the less, Barsaëntes fled towards the Indus, or into Gedrosia. But he was taken by some adherents of the conqueror, and returned to Alexander, who put him to death.

Admiral La Gravière figures that Alexander's column marched from Hecatompylos to a given point in Aria, a good deal over five hundred miles, in one hundred and ninety-eight hours, actual marching time. At ten hours a day, or twenty days, this would be at the rate of over twenty-five miles a day. Accurate or not, the figures are interesting, and it is certain that the Macedonians were extraordinary marchers.

It is probable that it was these untoward events in Alexander's march towards Bactria and his consequent countermarch to Aria which proved to him the necessity of caution, and determined him to put into practice the clean-cut strategy which preceded and succeeded Issus and Arbela, and fully to protect his rear before he proceeded on his way. Aria was of the highest importance. In it were the cross-roads between Iran, Turan and Ariana. Where the Ochus or Arius suddenly turns north, the great army roads, from Hyrcania and Parthia, from Margiana and Bactria, from Arachotia and India and the upper Cophen, meet and cross. At this point, about one hundred miles west of Artacoana, Alexander founded a city, Alexandria in Aria, and to-day among the people of this section dwells the remembrance of this wonderful king.

No doubt Alexander had made a study of the topography of this region, as far as it could be made, and had located as well as may be the roads and rivers, mountains and defiles, cities and peoples. He saw that he must positively not leave so great a section in a questionable attitude upon his flank. He therefore deferred his revenge upon Bessus for the moment, loath though he was to give him breathing spell in which to accumulate power and troops, and planned to make a southerly sweep so as to reduce to submission all the tribes north of the desert and west of the Arachotian ranges. This route implied an extra march of nearly a thousand miles. Then, and not till then, could he with safety advance over the great water-shed of the Parapamisus (Hindu-Koosh). In accordance with this plan, so soon as Craterus arrived, he advanced south to Prophthasia, meeting small opposition, except from the tedium and difficulties of the route.

It is on this march that Alexander is related to have encountered an inimical tribe, which, on being pursued, retired up the wooded slope of a mountain, the farther side of which was a sheer precipice. As he had little time to delay, and as the wind was blowing towards the mountain slope, Alexander contented himself with setting the woods on fire, and thus drove the barbarians over the precipitous cliffs. This is an illustration of his fertility of resource, if it is at the same time a demonstration of the cruelties of war.

Coin in the Bodleian Library, enlarged.

XXXII.

PHILOTAS. FALL, B. C. 330.

In Drangiana was discovered the so-called conspiracy of Philotas. There had been growing in the army a spirit of criticism which materially threatened its discipline. Philotas, among others, had been very outspoken. At this time a minor conspiracy, among obscure officials, to murder the king was discovered. Philotas knew of it and did not reveal it. He was tried by the Companions, and under torture confessed to what was treason, and implicated his father and others. True or not, he was found guilty and executed by the Companions. Parmenio, at Ecbatana, was also secretly executed. A number of others either fled, committed suicide, or were arrested and executed. Some were acquitted. The guilt of these so-called murders has been laid at Alexander's door. It is to-day difficult to decide the truth. But the effect was healthful to the discipline of the army, though Parmenio and Philotas were hardly to be spared.

It was in Prophthasia that Alexander discovered the so-called conspiracy of Philotas, son of Parmenio. This incident makes one of the saddest stories of his life. This was a matter intimately connected with the discipline of the army, and, as such, properly finds a place in our narrative. It should, perhaps, be mentioned that Alexander's plans, large and comprehensive beyond their grasp, were not generally understood by his Macedonians. Perhaps his *alter ego*, Hephæstion, was the only one to whom he unbosomed himself with perfect freedom. Some of the Macedonian generals, like Craterus, did their duty for duty's sake; others were very outspoken and hypercritical. This was a right they reserved to themselves. Freedom of speech, almost as we understand it, seems to have been indulged in as one of their political rights. But Alexander had gradually become less patient of such talk, as the talk doubtless grew in volume and openness. Perhaps the Eastern notions of royalty had already begun to take root in his mind, by nature and character and success so essentially imbued with the idea of one man power. Perhaps his Macedonians were suffering from the same ideas, and thought this people, which they had crushed in war, only fit to be further trodden under foot in peace ; and the fact that Alexander had begun to adopt in part the dress and ceremonial of the East, — if you like, largely from excessive vanity, but no doubt also for its excellent political effect on his Eastern subjects, who needed to see their new lord habited like their ancient ones, — had already given rise to much discussion and no little fault-finding among the simple Macedonians, and likely enough envy among those who wished to emulate the king's example, but could not. This fault-finding had not been decreased by Alexander's giving Orientals equally high places with Macedonians in the government of conquered provinces and near his own person, — though this, indeed, was altogether a political necessity, if he would keep what he had won, by satisfying instead of oppressing these peoples. The Macedonians, however, could not see why even the greatest among the peoples they had fairly conquered should now be set over them in authority. They felt that the least of the Hellenes was better than the greatest of the Persians ; it seemed to them as if the king were forgetting what he owed to them ; and they feared that he would end by treating them like the Asiatics.

The king had been often warned against an outbreak of this feeling, but had paid little heed to it. His mother, who always exercised great influence over him, had constantly protested against his reckless manner of trusting men against whom there was cause of suspicion, but without result. Still, Alexander must have been well aware of the existence of this disaffection, for the expression of it was open. He had been used to advice and criticism from Parmenio, from youth up; this was no novelty. But he felt that Philotas, though always brave in battle and constant in duty, had of late grown more and more antagonistic. Craterus, even, was not always like-minded with the king, though a pattern of what the soldier should be. Clitus was growing daily more estranged. In the war-councils these feelings had plainly come to the surface. All seemed to unite in desiring a cessation of conquest, a division of booty, a return home. Alexander stood alone with but Hephæstion by his side. So far the king had won his way with presents, without punishment. Now, largesses had lost their effect. Had the time come for other methods?

This spirit of criticism, if left to grow, tended to the destruction of discipline, with its thousand accompanying dangers. It is scarcely possible to imagine success in an undertaking of so gigantic and difficult a nature, so far from home, and against such vast odds as the one Alexander had in hand, unless the very essence of discipline could be maintained. It was evident that on the first outbreak of disaffection an example must be made. If Alexander failed to maintain an unquestioned authority, he was no longer king.

Parmenio was seventy years old. His youngest son, Hector, had been drowned in the Nile in the Egyptian expedition; the second son, Nicanor, who, as worthy chief of the hypaspists, had won the good will and admiration of all, had recently died. Philotas was the well-known leader of the Companion cavalry, distinctly the most brilliant command in the army. No family in Macedonia had earned the gratitude of the king in so high a degree.

The crime of Philotas appears to have been that he heard rumors of a certain conspiracy to murder Alexander, originating with some obscure members of the royal household, who were tired of the everlasting wanderings, and thought to relieve themselves by so bold an act; and that for two days, though constantly near the king, he neglected to speak of it. Unless there was some remarkable and easily stated excuse for this silence, it is very hard to explain. The plot came through other channels to Alexander's ears; the chief plotter, Dimnos, committed suicide at the moment of arrest. On being taxed with knowledge of the plot by the king, Philotas stated that he had considered it of so little import that it had made no impression upon him. This excuse Alexander apparently accepted, no doubt to be the more secure of arresting all the conspirators. Philotas was bidden as usual to supper. At midnight the king called together his most trusted officers, — Hephæstion, Craterus, Cœnus, Erigyius, Perdiccas, Leonatus, — and sent them out with suitable guards to arrest those to whom suspicion pointed — Philotas, chief of all.

Philotas had, in common with many other Macedonians, spoken in public with more or less acerbity of Alexander's growing Orientalism and vanity, and had also very naturally vaunted the services of his father and brothers and self, ascribing to his family in great measure Alexander's abnormal successes. More especially had he talked in this fashion to his mistress, whom Alexander, it is said, had suborned to reveal to him what Philotas had said in private. This espionage had been going on for over a year, and Philotas' doom was probably sealed long before the incident which was its immediate and alleged cause. Philotas was not without faults. He was overbearing as an officer, and is said to have been disliked by his men. He was no doubt open to criticism, if not censure, in many ways. But the fidelity to Alexander of the entire family had always been unquestioned till of late.

Next day a formal council of the generals was called, the king detailed the facts, and at once turned the matter over to the Companions for judgment, himself appearing as accuser.

To be so tried was probably Philotas' right, and appears to be a species of trial by his peers. But possibly the Companions inclined towards Alexander's behest in their action. They may have feared the king. They may have recognized that without discipline the whole army might be lost, — and discipline often means hardship, sometimes injustice to the individual. On the trial there was much testimony as to the conspiracy; according to many accounts, Alexander behaved without haste or prejudice; according to Plutarch, Curtius, Diodorus and Justin, Philotas was tortured to compel him to reveal who were his associates. Torture was a usual procedure, and need not be laid to Alexander's charge. It is alleged by some, one cannot but hope without truth, that Alexander witnessed this torture from behind a screen, and taunted the sufferer with cowardice. Brave though he was, Philotas succumbed under the ordeal, as many great souls have done, and perhaps untruly, and because he was tortured beyond endurance and the idea was then suggested to him, — implicated his father, and described a plot long subsisting, if not to assassinate the king, at least to take advantage of any accident to him to seize the reins of power. The confession was read to the army, which by a loud shout, immediate and unanimous, voted death to Philotas and Parmenio. Hereupon and at once, Philotas and all his confessed accomplices present with the army were put to death by the Companions with their javelins. Alexander sent an urgent messenger, Polydamus, to the generals commanding at Ecbatana, Cleander, Sitalces and Menidas, ordering that Parmenio suffer the same fate. Polydamus rode eight hundred and sixty miles in eleven days on camels, and reached Ecbatana long before the news of the trial.

Parmenio had written to his sons: "Care first for yourselves, then for your dear ones, thus we shall reach the end

we aim at,"—words of doubtful import. Alexander was
either convinced that the father must have been aware of the
son's plans, or deemed that Parmenio would be dangerous
after Philotas' death, his influence being great. He was at
the head of a large detachment — seven thousand men — and
in possession of the treasures at Ecbatana. On either hypothesis he must be put aside. The order was executed, as it
were, by assassination, and the worthy old man fell, one must
hope unaware that the dagger was directed by the hand of
the young king, to whom and to whose father his life's work
had been given, and for whom his life had been so often
risked. Perhaps it was impossible to successfully act above-
board, but the details of this Asiatic method of inflicting
death are too sad to relate. Despite all Alexander's care, it
is said that the suppression of this conspiracy in this bloody
manner was not accomplished without grave danger of mutiny,
for the army to a man was devoted to Parmenio, and the king
himself had always shown him the greatest respect and affection. Quintus Curtius ends his long account of the trial of
Philotas thus: "It is certain that the king here ran a great
risk both as to his safety and his life; for Parmenio and Philotas were so powerful and so well beloved, that unless it appeared plain they were guilty they could never have been
condemned without the indignation of the whole army. For
while Philotas denied the fact, he was looked upon to be very
cruelly handled; but after his confession, there was not any,
even of his friends, who pitied him." This, like much in Curtius, can be construed both ways, but inclines towards the
exculpation of Alexander.

Amyntas, son of Andromenes, commander of one of the
infantry brigades, and his three brothers (Polemo, a Companion, and Attalus and Simmias, brigade commanders), were
likewise accused of being associated with the matter. They

had been on very intimate terms with Philotas. Polemo fled to the enemy. The others, on trial before the Macedonians, bravely defended themselves, and were acquitted. Polemo was induced to return. It would seem that this acquittal of Amyntas by the same judges who condemned Philotas runs in Alexander's favor. Shortly after, Amyntas was killed in action. The other brothers remained in honorable service, and were entirely trusted by the king. Demetrius was also discharged from his post as confidential body-guard, on suspicion of being accessory to the fact; and Ptolemy, son of Lagus, was put in his place. Hephæstion and Clitus were made commanders of the Companion cavalry, hitherto under Philotas, which was divided into two regiments for this purpose. The king deemed it wise not to intrust his cavalry *d'élite* to a single man — even Hephæstion. It was subsequently reorganized. A separate squadron was formed of the sympathizers with Parmenio, and this squadron later greatly distinguished itself.

The murder of Parmenio, the brutality to Batis at Gaza, the treatment of Bessus and the murder of Clitus to be hereafter mentioned, are indeed black pages in the life of Alexander, though it may be more fair to characterize all these things as rather unhappy than guilty incidents. It must be remembered that Alexander dared run no risk, either personally or for the army, and that it was his peers and not his king who had found Philotas guilty, who pronounced judgment and conducted the execution. Some historians have doubted the existence of any conspiracy whatsoever, and have ascribed to Alexander's blood-thirstiness the whole disastrous drama; but a number of supposed conspirators either resorted to flight or self-destruction, which fact, so far as it goes, affords ground for believing the conspiracy to have been real, and not wanting in importance.

Perhaps no monarch has so much that is great and good to his credit, without being charged with more of evil, than Alexander. It is quite possible, by judicious extracts from all the ancient authorities, to prove Alexander a monster. It is equally possible to prove him superhuman in his virtues. He was neither. He had glaring vices, especially overweening vanity and often uncontrolled rashness of temper. But he had noble virtues as well, and a just estimate of all that is said of him by all the old historians, barring none, exhibits a personal character equal perhaps to any other man in history who enacted so eminent a rôle. But whatever the truth or the motives, that Parmenio and Philotas were grievous losses to the army, remains indisputable.

The Macedonians also demanded at this time the execution of the Lyncestian Alexander, whom the king had formerly shielded from death in Asia Minor, and who had since then been under arrest. This was carried out. Their zeal now outran their ancient spirit of antagonism. The king's danger had revived all their old enthusiasm for his person. The incident, terrible in its details, and much to be regretted, had none the less purified the atmosphere of discipline. The army was all the better for it.

Alexander.

(From a Medal struck at Apollonia.)

XXXIII.

THE CAUCASUS. FALL, B. C. 330, TO MAY, B. C. 329.

HAVING turned south, Alexander made a circuit through the land of the Ariaspians and Drangians, and the outskirts of Gedrosia, and then passed north through Arachotia towards the Caucasus. All the peoples on this route he reduced to subjection and tribute, — detaching forces right and left to thoroughly overawe the population, and garrisoning the towns. He again made some changes in organization to get his army into lighter order, for from now on he had small war rather than pitched battles to anticipate. Bessus lay behind the mountain barrier of the Parapamisus (modern Hindu-Koosh), feeling safe in the protection of its mighty summits. From Aria, Alexander could have crossed by an easy pass; from the Cophen region, to which his long circuit had brought him, he had before him passes higher and more difficult than any in the Alps. He started so soon as winter was fairly over, and, after incredible suffering and great loss, in fifteen days reached the farther side. Bessus fled from before him. Bactria and Sogdiana were the seat of an ancient civilization, with plenty of resources; but when Bessus abandoned Bactria, the whole country surrendered to Alexander, who thence crossed the Oxus, and marched on Sogdiana. Bessus' confederates then surrendered this prince in hope of pardon. He was later executed. Alexander marched to Maracanda.

ALEXANDER now marched (very likely through the valley of the modern Adoreskan River) into the land of the Ariaspians, a nation of horse breeders, who had afforded much assistance to Cyrus in his invasion of Scythia. He had a number of rivers to cross in his path, but the army had grown expert in such work, and there is infrequent mention of these, unless very large. They were taken as a matter of course. He found the Ariaspians an agricultural people dwelling in a fertile oasis surrounded by mountains or deserts. They were independent and self-governing on a model not unlike the Greeks. The king treated them with especial favor and honor, and accorded to them additional territory, which they had long desired, but were unwilling to go to war to obtain. He left them without viceroy or garrison, relying solely on their good-will and character for fidelity. Having dwelt with them two months, he turned northeast and marched towards Bactria, reducing the rest of the Drangians, and some northerly tribes of the Gedrosians on the way. Gedrosia was the farthest province of Persia on the southeast. It is now part of Beloochistan. Here, four years later, on his homeward march, Alexander lost the greater part of his army crossing the desert.

The Arachotians also submitted without constraint. Their territory ran as far as the water-shed of the mountain range which separated Persia from India. Menon was given a force of four thousand foot and six hundred horse, and made viceroy over the Arachotians. Alexander here founded another city of his name (modern Kandasar), to hold head against possible irruptions across the mountains from India, over which there were several passes debouching near this point. He then continued his march onward towards the river Cophen, and the land inhabited by the Indian tribes known as the Parapamisians, who dwelt at the foot of the Indian Caucasus. On this march across the range from Arachotia, the weather was severe — it was November — and the army suffered much privation in toiling through the snow, especially as they were short of breadstuffs. But the tribes were friendly, and afforded help in lieu of hindrance. They had food in abundance for themselves, but the inroad of an army taxed them beyond their ability to supply.

Alexander now learned that the Arians had again revolted, induced thereto by Satibarzanes, who, at the time of Alexander's return to Artacoana, had fled to Bessus, and had received from him a force of two thousand cavalry, with

which Bessus hoped that Satibarzanes would create a sufficient diversion on Alexander's rear to keep him out of Bactria. The king dispatched against them the Persian Artabazus, with the Greek mercenaries, including those who had
served under Darius, some six thousand all told, accompanied
by Erigyius and Caranus, with six hundred Greek allied
horse; ordering Phrataphernes, the viceroy of the Parthians,
to afford them all aid within his power. Parmenio's veterans,
some eleven thousand men, had now joined the army, leaving
Cleander, with the new levies from Greece, in Ecbatana.
This reinforcement enabled Alexander the more easily to
make the necessary detachment. The officers mentioned,
basing on Prophthasia, did their work with energy and skill.
In an obstinately contested battle, Satibarzanes was killed,
and his forces dispersed. This task completed, Artabazus,
Erigyius and Caranus rejoined the army.

Alexander was now in the valley of the Cophen (modern
Cabul) River. This valley, near Nicea (modern Cabul), is
some six thousand three hundred feet above the sea. To the
north of him lay the Parapamisus. There are now, and were
probably then, among others, three principal passes through
the range, leading to the Oxus valley beyond, — up the affluents of the Cophen, and down those of the Oxus. The northeast road leads to Inderaub (ancient Drapsaca) up the Pandshir Valley and over the Khawak Pass, thirteen thousand two
hundred feet in altitude. The west road runs up the Kushan
Valley and over the Hindu-Koosh Pass to Ghori. This was
the one by which Alexander returned. The southwest road
goes up the Ghorband Valley over the Hajiyak Pass to Ba-
mian, by a road over three hundred miles from Cabul. Alexander camped nearest the easterly passes, which are by far
the most difficult ones. He recognized that Bessus would
probably expect him by the easier route, and make prepara-

tions to defend its defiles. By the most difficult one he could scarcely travel at this early winter season, certainly not take his horses with him. He was forced to wait.

During this interval Alexander founded a new city — Alexandria ad Caucasum — near modern Beghram, some twenty-five miles northwest of Cabul. He chose the site with his

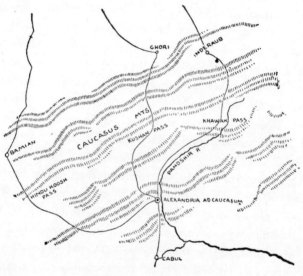

Routes over Caucasus.

usual discretion, at the point where the three roads branch off to the different passes to Bactriana. The city was built to keep his troops busy till the winter season had so far passed that he might cross, and to enable him to hold the pass he proposed to use. For the inimical tribes he was about to encounter might as easily cut off his retreat in case of disaster as now impede his advance. Alexander recognized, also, that beyond this range he was going into a real *terra incognita*, where varied and great and unknown perils certainly awaited him, and he took his measures accordingly. Here in his new post were left the Persian Proëxes, as viceroy, and Neiloxenus, a Companion, as his military associate.

By the experience of his late campaigns Alexander had learned that the fighting he would now be called upon to do would need much greater mobility in his troops than they had hitherto possessed. There was no more organized opposition to his sway on a large scale. There would be in the future no pitched battles to fight. What he would now have to encounter would be isolated bodies, such as that under Bessus, and much small war, demanding rapid marching and restless pursuit. He needed an army consisting of smaller units; he must have a greater percentage of light troops; he must utilize Oriental recruits in filling gaps, for sheer want of Macedonian reinforcements. For these reasons he was induced again to make sundry changes, partly, too, for that he had lost many of his old and trusted officers and must advance the younger to more responsible commands. From 329 B. C. dates the promotion of young lieutenants, and from now on his work was done with these.

Each of the eight ilēs of horse Companions had been already divided into two companies; and eight companies were now made into a hipparchy. Thus he had two hipparchies or regiments of eight companies each, instead of but one of eight ilēs. As before stated, Clitus was put in command of one; Hephæstion of the other. Later, again, when the army grew much larger, the Companion cavalry appears to have been extended to eight hipparchies, of say eight hundred men each. In the Indian campaign five hipparchs are named, — Hephæstion, Perdiccas, Demetrius, Clitus, Craterus and Cœnus with the agema.

The mercenary cavalry, which in 331 B. C. had reached Alexander four hundred strong under Menidas, was likewise increased to a hipparchy by additional recruits; it is not said

Oriental recruits, but that they were such is altogether probable; and a corps of mounted archers was organized. Important changes in the foot were made after the arrival of heavy
reinforcements to the army in Bactria. Alexander recruited
altogether a considerable amount of cavalry, — the Oriental
soldier being, as a rule, better suited to this arm of the service than to infantry duty. The army was beginning to
assume that new character which Alexander had always designed to give to his vast kingdom. It had consisted alone of
Macedonians, Greeks and European barbarians. He now incorporated in it Orientals to a high percentage, and began to
subject them to Greek training and habits. For war, Macedonian discipline was alone available.

In Alexander's army stood side by side both the civil and
military administrations. We look with astonishment upon
what this army did, and imagine that it could not have performed its extraordinary work, except by being divested of
every superfluity, and brought down to the scant proportions
of a mere fighting machine. And yet, with this army marched
the Court, with all its ceremonial and trappings, the directory
of the home and Persian governments, the treasury officials
and other civil functionaries, as well as the ordnance equip-
ments with their special officers, the engineers, the quarter-
master and commissary departments and the hospital corps.
These latter alone, with the changes of climate as the army
passed over its extraordinary course, from the tropical heat of
the desert plains to the arctic snows of the highest mountains,
must have called for endless labor. Tradesmen and sutlers
accompanied the army, speculators, men of science, litterateurs,
philosophers, many guests of the Court, priests and augurs, and
surely a great number of women. It was a moving capital.
All the more wonder that the king could control this vast cara-
van, and from it choose, at a moment's notice, a force which

could execute the wonderful marches and fight the splendid battles of which history gives us the details. How any one can look upon the man who could hold in his single hand such a huge aggregation of conflicting elements and make them useful, as a mere military adventurer, passes comprehension. Those who knew him in his own era and called him a demi-god came far more near the truth.

Alexander had now subdued all the tribes south of the Parapamisus, thus fully protecting his rear, and could safely cross the range to attack Bessus, whose main protection lay in this all but impassable mountain chain. He had received the bulk of the troops lately under Parmenio, which were largely replaced by reinforcements from the rear, and in addition some phalangites from Greece; and he had ordered thirty thousand selected Persian youths to be trained to fight Macedonian fashion, some of whom it is said he had already with him.

Bessus was the head-centre of all opposition. He had about him many of the fugitive chiefs from Darius' army, some relics of the Arbela infantry, about seven thousand cavalry from Bactria and Sogdiana, and several thousand Daäns; and had added to the difficulties which Alexander must encounter in the way of mountains and snow and lack of provisions all that he could by ravaging the land for several days' march on the north slope of the mountains. As already stated, he had sent Satibarzanes with two thousand cavalry to Aria, but with poor results. He had dispatched Barzanes to Parthia to foster insurrection in that province, but he was not yet heard from. He now collected his own forces, and for a while remained in Zariaspa. He hoped that Alexander might invade India rather than Bactria, or at all events fight shy of the terrible passage of the Caucasus. This would give him an opportunity of rising and operating in Alexander's rear.

The newly subdued countries could, he thought, be easily raised in rebellion. As a temporary expedient he sent out a number of small expeditions against Alexander's advance. Oxyartes of Bactria, Dataphernes, chief of the Daäns, Spitamenes of Sogdiana, and Catanes of Parætacenæ were in his company.

It is probable that Alexander's inquiring mind had possessed itself of all the information of the geographers of that day; was well aware of the extent and height of the mountain chain he was about to cross, and of the difficulties to be encountered in its passage; and that he knew something of the countries beyond the range. For the pursuit of knowledge, the love of adventure and the calls of trade had before his day carried an occasional Greek to distant points in India and Persia. He was intent on reëstablishing for his own benefit the ancient trade possessed by Phœnicia, which his own wars had tended to check. Silk, furs, iron and other merchandise had long been brought from here to the Mediterranean. There is clear evidence in the rapidity and certainty of his marches that his periods of inactivity were spent, not altogether in feasts and follies, as his severer critics would have it, but in studying up the countries he proposed to traverse. Moreover, he kept beside him, not only the philosophers, litterateurs and artists, but the engineers and scientists most celebrated in the world. No doubt he added to these the most available and best of native talent. And as Alexander was an enthusiast on the question of the fusion of races, he undoubtedly gave much time to the study of national as well as topographical characteristics. There is no disposition to deny Alexander's occasional, perhaps frequent overindulgence in the national vice of Macedon, any more than to veil some other of his failings, such as his inordinate vanity and greed of adulation. But altogether too much stress has been laid on these. So much attention has been called to Alexander's vices that the true perspective of his portrait is in danger of being lost. He had vices, but they became prominent only at intervals; his life was, with rare exceptions, one prolonged period of toil and danger. Perhaps no great man has ever had less of the mean or evil in proportion to the great and good than Alexander; and in sketching his character, it is certainly safer to draw our colors from the materials of the ancient authorities, rather than from the speculations of the modern critic.

Alexander started as soon as the severest weather was over, and before the snow was fairly off the ground. It was many weeks earlier than he should have started, but he could no longer constrain himself to wait. The army marched, with great suffering from cold, hunger and exertion, up the Pandshir Valley, and climbed to the height of the pass at modern Khawak. This is four thousand feet higher than the Stelvio, which is the highest pass in the Alps, and is within two thousand feet as high as the summit of Mont Blanc. Many soldiers had no force to follow the army, says Diodorus, and were abandoned on the way; some lost their sight from the effect of the sunlight on the snow. The villagers along the route were friendly, but had no provisions. A few cattle were their only wealth. Finally the column began the descent.

The ancient historians dismiss this remarkable march with a few words; but it has no parallel, except Hannibal's crossing the Alps, and it is the first undertaking of the kind of which we have any record. Hannibal, from unexpected delays, started too late in the fall; Alexander, from overeagerness, started too early in the spring. Both contended with heavy snows, and suffered from all their attendant trials.

The villagers had consumed or concealed all their winter

supplies, mainly wheat, but scant at best; there was no wood for camp-fires. The rocky mountains were covered solely with a scrub growth of turpentine bushes. The only obtainable food consisted of a few roots, an occasional fish, and the beef cattle of the trains, which latter were eaten raw or seasoned with silphium (asafœtida), growing here in abundance. The farther down the mountain the column got, following an affluent of the Oxus, the worse off the men were, for they ran into the devastated region, where all the houses had been burned and the flocks driven away. On the south side, which they had ascended, the snow-line was but ten to twelve miles below the summit; on the north side the march was nearly forty miles through deep and treacherous snow-banks. And we must not imagine that the roads approached the magnificence we see in the great military turnpikes of the Alps. Over the snow there were practically no roads.

On the fifteenth day, after incredible suffering, the army reached the first Bactrian town, Drapsaca (modern Inderaub). Here the men were given a rest. We do not learn the loss in this terrible march. That the horses largely perished is stated. We are left to conjecture the loss in men. The more awful march through the Gedrosian desert, which the bulk of the army never lived to cross, has no losses given. Only those killed in battle were wont to be honored by mention, few indeed compared to the men who perished in exposures such as these. The route from Susia, before Alexander turned south to Drangiana, would have been in comparison easy. And this, as we have seen, was his first-chosen path; but the dangers from the southerly provinces forestalled his intention, and having reached the Caucasus at a point so far to the east, he had practically no choice but between passes in this part of the chain, and had selected this one for the reasons given.

Bactria and Sogdiana were the seat of an ancient and well-developed civilization, and had since their conquest been the eastern bulwark of Persia.   Never entirely reduced to possession by the Great King, they had none the less joined his standard, while retaining their own liberties ; and, in the last

Bactria and Sogdiana.

campaigns, Bessus had been rather a confederate than a subordinate of Darius.   That Bessus had brought the Scythian Sacæ to Arbela as "allies of the Great King" looked as if Alexander might have to encounter these wild peoples as well.

From Drapsaca, Alexander rapidly advanced over the passes in the lower ranges without opposition to Aornus, and thence over the fruit-bearing plains towards Bactra or Zariaspa. Bessus, who had believed himself well secured from invasion by the mountains and the devastated land on their northern slopes, awoke suddenly to his danger. On the first sign of Alexander's appearance he retired behind the Oxus (Jihoun or Amou), burned all the boats he used in crossing, and took refuge in Nautaca, in Sogdiana. When his Bactrian cavalry saw that he would not stay to defend his own satrapy, it dispersed, every man to his home. But the Sogdianians and Daäns still remained with him.

Reaching Zariaspa, Alexander took it at the first assault. Artabazus and Erigyius having returned from the Arian expedition, the king appointed the former viceroy over Bactria, and placed Archelaüs, a Companion, in command of a suitable garrison at Aornus, which, situated at the mouth of the defiles, was chosen as a depot. The apparent subjugation of the region between the Parapamisus and the Oxus had been as easy as the toil of crossing the mountains had been severe.

The spring of 329 B. C. saw Alexander ready to undertake the conquest of Sogdiana. This country was peculiarly adapted to offer easy and stanch resistance to the Macedonian advance. Maracanda, the capital, was situated in a populous and rich plain, protected on the west by deserts, on all other sides by mountain barriers, and was difficult of access. It could be easily defended, and Sogdiana was, besides, not only able to raise a considerable army, but was so placed as to enable a force to debouch into Aria, Parthia, and Hyrcania at will, and operate on Alexander's rear. The Daäns and Massagetans, and the Scythians beyond the Jaxartes, were always ready for plundering raids; and some of the Indian kings, indeed, are said to have promised to take part with Bessus, whom they could reach by passes leading from the headwaters of the Cophen affluents to the headwaters of the Oxus. With the mountains and the desert to afford temporary refuge, it was hard to see how Alexander could subjugate Sogdiana. It was the sort of task in which Napoleon failed in Spain.

From Bactra, whose vicinity is fertile, the route to the Oxus was over a barren tract, which made the marches more difficult. There was not a brook for fifty miles, and the weather was, for the season, extremely hot and dry. The difficulty of the march may not have been recognized beforehand, for a large percentage of the men fell in their tracks; but when the Oxus was reached, water was carried back to the sufferers, and many were thus rescued. It is said that Alexander never took off his armor, nor rested from personal endeavors until the last live man was thus brought in; but Diodorus puts the loss higher than that of any of his battles.

The Oxus was the largest river Alexander had yet encountered. It was deep, about three quarters of a mile wide, full and rapid, and with a sandy bottom that would not readily hold piles. There was little timber growing in the vicinity; it would take too long to collect materials for a bridge or for new boats, and Bessus had destroyed all the old boats on the river for a long distance up and down. But Alexander must cross by some means; and he again utilized his tent-skins, as he had done at the Danube. These he filled with straw and other light floating material, and stitched up so as to be watertight. Using them as floats for rafts, or a flying bridge, or as floats for the men themselves, he leisurely put his army over in five days. There was no opposition. This use of floats for men is both ancient and common. To-day, fishermen in these parts are said to cross rivers with earthern vessels as floats, and to fish on the way.

Before crossing, Alexander allowed a number of old and worn-out Macedonians, and the reënlisted Thessalians whose time was up, to return to Macedonia. Each horseman is said to have received a sum equivalent to two thousand two hundred dollars, each foot-soldier five hundred dollars. These bounties vary so considerably that no rule of distribution can be deduced from them. He also sent Stasanor, a Companion, into Aria, to displace Arsames, the viceroy, whom he thought disaffected; for Bessus had been tampering with him.

After crossing, Alexander made a forced march towards Bessus. The latter had quite lost the confidence of his associates by his constant retreats, and by his weak management since the murder of Darius. The king had gone but part way when he was met by messengers from Bessus' chief abettors, Spitamenes, Dataphernes, Catanes and Oxyartes, who, probably overawed by Alexander's evidently offensive intention in crossing the Oxus, and anxious to make their peace with the conqueror, had deemed any treachery justifiable, and had revolted from Bessus and seized his person, as he had done Darius. They now promised to surrender him if Alexander would send them a force to aid in the work. Alexander sent Ptolemy, son of Lagus, with three squadrons of the Companion cavalry, the lancers, the infantry of Philotas, one thousand shield-bearing guards, the Agrianians and half the archers, — some six thousand men all told, — by forced marches towards Sogdiana, he himself following more slowly to rest his men. This force seemed ample to compel the surrender if declined. Ptolemy made what is stated as a ten days' march in four (*i. e.* one hundred and fifty miles in four days, or thirty-seven miles a day) and reached the camp where the barbarians had been the day before. Spitamenes and Dataphernes were loath to make the surrender of their late companion themselves, but arranged the matter so as to isolate

Bessus in a village by himself, and then retired. Here Ptolemy seized Bessus. This wicked but unfortunate prince, when he was brought to Alexander, naked, confined in a wooden collar, and led by a halter, was ordered to be subjected to the indignity of scourging, and was then sent to Zariaspa. He was later executed. Spitamenes, Dataphernes, Catanes and Oxyartes appear to have been pardoned, for we are not told that Alexander put any viceroy over their heads.

In this province Alexander was able to remount a large part of his cavalry, a matter of prime necessity, for many horses had been lost in the crossing of the Caucasus. He then marched to Maracanda, the capital (modern Samarcand), where plentiful supplies could be got from the rich and fertile valley, known to-day as Al Sogd, and often called the Mohammedan paradise. Here again he left a garrison. The territory in the south had practically submitted. But as Alexander advanced north, he encountered more serious signs of opposition.

A Scythian Prince.

XXXIV.

THE JAXARTES. SUMMER, B. C. 329.

ALEXANDER now marched on Cyropolis, near the Jaxartes, the farthest point attained by Cyrus in his conquests. In one of his mountain battles he was again wounded, but still continued his activity, carried in a litter. Arrived at the Jaxartes, Alexander founded another namesake town on its banks. He was anxious to make this section of his kingdom self-governing, but his efforts in this direction were misunderstood, and an uprising ensued. Alexander took the matter sharply in hand, moved against and destroyed seven cities, to which the rebels had retired. But he was again wounded by a sling-stone. He then crossed the Jaxartes, and defeated the Scythians in so marked a manner that they were glad to make a permanent peace. This was a happy outcome, for all Sogdiana was now in open revolt in his rear, and Alexander had got himself into the most dangerous situation he ever occupied.

ALEXANDER marched on Cyropolis (not far from modern Khojend), the last city of the satrapy, and named after its celebrated founder. It was not far from the banks of the Jaxartes ("Great River"), which Alexander mistook for and called the Tanaïs, as it was the Araxes of Cyrus. Arrian, in his narrative, frequently strays off into geography. In this he is often and naturally inaccurate. But his own errors, though committed centuries later, help us to understand those into which Alexander still more naturally fell. His incomplete knowledge, however, by no 'means interfered with the king's taking advantage of every natural and artificial means for attack, defense and permanent occupation.

Hereabouts, in crossing some passes in the Scythian Mountains, through which ran the road from Maracanda to Cyropolis, one of the Macedonian foraging parties, having lost its way in the defiles, was ambushed and cut to pieces by the barbarians, who then escaped to a part of the chain in which were several fastnesses or easily defended positions, some thirty thousand armed men in number. Alexander determined at once to punish this act. He took his lightest troops, pursued the barbarians, and attacked them vigorously in their principal retreat. This was exceedingly strong, so much so that Alexander made many ineffectual assaults on them, though indeed these barbarians, like all the other tribes he met in arms in this region, rarely fought hand to hand, but relied mainly on missiles cast from a distance. Alexander himself — leading his men with his accustomed recklessness — received a wound in the leg from an arrow, which broke the fibula. This accident so inflamed the anger of the troops that nothing could resist their onset; a fresh assault resulted in the capture of the place. Many of the barbarians were massacred, more cast themselves down the rocks ; out of thirty thousand men not more than eight thousand escaped from the holocaust to tender their submission. Alexander was for some time obliged to travel in a litter, which the different bodies of cavalry and infantry alternately vied to escort. This enforced rest must have been irksome indeed to the king, especially as there was abundant call for all the activity, mental and physical, of which he was capable.

About this time also occurred the massacre by Alexander of the descendants of the Branchidæ, who had surrendered to Xerxes the treasures of the temple of Apollo at Miletus, and to escape the vengeance of the Greeks had accompanied the Great King into Persia, and been by him settled in Sogdiana. Here they had kept themselves free from mixture with the barbarians for one hundred and fifty years. Alexander deemed it wise to exterminate this people. Such an act, unpardonable according to our ideas, can be only explained by the natural inhumanity exercised in that age by

every one to his enemies.   Or perhaps, as the act was in the
nature of a religious retribution, the massacres of the era of
the Reformation make a parallel which better elucidates, if it
does not palliate, the cruelty.

The territory (modern Ferghana) in which Alexander now
stood, between the rugged range of the Scythian Caucasus
and the wide and deep Jaxartes, had always been a marked
boundary between the then so-called civilized world and the
Scythians, as were named the wild and roaming tribes beyond,
— now the Tartars; and in fact it plays to-day a somewhat
similar rôle.   On the south and east were difficult mountain
ranges; on the north the rapid river; on the west alone was
it open to assault.   There was no present inducement to Alexander to move beyond this boundary, while the riches of India
awaited his conquering progress.   He desired but to establish
a point from which he could in future proceed against the
roving barbarians, if he so wished; which point would also
have its commercial value in whatever intercourse could be
had with them.

There had been from time immemorial a series of fortified
towns or posts not very far apart along this border.   There
appear at this time to have been seven prominent ones, of
which Cyropolis was the most important.   Alexander garrisoned these towns, occupied the defiles in his rear so as to
secure his line of retreat, and camped at the last narrows of
the Jaxartes, where it turns northward into the flat, sandy
plains of modern Tartary.

Alexander's desire to remain at peace with the Scythians
seemed at first about to be realized.   While near the Jaxartes
an embassy came to the king from the so-called Scythians in
Europe, and another from those in Asia, known as the Abian
Scythians, which latter Homer lauds as the most just nation
on earth, probably from their being poor and unambitious,

and desiring nothing of their neighbors.   With these embassies, on their return, Alexander sent Companions, with instructions, ostensibly to convey his friendly greetings, but really
to observe the country, its topography, riches, strength and
military conditions.   To supplement these friendly advances,
Alexander determined to found a city near the Jaxartes, as a
base for future expeditions against the Scythians, should this
be desirable, as a bulwark against their incursions, and
because the city, he thought, would naturally grow to be an
important one on account of the thickly-settled country, and
his own royal patronage.   This city, probably modern Khojend, though indeed its locality is in dispute, still remains to
testify to Alexander's good judgment in selecting its location.

Alexander seems to have entertained different notions as to
the best methods of governing this trans-Caucasian country,
from what he had so far practiced with his Asiatic conquests.
He had conceived the idea of giving this people a larger
share in its own government, and thus attaching it the more
firmly to his interests.   For this purpose he called the Sogdianians together to a conference to decide upon the best
interests of the country; but instead of conciliating them,
this well-intentioned step and the planning of a fortified city
gave rise to the suspicion that Alexander proposed to gather
together all their chiefs, and by assassinating them, at one
blow to deprive the country of its leaders as a first means of
reducing it to servitude.   With this idea they revolted, instigated, no doubt, by Bessus' treacherous associates, seized
upon the Macedonian garrisons in the seven towns above
named, and slew the soldiers.   They then shut themselves up
in these towns, all of which were fairly well fortified.   Sim-
ultaneously with this occurred a revolt of Spitamenes in Maracanda, and several uprisings in Bactria, all apparently having
the same suspicion at the root, or at all events community of

action. It is not unlikely that in surrendering Bessus to Alexander, the conspirators imagined that Alexander would leave the region, — for the capture of Darius' murderers was the alleged object of his presence, — and that they would then be free to resume their sway; and when they saw that Alexander proposed to subdue the whole country, they fomented the revolt which now broke out. They were not slow to see that Alexander had placed himself in a danger-ous position.

Alexander's general military situation was indeed more

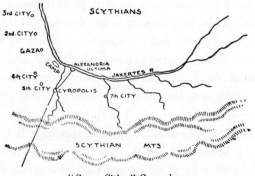

"Seven Cities" Campaign.

perilous than at any other time. Farther from his base than ever before or after, with limited numbers, many unrea-soning, inflammatory and warlike tribes at his back, and with an almost impassable mountain range in his rear, where his enemies could easily arrest his retreat; with the Scythian hordes ready to cross the river, intent on spoil, in fact eagerly watching this very chance, for with the details of the upris-ing they were probably familiar, — nothing but the utmost vigor and instant action could save him, coupled with the errors which would probably be committed by the natives.

Upon learning of the local uprising, Alexander took his measures on the minute. He had not yet heard of the insurrection in his rear, nor was he probably aware of the extent of the matter. But he determined to suppress the one in his front in short measure. He instructed each company to get ready its scaling ladders. He sent Craterus by a forced march to Cyropolis, the largest of the towns of the country, with instructions to blockade it with a stockade and ditch, to build siege engines on the ground, and to keep up such active demonstrations as to prevent any aid being rendered the other cities by this one. Cyropolis was surrounded by stone walls, and had a citadel with a large garrison.

The king himself marched to Gaza, the nearest city to the Macedonian camp. This was defended only by an earthen and conglomerate rampart. No sooner on the ground than he began operations. With his archers and slingers, and the smaller military engines he had brought with him, the walls were speedily cleared, and the phalangites then advanced to the assault with their ladders. It was but short work; the town was taken at the first rush, and every man put to the sword. The women and children were reserved as plunder, and distributed among the soldiers; the town was razed. The second city, probably at no great distance, was taken in like manner on the same day, and suffered the like fate. This was indeed a marvelous day's work, well exhibiting Alexander's tireless energy. The third city fell the next day.

While all this was going on, Alexander had established a cordon of cavalry around the two nearest other towns to prevent the population from taking to flight and reaching the uplands. When by the smoke from the burning cities and by the report of some who escaped, their fate was known, the inhabitants of the two other towns endeavored, as Alexander had anticipated, to secure safety by flight; but they were remorselessly cut down by the cavalry which was around them on every side, and nearly all perished. Thus five cities were taken and destroyed in two days. This fatal reverse was chiefly due to the fact that the barbarians had committed the imprudence of discontinuing the desultory warfare in which alone they were preëminent, and in taking to one in which they were no match whatever for the Macedonians.

Thence Alexander moved on Cyropolis, which Craterus had already blockaded. The stoutest hearted and most notable of the barbarians had gathered there, and the place was surrounded by so strong and high a wall, that it could not be taken by a *coup de main.* Some fifteen thousand soldiers, and many of the lesser chiefs, had rendezvoused there. While Alexander was preparing his engines to batter down the walls, a work of some days, as their heavy timbers were usually cut on the ground, he noticed that a small confluent of the Jaxartes, on which the city was built and which ran under the city wall, — or, according to Arrian, a small channel which was full only during the freshet season, — was dried up to such a degree as to afford a passage into the town. He sent the Companions, the shield-bearing guards, the archers and Agrianians to the nearest gates, and he himself headed a small party; and, while the attention of the inhabitants was taken up on the farther side of the city by the severity of the fire from the engines and light troops, which he ordered to be redoubled in vigor, he secretly made his way along the channel into the town, on the other side, and speedily forced the gates at the place where he had stationed his *corps d'élite.* Through these gates the expectant Macedonians rushed in. and captured the city. But the barbarians would yet not yield. Though they saw that the city was gone, they must fight for their lives. A fierce struggle ensued, in which Alexander was again wounded by a sling-stone on the head and neck, and Craterus by an arrow. The number of wounded was exceptionally large, including many officers. The barbarians were driven out of the market-place, where they had made their stand; the defenders of the walls were swept away, and the rest of the troops from the farther side joined Alexander. About eight thousand barbarians were slain; the rest, some seven thousand in number, fled into the citadel; but after one day's siege they were forced to surrender for lack of water. The seventh city was also taken at the first assault, and most of its inhabitants perished.

Many of the survivors were imprisoned in chains. Alexander proposed to transport those who were known as leaders out of the country, to prevent their encouraging future sedition. The cities were uniformly razed to the ground. Whether this course was justifiable or not will always be the subject of dispute. It seems unnecessary to go over the ground again. But it is to be noticed that Alexander invariably treated those who submitted with as marked and constant generosity as he did those who revolted after submission with the utmost, almost savage, severity. In his late situation, it had been with him a case of life and death, and not merely of present subjection and future submission of these tribes. He had been and still was in a *cul de sac* from which there was no escape if the plans of the barbarians were not utterly thwarted. But, by his rapid and vigorous measures, Alexander had now opened the road back to Sogdiana. This was a first but only a partial gain.

Meanwhile, the Scythians, quick to act on hearing of the uprising, arrived with an army on the other bank of the Jaxartes and camped, ready to take a hand if a favorable chance should occur, and, meanwhile, taunting the Macedonians from what they considered a safe distance. Alexander now first learned that Spitamenes had again risen, and had begun to besiege the garrison at Maracanda. The Massagetæ, the

Daäns, the Sacæ were reported to have joined in the insurrection; and Oxyartes, Catanes, Chorienes, Haustanes and

Scythian Archers.

many other noted chiefs were fostering it. Alexander understood that this was still part and parcel of the insurrection of the seven towns, and now fully comprehended the gravity of his situation. But he also saw that he must protect himself against an invasion of the Scythians before he could turn on Spitamenes. He was therefore fain to content himself with sending against the rebels a force under Andromachus, Menedemus, and Caranus, consisting of eight hundred Greek mercenary cavalry and fifteen hundred Greek mercenary infantry. To these he associated (Arrian says placed over them) an interpreter, Pharnuches, who had shown himself clever in dealing with the barbarians. For he believed the population in bulk to be more inclined to peace than war. This force, at all events, he felt could create a diversion sufficient to enable him to finish the Jaxartes problem before turning southward.

It was plain that the Scythian question must be settled before the Bactrian. Alexander could not turn back from the Jaxartes except distinctly as conqueror. The body of Scythians on the other shore was as yet small, but vast hordes were probably assembling on the desert in their rear. Should he retire without making them feel the weight of his hand, he would have the most troublesome of enemies on his heels, so soon as he retired. Now, as always, Alexander took the broadest views of the military problem before him. The details were secondary. To compel a favorable outcome to these he could take such action as the immediate circumstances warranted.

In three weeks Alexander had fortified his intended city on the Jaxartes, Alexandria Ultima, and settled therein some Greek mercenaries and Macedonians who had grown unfit for military service, such barbarians as chose to join the colony, and such of those who remained over from the seven destroyed towns as he deemed safe to leave behind. Among the denizens of the new city were some captives purchased by Alexander. These were drafted into the ranks to serve as garrison. The Hellenes must have felt much in the position of abandoned sentinels. Having celebrated the foundation of this most distant of his namesake cities

Scythian.

by the usual games and sacrifices, Alexander turned his attention to the Scythians. These barbarians were growing restless and audacious, and had endeavored to interrupt his building operations from the other side. They assembled in groups and taunted him with fear to cross and attack the Scythians, whom he would find, they gave him to understand by unmistakable signals, different from the weaklings he had so far met; and generally acted in a manner showing their need of a salutary lesson.

In offering the sacrifices which always preceded an advance, the soothsayer Aristander pronounced the signs of the victims to be unfavorable to success. Alexander contented himself with waiting a while, which he was the less reluctant to do, as probably his wound was not yet quite healed. Again shortly sacrificing, with the purpose of crossing the river, the victims proved on this occasion to portend personal danger to himself; but the king declared that he had better incur grave risk than be a further laughing-stock to the barbarians, and resolved to delay no longer.

Alexander no doubt was superstitious. He came honestly by it. His mother was the triple essence of superstition. But he was far from being a bigot. His determination always overrode his belief in the portents. " We have not always in war a choice of circumstances," quoth he. " I could desire, no doubt, more propitious auguries to fight under ; but necessity goes before the counsels of reason. If we allow the Scythians to insult us unpunished we shall add courage to the Bactrians. Our rôle is attack. That day on which we put ourselves on the defensive will see us lost."

But despite these brave words, Alexander was, according to Quintus Curtius, far from easy. Unlike the night before Arbela, he could not sleep, but incessantly gazed at the many watch-fires on the farther bank. Nor is this unnatural. At Arbela he slept, conscious of his own ability, the courage of his handful of men, and of the fact that here was a fair field and no favor. At the Jaxartes he was caught in the meshes of a danger of unknown extent. He was absolutely compromised by the revolted provinces in his rear, and saw in his front a problem perhaps as awkward as any he had yet faced. But his conduct, as we shall see, partook in no sense of the weakness usually associated with overanxiety.

In dry seasons the Jaxartes was fordable here. But Alexander's only present means of crossing was skins, used, as at the Oxus, as floats for the light troops and to float rafts for the cavalrymen and phalangians. The horses were swum over. Alexander was just recovering of his wound. This was his first appearance in command, and he was greeted with affectionate enthusiasm. To protect the crossing he brought up his artillery, and trained it on the barbarians across the river. A number were shot down, and one of the killed, apparently their chief or champion, was shot by a shaft through his wicker shield and linen breastplate. Astonished beyond measure at being struck by missiles from such an incredible distance, the Scythians retired to a more respectful position back from the banks. This is the first record of the use of artillery to protect the crossing of a river in offense.

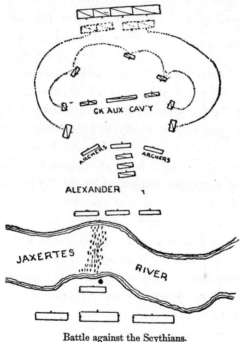

Battle against the Scythians.

Alexander led the way on the first raft, with the trumpets sounding, while the men made breastworks or tortoises of their interlaced shields, and used their missiles freely during the passage. The archers and slingers were first got across, and skirmishing gallantly with the Scythians, prevented their approaching the river, while the phalangites and cavalrymen were ferried over. The horses of each party swam behind the boats.

Alexander now engaged the enemy by sending forward a

regiment of Greek auxiliary cavalry and four squadrons of

Scythians.

lancers, in all one thousand two hundred strong. These the Scythians smartly attacked, and by riding in circles around them, according to their method of attack, without coming to close quarters, wounded many with their arrows and darts, and threatened them with defeat. Seeing his men close pressed, Alexander, covered by the archers, Agrianians and light troops under Balacrus, led forward the cavalry in one body, and compelled the Scythians to forsake their skirmishing tactics and form line. Then, throwing part of the light horse about their flank, he himself headed three squadrons of Companion cavalry and the horse lancers, and advanced sharply on the enemy in column. The Scythians, finding themselves unable to use their peculiar skirmishing tactics on account of the rapid manœuvres of Alexander's columns, lost head, and, unequal to the task of a clash with the Macedonians, were speedily dispersed, encountering a loss of one thousand slain. There were one hundred and fifty of them captured.

Pursuit was at once undertaken. The heat was very oppressive, the distance great, and the men, suffering from thirst, drank largely of stagnant water, there being no other to be had. Alexander did the like, and shortly after, while following up the enemy, he was seized with a grave sickness as a result, and thus the prophecy of the victims was fulfilled. The pursuit was arrested. The king was carried exhausted back to the camp, and his life for some days was in much danger. But his rugged constitution came to the rescue, and he recovered. The battle at the Jaxartes had cost one hundred and sixty killed, and one thousand wounded, a loss of nearly twenty per cent., for not exceeding six thousand men had been engaged. Much booty, including eighteen hundred camels, had been taken.

Alexander's victory over the Scythians had by good fortune the desired result. Not long after, envoys came from the Scythian king, with an apology for the conduct of the troops at the river, alleging that this was but a band of marauders and freebooters, with whose lawless acts the Scythian state had nothing to do. The king tendered his fealty, and undertook to perform whatever Alexander should prescribe. As Alexander had no desire or time to engage in operations beyond the Jaxartes (for he must turn at once on the Sogdianians, and moreover his vanity was satisfied with having advanced as far as Cyrus), he was pleased to give credit to the message of the ambassadors, and sent them back with a courteous answer, releasing without payment of ransom the prisoners he had taken. This generosity, coupled to the king's remarkable feats of war, which they had both seen and heard of, gave to his name among the Scythians the same halo with which their brethren beyond the Danube seven years before had surrounded it. This reputation was Alexander's surest defense against these tribes.

Alexander the Great.
(From a Mosaic in Naples.)

XXXV.

SPITAMENES. SUMMER, B. C. 329, TO FALL, B. C. 328.

THE Scythian campaign had given the Sogdianians time for preparation. Spitamenes was the ruling spirit of the insurrection. He had unsuccessfully tried to seize Maracanda. Alexander dispatched a force against him. These men drove him into the desert, but being poorly led, Spitamenes turned upon them, surrounded them near the Polytimetus, and massacred them, to the number of over two thousand. Alexander, when he learned of this disaster, had just completed his Jaxartes programme. By a forced march, he reached the scene in four days. But Spitamenes fled. Alexander took bitter revenge by devastating the land. The winter was spent in Zariaspa with many feasts but more labor. A dozen new cities were started, and Sogdiana again colonized. Considerable and much needed reinforcements reached Alexander in Zariaspa, and embassies from many and distant nations came to him. He began to plan for his Indian campaign; but the Sogdianians again rose under Spitamenes, and intrenched themselves in the mountain strongholds. Another campaign became essential. Alexander divided his troops into five flying columns, and traversing the land in length and breadth, stamped out the insurrection once for all, and rendezvoused at Maracanda. Spitamenes, with a force of nomads, was still afoot and threatened much trouble, but between Craterus and Cœnus he was defeated, and finally murdered by his own allies. He was the last of the rebels.

ALEXANDER'S delay at the Jaxartes had given time for the Sogdianian revolt to make much headway. In part by threats, in part by cajolery, Spitamenes had induced the entire population to join the insurrection. They were like clay in the hands of the potter. The delay had been unavoidable; but so soon as the Scythian question was settled, Alexander lost no time in turning towards Maracanda.

Spitamenes with his immediate command had been able to make but small impression against the garrison of Maracanda. The Macedonians had not only held him at bay, but had made a successful sortie upon him, in which they had punished him severely, and had again retired to the citadel without loss. And when Spitamenes learned that the forces which Alexander had dispatched against him to Maracanda were near at hand, he retired from the vicinity of the capital in a westerly direction. The commanders of the relief party, on its arrival at the theatre of operations, not content with what had already been won, but anxious to distinguish themselves, followed Spitamenes up in the hope of punishing his audacity; and, in fact, they seriously harassed his rear during the retreat, which he now continued towards the desert. But emboldened by their success, they were unwise enough to advance well into the steppes, and to attack a body of nomad Scythians, whom they suspected of being Spitamenes' allies, or at all events of having given him aid and comfort. These people, angered by the act, did in reality join forces with the Sogdianians, and sent them a reinforcement of six hundred of their best horse.

Spitamenes, seeing that the Macedonians were illy led, determined to risk the offensive. Selecting a level plain near the Scythian desert where he could fight in open order, — a formation which allows the great individual bravery of the Oriental cavalry to have full play, — he declined to come to close quarters, in which the Macedonians were easily his superiors, but rode round and round the phalanx, discharging darts and arrows, and making feints at all points. His troops did not once attempt to stand their ground when the Macedonians charged home upon them. From the onsets of the Macedonian horse they continually fled, but again turned when the pursuit halted, and tired it out by unceasing activity, as with their great preponderance of force they could easily do. Their horses were fresh, while those of Andromachus were exhausted by their long march to Maracanda, and had been but half fed for many days. The Macedonians had got themselves where they could neither advance nor retreat; for the Scythians were constantly on the alert, and afforded them no rest. Many were killed and wounded in this desultory fighting.

Pharnuches, who was brought up to diplomacy rather than to arms, refused any longer to head the expedition; the other leaders declined the command of a matter already past cure. There was neither head nor purpose. The only recourse of the Macedonians was to form square, and march towards the river Polytimetus (modern Sogd-Kohik), where they saw a wooded glen which might afford them shelter. But there was lack of common action. Caranus, commanding part of the cavalry, attempted to cross the river, but failed to notify Andromachus of what he was about to do; the infantry followed Caranus heedlessly; the men became demoralized, missing the strong hand, and began to break ranks at the ford. Seeing this, the barbarians, who had kept close on their heels, and pressed in hard, waiting for just this chance, now attacked the force in front, flank and rear, and from both sides of the stream, crossing over above and below the Macedonians, and threw the phalanx into complete confusion. The retreat became a *sauve qui peut.* Most of the soldiers who had not been killed or fatally injured made their way to a small island in the river. Here they were surrounded at a safe distance by the barbarians, and all slain by arrows, except a few who were kept for trophies, subjected for a while to the bitterest slavery, and later killed. Some sixty horse and three hundred foot are all who are said to have got away.

In this pitiful campaign, the account of which varies but slightly in Arrian and Curtius, and which is so unlike what we are used to see under the Macedonian standard, two thousand men were lost to Alexander, — more than the entire number killed in the battles for the conquest of Persia. It is but one more proof that success in war depends not alone on men, but needs a man. Alexander was to blame in the selection of his commander. Spitamenes returned in high spirits to Maracanda, and prepared to besiege the citadel a second time, with far greater prospect of success.

On learning of this untoward event, Alexander, chagrined beyond measure at the disgraceful check, at once prepared to put his own shoulder to the wheel. He had finished the Jaxartes problem, and could leave this outpost safely now that the new city was fairly started. He took half the Companion cavalry, the shield-bearing guards, archers, Agrianians, and light phalangians, and headed towards the valley of the Polytimetus, leaving Craterus to follow with the bulk of the army. The king, who was never slow in his movements, this time marched one hundred and seventy miles in three days, and on the morning of the fourth day reached Maracanda. But Spitamenes, on the first notice of Alexander's presence, abandoned the siege of the city, and fled. Alexander pursued him well into the desert, where Spitamenes crossed the Polytimetus, but he could not overtake him. The king's path lay near the late battlefield. Here he buried, with as much ceremony as the time allowed, all the soldiers whose remains had not disappeared, and in retaliation for the loss of his men he laid the whole district waste. The miserable Sogdianians, suffering for another's guilt, had retired into every place of safety, and had fortified every town and hamlet. They could expect no mercy; nor did Alexander show any. He swept over the length and breadth of the land like a blizzard, burning and destroying villages and farms. He slew all the barbarians who had taken part in the campaign, most of whom had fled to the fortified places. These were each in turn reduced and razed. In this frightful retribution one hundred and twenty thousand men, not counting women and children, are said to have perished. Only Cæsar's massacres in Gaul exceed the frightful score of this devastation.

Alexander then left Peucolaus with three thousand men in Maracanda, and returned to Zariaspa, where he intended to remain for the coming winter. The people of Bactria, after the fate of Sogdiana, needed no further effort to reduce them to subjection. The revolt had not progressed far in this province. Little more is mentioned about it. Clemency succeeded cruelty, says Quintus Curtius, and had a good effect. But some of the leaders in the late insurrection had fled into mountain fastnesses, where they deemed themselves secure from pursuit.

During this winter Alexander had his headquarters and camp at Zariaspa. The reinforcements which reached him here were considerable. We know that there was quite an amount of trouble in the rear among the newly-appointed satraps and other civil governors ; it could scarcely be otherwise ; and the fact that these detachments were able to march through the length and breadth of the land, despite these turmoils, points conclusively to the excellence of the chain of military posts which Alexander had established in the succession of cities he had founded on the way.

Military activity at Zariaspa was shared with the toils of state, and both alternated with games and feasts. Alexander is said by Curtius to have founded six cities in Bactria and Sogdiana ; by Justin, twelve. The general convention which had evoked the insurrection was now held. It was here that Bessus was tried before the assembly of notables, convicted and mutilated by cutting off his nose and ears. He was then sent to Ecbatana, probably exhibited as an example on the way, and was there executed. This was the Oriental method of procedure.

To show that modern critics have not been the first to

discover weaknesses in Alexander's character, the following
extract from Arrian, his most accurate historian and chief
laudator, is of interest : " I do not commend this excessive punishment ; on the contrary, I consider that the mutilation of
the prominent features of the body is a barbaric custom, and
I agree with those who say that Alexander was induced to
indulge his desire of emulating the Median and Persian
wealth, and to treat his subjects as inferior beings, according
to the custom of the foreign kings.   Nor do I by any means
commend him for changing the Macedonian style of dress,
which his fathers had adopted, for the Median one, being, as
he was, a descendant of Hercules.   Besides, he was not
ashamed to exchange the head-dress which the conqueror had
so long worn for that of the conquered Persians.   None of
these things do I commend ; but I consider Alexander's great
achievements prove, if anything can, that supposing a man to
have a vigorous bodily constitution, to be illustrious in descent, and to be even more successful in war than Alexander
himself ; even supposing that he could sail right round Libya
as well as Asia, and hold them both in subjection as Alexander indeed designed to do ; even if he could add the possession of Europe to that of Asia and Libya ; all these things
would be no furtherance to such a man's happiness, unless at
the same time he possess the power of self-control, though he
has performed the great deeds which have been supposed."

It cannot be denied that the Persian habit was constantly
on the increase with Alexander, as how could it be otherwise
if he was suitably to maintain the godlike character which
these Eastern peoples would not believe in without their accustomed pomp and circumstance ?   And was not this blind
but most natural belief a great part of Alexander's stock in
trade ?   No doubt history would show us a more perfect man,
if, with all his wonderful ability and native truth and gener-

osity of character, Alexander had kept up his Macedonian simplicity. But Alexander, though a perfect captain, was by no means a perfect man. And was Macedonian simplicity either natural or politically wise? His ancient domain was but a small spot even on the map of the then world, the greater part of which he had already conquered. What more proper in almost every sense, than his adoption of the habits, dress and customs — in part, at least — of those peoples which made up all but a limited percentage of his empire, though, indeed, it was by his Macedonian simplicity, discipline, intelligence and superior skill that he had attained his extraordinary preëminence.

The reinforcements above referred to, which reached Zariaspa during this winter from Greece, were under Nearchus, satrap of Lycia, and Asandrus, satrap of Caria, Asclepiodorus, viceroy of Syria, and Menes, his deputy, Epolicus, Menidas, and Ptolemy, the Thracian strategos, and amounted in all to seventeen thousand foot and twenty-six hundred horse. This accession of troops was sadly needed to repair the gaps rent by the last campaigns. For north of the Parapamisus, the warlike tribes of herdsmen and mountaineers, of whom every one was a soldier, by no means succumbed to one or two battles, as did the peaceable inhabitants of the more western countries, who were accustomed to be ruled and to pay tribute; of whom but a few bore arms, and the rest were artisans and farmers. In fact, without these reinforcements, the king would shortly have been in an untenable position. They were the leaven of a considerable lump of new troops. "When," says Admiral La Gravière, "the Emperor Napoleon camped under the walls of Moscow, there is no strategist but what would pronounce his position very hazardous, and would be tempted to accuse it of adventurous temerity; the temerity was much greater on the part of Alexander the day when he came and established himself between the Oxus and Jaxartes. Never had the king of Macedon manœuvred on a theatre so perilous." But Alexander's temerity was forced on him. To penetrate into Russia so far as Moscow was an optional proceeding with Napoleon. The conquest of Bactria and Sogdiana was a prerequisite to Alexander's holding the plateau of Iran. And once on the borders of Scythia, there was no alternative. From the Jaxartes it was a question of successful withdrawal without losing what was already won or of absolute destruction. His temerity was rather exceptional boldness of action.

Phrataphernes, satrap of Parthia, and Stasanor, satrap of Aria, now arrived and brought in chains Arsames, late satrap of Aria, Barzanes, an adherent of Bessus, to whom the latter had assigned Parthia, and some others. These were the last of the ringleaders who had betrayed Darius. With them in arrest, opposition in the rear might well be said to have been crushed out.

The Companions whom Alexander had sent to the European Scythians now returned with another embassy, for the old king was dead and his brother was reigning in his stead. The latter desired to make a friend of Alexander. He sent such presents as the Scythians deemed of the highest value, and invited him and his officers to unite in marriage with his own family. No doubt he looked on this as an equal alliance. He offered to come to receive Alexander's orders, if the king so desired. Alexander also received a deputation from the Chorasmians, who dwelt between the Caspian and Ural seas, headed by their king, Pharasmenes, and fifteen hundred horse-guards, asking for a treaty, and offering him guidance and provision in case he wished to make a campaign against the Amazons, whose land they said was next beyond their own. Pharasmenes feared lest Alexander should think he also had abetted Spitamenes. Alexander received both these embassies with courtesy and sent them away satisfied, having made friendship between them and Artabazus, whom he had appointed viceroy of Bactria.

Alexander had early imagined that the Caspian Sea was a part of the ocean, and that as such he must eventually subdue its borders in order to complete the boundaries of his ideal empire. But he had now learned from the reports of his own officers and from those of the barbarians that the ocean was nowhere near the Caspian, and that untold stretches of country beyond were inhabited by the people he called Scythians. He was therefore content to make alliances with and to erect obstacles against these tribes rather than seek to extend his conquests into their territory. His limitation of his own borders was always conceived on a scale full of common sense. He told Pharasmenes that he must first conquer India; but once lord of all Asia he would return to Greece, and thence advance through the Hellespont, the Bosphorus and Euxine Sea. He would then gladly ask his alliance and aid. Alexander was very anxious to get matters to rights in Bactria and Sogdiana, for his mind was set on the conquest of India, and he was impatient of these seemingly never-ending delays.

Alexander's plan of conquest was well matured; its scheme was compact and intelligent. Few things show Alexander's grasp of his gigantic problem better than the fact that he limited the boundary of his conquest of Persia by the water-shed of the upper Euphrates and Tigris, of Ariana by the Oxus and Jaxartes, and made his eastern limit the Indus and Hydaspes, fortifying these rivers with suitable cities, or military posts, as a barrier against the tribes beyond, and erecting a yet better barrier against them by his control over the bordering nations.

But the campaign against India was destined to be delayed.

While Alexander was preparing for this campaign, the Sogdianians again rose against Peucolaus, the satrap Alexander had appointed over them. Their late punishment had made them desperate rather than tamed them, and many bands had taken refuge in the uplands, whither some of their chiefs had previously fled, and had there intrenched themselves in strongholds of every nature, — the castles of their chiefs, villages, defiles, mountain heights, forests. A new problem, and a worse than ever, seemed to have been thrust upon Alexander. The more desperate the people the more dangerous the situation. Peucolaus, with his three thousand men, could not even attempt to reduce this insurrection ; he could scarcely protect the valley of Maracanda ; and Alexander himself, after leaving suitable garrisons in Alexandria Arachotia, ad Caucasum, Ultima, had kept not exceeding ten thousand men with him, of which he could dispose for a campaign against these people. He was handicapped. Happily Spitamenes was in the land of the Massagetæ, and not on hand to head the insurrection. And it may be characterized as another instance of "Alexander's luck" that about this time, mid-winter, the reinforcements above mentioned reached him.

It was in the early part of the year that the army broke up from Zariaspa, where were left in garrison some convalescent Companions, eighty mercenary cavalrymen and a few pages. Alexander sent the brigades of Polysperchon, Attalus, Gorgias and Meleager, now reinforced, in several detachments among the Bactrians to hold them in subjection, and to reduce to control that part of the land which was still in questionable humor ; and in order to cover as much ground in as short a space as possible, and have done with the matter once for all, divided the entire rest of his army into five flying columns, under Hephæstion, Ptolemy, son of Lagus, Perdiccas, Artabazus and Cœnus, and himself. There being

none but isolated bodies to contend with, this was a safe
enough proceeding. As the king approached the Oxus and
camped, a spring of water and oil (no doubt petroleum)
sprang up or was discovered beside his tent. From this circumstance the soothsayer, Aristander, foretold that victory,
but dearly bought, would be his meed in the present undertaking.

There are unfortunately few details of this campaign preserved to us. The Sogdianians had again committed the fatal

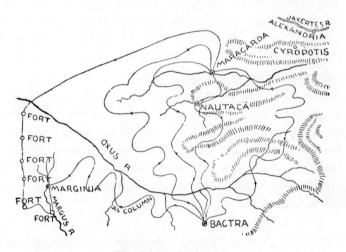

Five Column Campaign.

imprudence of taking to their fortified towns instead of relying on their usual desultory warfare, which it would have
puzzled the Macedonians infinitely more to meet. These five
columns swept to and fro across their land, very likely up and
down the Oxus and the Polytimetus and their affluents, reducing place after place, some by force and some by terms of
surrender, going as far as the Margus River and beyond,
and finally rendezvoused at Maracanda. According to Quintus Curtius, Alexander's column moved down the Oxus, and

thence up the Margus, as far as Marginia or Antiochia (modern Merv). Here he built six fortresses, two facing south and four west, to hold in check the Daäns from the vicinity of the Caspian Sea.

These several insurrections followed by their frightful retribution must have brought the Sogdianian land to the very verge of ruin. It had been essential that Alexander should subdue it thoroughly; it became essential that he should again populate it; for the wars had transformed what had been a garden to the semblance of a desert. This duty Alexander committed to Hephæstion, who founded new cities, moved fresh inhabitants into them, and built up and fostered the agriculture of the land in every possible way. But it must have taken many years to bring back the thrifty condition of Sogdiana.

Although occurring some months later, the fate of Spitamenes may as well be detailed here.

Many places in the mountains on the north and east still remained unsubdued, and Alexander naturally feared that Spitamenes might again appear to fan the flame. Only a leader was wanting. From Maracanda, therefore, Alexander sent the column of Artabazus and Cœnus into Massagetan Scythia, whither he had heard that Spitamenes had fled, and assuming personal direction of the others, marched on the rebellious towns in Sogdiana, which were as yet unsubdued. After a campaign of marvelous marches, he reduced them to a full sense of their helplessness, and again returned to Maracanda. No details of this campaign exist.

Spitamenes had collected a force of six hundred Massagetan horsemen in addition to some of his old troops, and with these he made a descent on an outlying fort in Bactriana, garrisoned by Macedonians. This chieftain by no means lacked ability. He manœuvred so as to induce the garrison

to leave the fort, waylaid it by a cunning ambush, captured
the place, and slew every man.   Emboldened by his success,
he advanced, burning and ravaging, to Zariaspa.   He had
collected much booty, but declined to attack the town.   A
few convalescent Companions, as above stated, constituted

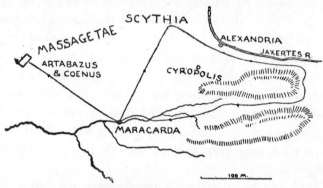

Final Sogdianian Campaign.

the paltry force at Zariaspa with a few attendants; but with
them was Peithon, son of Sosides, Aristonicus, eighty Greek
mercenary horsemen, and a few pages.   These, though a
mere handful, were not to be dismayed.   They sallied out,
fell opportunely upon the Scythians, gave them a sound beat-
ing, took away their booty, and slew a large number of them;
after which handsome work they were returning to Zariaspa,
supposing themselves beyond danger, and probably in loose
order, when they fell into an ambuscade, and lost seven Companions and sixty mercenary cavalrymen.   Aristonicus was
killed.   Peithon, wounded, fell into the enemy's hands.   The
city barely escaped capture.   Spitamenes threatened to make
trouble, when Craterus (where he was at the moment does
not appear), hearing of the situation by couriers, marched
against this chieftain, and he, conscious that he could not
meet regular troops, fled towards the desert with about one

thousand horsemen in his company. Craterus overtook him, and defeated him with a loss of one hundred and fifty men. The rest escaped.

About this time Amyntas was made viceroy of Bactria in place of Artabazus, who, ninety-seven years old, felt compelled to retire for age. This place had been intended for Clitus, whose unhappy fate will be detailed in the next chapter. Cœnus was left in Sogdiana for the winter with his own brigade and Meleager's taxis, four hundred Companions, the horse archers, and Amyntas' old command of Bactrians and Sogdianians. It was made the peculiar duty of Cœnus to watch for Spitamenes, who, finding Bactria too hot to hold him, was now wandering about the outskirts of Sogdiana.

While Hephæstion returned to Bactria to make arrangements for provisioning the troops during the coming winter, Alexander moved across the Polytimetus to Xenippa in pursuit of a number of the Bactrian and Sogdianian rebels. The Xenippians, fearing to be mixed up in the matter, refused their countrymen the usual hospitality. Some two thousand in number, these were compelled to turn and defend themselves, and after a severe struggle, in which they lost eight hundred men, they were obliged to sue for peace.

After this success, Alexander moved on the rock fortress of Sisimithres, the location of which is undetermined, but by some authorities is put at a distance of several hundred miles from Maracanda; and after much toil and danger — the march to the fort being as severe as the work of taking it — this also succumbed by capitulation.

Meanwhile, Spitamenes determined to make one last effort in Sogdiana. In addition to his own renegades, he had collected a force of three thousand Scythian horsemen eager for booty. These people, having no homes or cities, and ground down by poverty, were always ready for raids in which there was a prospect of profit. With this force, Spitamenes advanced to Bagæ, near the boundary of the Massagetans and of Sogdiana. Cœnus, always ready for duty, marched out to meet him, and in a sharp combat defeated him with eight hundred killed to his own thirty-seven. The Bactrians and Sogdianians with Spitamenes, recognizing the helplessness of their cause, and out of patience with this luckless leader, surrendered in a body. The Scythians, after plundering their baggage, fled with Spitamenes toward the desert. But many returned to Cœnus, and gave themselves up. Learning shortly after that Alexander was on the march toward them, these same Scythians slew Spitamenes, and sent his head to the king as a matter of conciliation. Quintus Curtius says that his wife murdered Spitamenes, and brought his head to Alexander. The death of this persistent, treacherous and wily foe gave final promise of peace to this territory. Only Dataphernes was left of all the conspirators, and him the Daäns surrendered. Alexander was able to undertake substantial measures towards replanting a country which has been called the Garden of the Orient, but which had been absolutely desolated by the war.

Alexander.
(From a Coin in the British Museum.)

XXXVI.

CLITUS. WINTER, B. C. 329–328.

A⊤ Maracanda there was an attempt by some of the Greeks and Persians, much to the annoyance of the Macedonians, to introduce the custom of prostration on approaching Alexander, who had already begun largely to imitate the dress and manners of the Persian monarchs. This was partly a political desideratum, partly a very natural growth of vanity on Alexander's part. At a feast here, when much fulsome flattery had been indulged in, Clitus, excited with wine, let his natural repugnance to such servility get the better of him, and indulged in insulting and treasonable language. Alexander, at first patient and cool, finally allowed his anger to control him, and, seizing a spear, ran Clitus through the body. Repentance, however sincere, came too late. This same mood gave rise to a conspiracy of the pages, which was discovered and suppressed; and to the execution of the philosopher Callisthenes, for indulging in too much free speech. The discussion of this subject is not properly part of this volume.

I⊤ was at Maracanda, as Curtius informs us, during the winter preceding the death of Spitamenes, that the habit of intemperance to which Alexander, in his hours of leisure, was becoming too much addicted, began to produce its most lamentable results. The murder of Clitus at a drunken bout, for words spoken in the heat of wine, can be traced only to a lapse in self-control due to excess of vanity, and to rage largely the effect of overdrinking. The fact that such lapses were rare, and that they did not interfere with work to be done, cannot be warped into an excuse. This incident, unlike the conspiracy of Philotas, has properly nothing to do with the military history of Alexander; but it has been given so great prominence by most historians that it cannot well be skipped, especially as Clitus was one of the most distinguished of the

Macedonian leaders. The devotion of some pages to the matter will therefore be pardoned. As a touch in Alexander's portrait, the story is perhaps essential.

Alexander's assuming some portions of the Oriental dress and manners, and encouraging, or at least allowing, the Eastern custom of prostration on approaching his person, was no doubt partly another symptom of weakness as derogatory to his character as his occasional fits of intemperance; although the latter had no connection with political requirements, the former had. It was such lapses from moderation which gave rise, also, to the conspiracy of the pages and the execution of Callisthenes, the philosopher, and of Hermolaus.

Alexander had no doubt begun to suffer in personal character from his almost superhuman successes. His moral force had in nowise declined; but some of the petty traits of human nature had struggled through to the surface. This was natural enough. We have seen how violent were the passions and how strong the superstition he inherited from his mother. These had been increased by his career of victory to a very material extent. The priests of the oracle of Jupiter Ammon had deemed it wise to declare him descended from a god, and though it is improbable that Alexander actually gave credit to such an idea, he saw fit to use the oracle for political effect. His remarkable campaigns might well have inflated his ideas to the point of real belief in this oracular dictum; but there are many hints to the effect that among his friends he laughed at the proposition. He had begun to adopt the Eastern dress and customs for perfectly valid political reasons, but he had gone beyond the necessary or advisable, and had recently come to require a servility which his liberty-loving Macedonians gravely resented. To those who remembered the honest greatness of Philip, Alexander's claim to be descended from other loins than his had always been a distasteful morsel. And at an unhappy feast in Maracanda, on the day sacred to Bacchus, but when Alexander chose rather to sacrifice to Castor and Pollux, when the Macedonian habit of overdrinking had no doubt been indulged in by all to a much too great an extent, the first serious outbreak of this change of mood occurred.

Flatterers had been extolling Alexander, singing his Æacic lineage, and comparing him to the demi-gods. Clitus, son of Dropidas, the "black" one, commander of the agema of cavalry, no doubt strongly under the influence of liquor, but retaining sufficiently his ancient Macedonian manliness to be stung to the quick by this slur on his old and beloved king, harangued the party in the opposite strain, and told Alexander to his face that he owed his victories to the army Philip had created, and to the generals Philip had trained ; that Parmenio and Philotas, now dead by his hand, had done as much as — more than Alexander ; and that he, Clitus, had saved Alexander from death at the battle of the Granicus, — as was true. Of the two, Clitus was apparently the more heated by his drinking. It is alleged that Alexander stood these taunts with great patience and self-possession for some time, turning to a neighboring Greek with : "Do not you Greeks feel among us Macedonians like demi-gods among beasts?" But if Clitus' words and manner were to the last degree insulting to the man, how much more to the king? Nothing better illustrates the meaning of the word "Companion" than Alexander's tolerance of so much. No monarch of modern times ever allowed a subject so much laxity of tongue. At all times in the world's history, such intemperate language would be treason punishable with death. Finally, infuriated at the continued flow of such language, Alexander started to his feet. Clitus was removed by his friends. Harmony was about to be restored. But on Clitus returning into the hall with a fresh taunt, Alexander, after vain attempts to restrain him by his companions, seized a pike and ran Clitus through the body. His subsequent grief was as violent as his fatal act, but repentance, though creditable to his feelings, was no excuse for his murderous transport of rage.

In this place it may be as well to say a word about the alleged desire of Alexander that prostration should be practiced before him as was usual before Persian monarchs. The Orientals at the court naturally continued to Alexander that obeisance which they were habituated to practice to their own sovereigns. It was not less naturally irksome to them to see that the Greeks and Macedonians approached this humbler of the Great King as if he were indeed but a companion. Whatever the really strongest underlying motive may have been, this difference led to difficulties which the wisest policy might have been puzzled to remove. It is certain that many of his nearest Macedonian friends had agreed that the Eastern habit of prostration should be introduced among all. The bulk of the Macedonians held this practice in abhorrence, though some few Greeks and Macedonians had already adopted it. At a banquet in Zariaspa, no doubt with Alexander's privity, there was an attempt made by a party of which some noted Greek philosophers and literary men were members, to introduce the custom by a surprise, in the hope that once adopted by the majority, under whatever circumstances, the active opposition to it would cease. In the speeches at this banquet, Alexander was compared by the philosopher Anaxarchus to Bacchus and Hercules, and those who favored the plan, joined in this fulsome adulation, as well as actually prostrated themselves. Most of the Macedonians were disgusted at both speech and act, but remembering the fate of Clitus, deemed it prudent to abstain from criticism.

Especially two philosophers were prominent in Alexander's

court: Callisthenes, who told Alexander that not his descent from Zeus, but what he himself should write in history would make him famous or the reverse ; and Anaxarchus of Abdera, who was of quite another mould, a man of the world, practiced in flattery, and wont to eulogize to over-satiety. It was he who, after the murder of Clitus, told the king in the way of comfort that the son of Zeus could do no wrong. The philosopher Callisthenes was bold enough to take this matter of prostration up. He was the pupil and nephew of Aristotle, at whose request indeed he had accompanied Alexander, as witness of his deeds, and their future historian. There was always a large number of artists, historians, philosophers and actors among other professional men in the suite of Alexander, who delighted to have those about him who could record and illustrate his deeds, and sincerely enjoyed their society. Callisthenes on this occasion, though invited by Hephæstion to join the rest in performing the act of worship, refused, and gave publicly the reasons of his refusal. Nothing was said or done at the time. This act was imprudent, no doubt, but full of moral courage. Callisthenes became a marked man.

About this same time there was a plot among the pages, led by Hermolaus, son of Sopolis, whom the king had punished for misbehavior with stripes and dismounting, probably aware that Hermolaus was imbued with too much of the extreme Macedonian spirit. Hermolaus and Sostratos, son of Amyntas, plotted to murder Alexander the next time the turn came to them to watch at his bedside. Four others joined the conspiracy. But on that night, as it happened, Alexander sat late at supper, induced thereto, it is said, by the advice of a female soothsayer who followed the camp, and the plot fell through. Before the next opportunity arrived, the plot was divulged. The guilty pages were seized, and implicated Callis-

thenes.   The army, as usual, judged and executed the pages.
Callisthenes, not a Macedonian, was kept imprisoned, and is
said by Aristobulus, to have died in prison; by Ptolemy, to have
been hanged.   The antagonism of Callisthenes, Alexander is
said to have ascribed to his old teacher, Aristotle, whom he
now remembered with feelings of not unmixed affection.
These are among the pages which are well quickly shut.   So
restless under freedom of speech had Alexander become, it
has been observed, that it is hard to say whether his periods
of rest were not more dangerous to his friends than his
marches and campaigns to his enemies.

Perhaps all this is out of place in a volume which makes
no pretense to being a history of the man or king Alexander
or of his times, but is merely a narration of the deeds of the
soldier, as illustrative of the growth of the art of war.   It is
difficult, however, to pass over such grave personal incidents,
or to divorce the man with his weaknesses from the captain
with his glorious achievements.

Alexander.

(From a Coin in the British Museum.)

XXXVII.

ROXANA. WINTER, B. C. 328–327.

HEADQUARTERS for the winter were at Nautaca. Complaints of mismanagement began to come in, and a number of changes were found to be necessary among the satraps of the provinces in the rear. Bactria and Sogdiana were now definitely reduced, except a few rocky fastnesses to which some of the unreconstructed chiefs had retired. Oxyartes had fortified himself in the Rock of Arimazes. The march thither was very laborious, and the place seemed beyond capture; but it was taken by the bold feat of some Macedonian mountaineers, who escaladed the perpendicular sides of the rock, and terrified the garrison into surrender. Here Roxana, daughter of Oxyartes, was captured; her beauty and grace led Alexander an equal captive, and he soon after married her. Thence Alexander moved by an equally toilsome and longer march to the Rock of Chorienes on the upper Oxus. This was also surrendered after the bold bridging of a difficult ravine. Both Oxyartes and Chorienes Alexander made his friends and viceroys. Craterus finished the remaining work by defeating in battle both Catanes and Austanes. Sogdiana was completely subdued, and the entire region beyond the Oxus was left under a freer form of government, the rulers and people being given a species of independence.

WINTER was approaching. The various detachments under Cœnus and Craterus now rejoined Alexander at Nautaca, where he had finally taken up winter-quarters. Phrataphernes, from Parthia, and Stasanor, from Aria, likewise reported. A number of changes were made in the command of the satrapies. Phrataphernes was sent to replace and arrest Autophradates, satrap of Mardia and Tarpuria, who had neglected to repair to headquarters when ordered so to do. Stasanor was sent to Drangia in command. Atropates replaced Oxydates in Media. Stamenes was made satrap of Babylonia, vice Mazæus, deceased. Sopolis, Menedas, and Epocillus were sent to Macedonia to recruit.

Arrangements looking to an Indian campaign were seriously begun. It was hoped that this might be undertaken early in the coming summer, so soon, in fact, as the melting of the snows should have sufficiently opened the mountain passes.

Bactria was quiet. Sogdiana had been reduced to submission, and thenceforth remained so. The exceptions were only one or two strongholds, where the last relics of opposition had collected. But these in nowise affected the general sentiment of the country. Oxyartes, an influential Bactrian, had conveyed his family for safety to the Sogdian Rock, or Rock of Arimazes, in Sogdiana, a fastness which was supposed to be quite impregnable, and was victualed for a long siege. The snow furnished abundance of water.

Alexander opened operations early. The march was full of difficulties. Storms were very severe. One is mentioned by Quintus Curtius in which one thousand men perished from cold and exposure; and Diodorus details the energy and courage displayed by Alexander in cheering his men to those exertions by which alone they could save themselves. The severity of the climate corresponds with what travelers tell us of this trans-Caucasian region to-day.

The snow was not yet off the ground when Alexander appeared before the place. This rock was very high; its sides were almost perpendicular, and an assault promised utter failure. It was absurd to attempt one. How to begin siege operations was a question no one could answer. There seemed to be no approach; the one road up the rock could be held by a dozen men. The snow made treacherous footing for the Macedonians if they attempted to climb the rock. But the difficulty of the situation made the king all the more determined; "for," says Arrian, "a certain overweening and insolent boast uttered by the barbarians had thrown him into a state of ambitious pertinacity." On being summoned to surrender, with promise of free exit and safety, the garrison laughingly replied that they feared only winged soldiers. This whetted Alexander's ambition.

The fortress was probably built on a rock jutting out from the side of a mountain, — for there was a precipice overhanging the fortress. But its sides were perpendicular. If

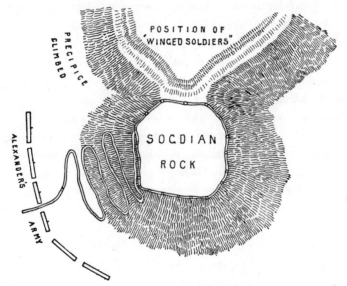

Sogdian Rock, or Rock of Arimazes.

this precipice could be gained, it would dominate the enemy's position. Alexander sent a herald through the camp, offering prizes to such men as would essay to scale the rocks; twelve talents (fourteen thousand five hundred dollars) to the first who succeeded, nine to the second, and so on, down to three hundred Darics (eleven hundred dollars); and excited the ambition of many. Of those who were expert climbers, having learned in sieges and mountain training how to scale walls and cliffs, three hundred in number volunteered.

They provided themselves with ropes, took their iron tent pegs, and selecting the most dangerous, because least watched, spot, began the ascent at midnight, by driving the pegs into the crevices of the rocks, or into the ice or frozen ground. The operation was hazardous in the extreme, and thirty of the climbers fell and were killed. The inaccessibility of the ledges is shown by the fact that none of the bodies could be recovered for burial. But by dawn the heights were occupied, and the men made great parade of themselves, waving their white scarfs in token of success.

Alexander now pointed out his "winged soldiers" to the garrison, sent a herald towards the gate, and again called on Oxyartes to surrender. The position gained may not have had any peculiar value in compelling this; but, astonished beyond measure at being thus outdone, and imagining the men on the rocks above to be much more numerous than they actually were, and fully armed, the whole thing savoring, moreover, of the supernatural, with which Alexander's name was uniformly connected, the demand was complied with.

Among the many captives, male and female, was the daughter of Oxyartes, Roxana, said by the Macedonians who saw her to be the most beautiful woman of the East, since Statira, wife of Darius, was dead. She fell as captive to Alexander. But the king is stated to have fallen an equal and honest captive to her charms. He treated her with all becoming dignity, — as he had Statira, — and shortly afterwards married her. This side of Alexander's character is wholly admirable. Oxyartes was not only forgiven, but received into highest favor.

One other place remained, the Rock of Chorienes, in the land of the Parætacians, which was the mountainous region of the upper Oxus. Here Chorienes himself, and many other chiefs, had retired for refuge. There is a great deal of disagreement as to where the Rock of Chorienes was situated. It has not been any more positively located than hosts of other places where Alexander performed his remarkable exploits. Though its conformation is carefully described by the ancient authors, its whereabouts are not given. This region, indeed, is not well known to geographers. Colonel Chesney locates this rock, or the "Rock of Oxyartes," near the southeast shore of the Caspian Sea. Droysen puts it on the upper waters of the Oxus, seven hundred miles farther east. There is no means of reconciling this extraordinary disagreement, nor object in trying so to do, but probably the rock was to the east rather than to the west of the Sogdo-Bactrian country.

The march to this fortress was, in any event, over snow-clad mountains, and was a most severe one. The men suffered terribly from cold storms and lack of food. Many were frozen, many died of exposure. The king, as usual, shared the labors of his men in every sense, but could not lessen their sufferings. It seems that a march to the westward, where the land was less in altitude, would not have been so severe at this time of year. For it was early spring.

These mountain marches of Alexander are all in the highest degree remarkable. He appeared able to surmount any and all difficulties. The pity is that we know so little about their details. Anecdotes survive when important details have failed of record. It is related that one day on this march, when the king was warming himself at the camp-fire, a Macedonian, almost frozen stiff, was brought in. The king himself helped to take off his armor and gave him his own place at the fire, where the man revived. Coming to consciousness, the soldier was wonder-struck and frightened to find himself in the king's place. "Look you, comrade," quoth Alexander, "among the Persians, to sit on the king's seat entails death. To you, a Macedonian, it has brought life."

This remarkable rock of Chorienes is described as about

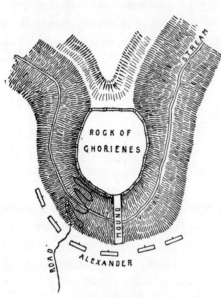

Rock of Chorienes.

seven miles (sixty stades) in circumference at the base. A difficult, narrow, winding road, artificially made, easily defended, and something over two miles (twenty stades) long, was its sole outlet. This was not easy of ascent, which must be made in single file, even when no one barred the way. The only height near by, from which the rock could be approached, was separated from it by a deep ravine through which rushed a violent mountain torrent. This must be bridged by a causeway in order to get near the walls. Arrian says the ravine ran all round the rock. The place in question was probably the only spot high enough to operate from. Though it was deemed entirely impracticable, Alexander nevertheless undertook the task. From the height mentioned, the soldiers were obliged to use ladders to descend into the ravine, the walls of which were very steep. These ladders were made by cutting down the pine-trees, which were here abundant and lofty.

Once in the ravine, Alexander began to build up a sort of

trestle-work of covered galleries, the whole army working at it, one half by day, under superintendence of Alexander, and the other half in three watches by night, under the somatophylaxes Perdiccas, Leonnatus, and Ptolemy, son of Lagus. With all their efforts, but thirty feet could be built during the day; at night the stint was less. In the narrowest part of the ravine they drove piles, close enough to sustain great weight. On these they constructed a sort of bridge of hurdles, woven of willows and osiers, and this was covered with earth. The barbarians began by deriding these efforts; but when they saw the structure rise, and covered in such a manner with screens and roofs, that, although below them, they could not harm the Macedonians; while these, from engines and with bows and slings, covered them with missiles, — which, being of better material and construction, killed and wounded many, — they changed their tone. Chorienes sent to Alexander, asking that he might see and consult his ancient ally, Oxyartes. This was granted, and Oxyartes, quoting his own case as example, so entirely impressed Chorienes with the idea of Alexander's justice, as well as his ability to do anything he set his hand to, that Chorienes concluded to surrender. He came to Alexander, who received him with the utmost kindness, entertained him in his own tent, and sent messengers to receive the surrender. Next day the king, accompanied by five hundred hypaspists, inspected the rock and fortress. So large a store of victuals had Chorienes in this fastness, that he was able for a period of two months to ration Alexander's entire army, giving them corn, salt meat, and wine; and this consumed but a tenth part of the stores laid up in the rock. The aid was opportune, for Alexander was sadly lacking in supplies, and during the siege much snow had fallen, making the hardships of the operation excessive. Alexander made Chorienes his friend, and continued him in command as his viceroy of all he had ruled before.

Alexander now returned to Bactra, and dispatched Craterus with six hundred Companions and four brigades, his own and those of Polysperchon, Attalus and Alcestas, against the only two remaining rebels in this Parætacenian mountain district, Catanes and Austanes. Craterus did his work well. He was growing to be one of Alexander's best generals. These chiefs were defeated in a bloody battle, in which Catanes and sixteen hundred men were killed, and Austanes was captured. This event ended the subjugation of the territory. Craterus returned to Bactra. Spring had now come.

For two years Alexander had been laboring to reduce this trans-Caucasian territory to a condition something like submission. He had found the people of an entirely different stamp from the inhabitants of the plains. In this most eastern land he had encountered the fiercest opposition ever made to him, and he had all but reduced a flourishing land to a desert — to a condition which only the care of years could improve — before he could call it his own. He found, too, that different measures were desirable to keep this land in subjection from those employed elsewhere. Alexander endeavored to leave the trans-Oxian region under a sort of dependent king. There are few details given of just what was done, or who was left in power. Sogdiana, filled with newly grounded Greek cities, and having Bactria and Margiana as a sort of reserve force in its rear, made a perfect bulwark against the incursions of the roving Scythians. Alexander carried with him no less than thirty thousand youths from Bactria and Sogdiana to serve not only as soldiers, but equally as hostages for the good behavior of their native land. It is far from improbable that the marriage with Roxana was as much a bold stroke of policy as it was a case of love at first sight. For her father's great influence could perhaps accomplish more towards keeping the population quiet than his own arms. By his union with Roxana he began in his own person that blending of the Occident and the Orient which was his favorite scheme. It was also from this idea that grew his assumption of a part Eastern dress and habits and the public insistence upon his descent from the gods. But this, however essential for the Eastern ear, he was, it is said by many, wont to scoff at with his closest friends.

The Macedonian soldier had changed too, in these six years' campaigns. From the independent but simple and well-disciplined shepherd-soldier, he had grown to be, as it were, one of the owners of the boundless wealth and luxury of the mighty East. As such he had acquired a self-esteem, an overweening sense of his own importance, which under any other commander would have been fraught with grave danger; but underlying this feeling was a still stronger sentiment, which may indeed be said to have been his one impulse, — a passionate love for his godlike young king, for the chief who was foremost in all dangers; superior to all in his personal gallantry, his superhuman endurance of fatigue, hunger, thirst; who was kinsman of the common soldier while he was easily lord of the phalangiarch; who, from his personal beauty to the gigantic grasp of his intellect, from his heroic daring to his divine military genius, was distinctly the first of soldiers — the first of men. No wonder, indeed. And while these Macedonians might criticise and bluster and browbeat, there was yet never a moment during Alexander's whole reign when, from the least to the greatest, each and every man in his army would not without thought or hesitation have laid his life at the feet of his beloved chief. This wonderful superiority, indeed, is the reason why Alexander's lieutenants have themselves less personal prominence; their own individ-

ual rays were swallowed up in the greater refulgence of the
central light.   " Thus the noble Craterus, who, as it is said,
loved the king; the gentle Hephæstion who loved Alexander;
thus the ever reliable and duty-doing Ptolemy, son of Lagus;
the quiet, through and through faithful Cœnus; the calculat-
ing Lysimachus."   The Macedonian hoplite, the artist, poet,
philosopher who followed the camp-court, the Persian noble,
each stands out in history in bolder personal relief than the
most efficient of Alexander's generals.   It is wont to be thus
with all great captains.

Alexander.

(From a Statue in the Glyptothek in Munich.)

XXXVIII.

THE COPHEN COUNTRY. MAY, B. C. 327, TO WINTER.

DURING the spring of B. C. 327, Alexander set out for India, a sort of fairy-land to all Greeks. From some Indian princes who had come to him with embassies of peace he had discovered that the Cophen cuts its passage through the mountain ranges to the Indus, in a narrow defile which formed, as it were, the Gates of India. With some hundred thousand men he left Zariaspa, and crossed the Caucasus to Alexandria. Thence, in two columns he advanced down the Cophen. The lesser column marched down the south bank, subduing the narrow strip of land between the river and the mountains, with orders to meet the king at the Indus. With his own column he moved along the north bank, and by sending detachments up each valley, and holding its outlet, he subdued the peoples of these mountains. This campaign in the mountain snows was very severe on the men, and cost much toil. A number of minor battles and sieges were among its features, and Alexander showed again and again how remarkable he was as a mountain fighter. He was twice wounded during this campaign. At Massaga, especially, he had a difficult problem, being repeatedly repulsed by Indian mercenary troops from the walls of the city. Finally all the barbarians abandoned the cities, and fled for refuge to the Rock of Aornus.

SPRING being well advanced, Alexander began to make definite arrangements for his expedition to India. Only Bacchus and Hercules had preceded him on this route. This country had always been a species of fairyland to the western nations. Shut out from access on the north and west by the greatest of mountain chains, it was a rare person, in the days of Alexander, who had ever reached the land of Brahma. Its wealth and glories were known only from the tales of merchants. Probably then at the height of its glory, these reports had been enough to excite the cupidity as well as the curiosity of Alexander, beyond any other land, and having got so near, he was bound to tread its sacred soil. He had discovered by good fortune, added to his native keenness, the best gate through the protecting mountain chain from Persia to the Indian plains, viz., the roadbed of the river Cophen, which plows between walls of rock through a narrow precipitous valley, from the parched uplands of Central Asia to the smiling levels of India. As Strabo expresses it, Alexander discovered India, and in view of the ignorance of geography at that day, the phrase is not inappropriate. At the outlet of the Cophen valley, the Five Rivers make a fresh boundary to the interior, and beyond them, Alexander knew, lay the head waters of the Ganges, the holy stream of India. Of the Ganges, Alexander had no doubt heard more than of any other feature of the country, and he believed that he could easily reach this river, which, as he heard, would conduct him to the great ocean, the confines of the world.

The Aryans had wandered from the upland plains, where they originated, through this very pass. Some had gone as far as the Ganges; some no farther than the Cophen valley. When Assyria grew strong, she conquered the Aryan uplands, still inhabited by a part of the race, but "Semiramis saw," it is related, "the camels of the Western steppes fly from before the elephants of the Indian East at the bridge over the Indus." The Medes came after the Assyrians, then the Persians. Cyrus claimed fealty from Gandara; Darius sent a Greek to the Indus, who sailed down the river to the sea, and then returned through the Arabian Gulf. A few Indians served at Gaugamela under Bessus and Barsaëntes; but beyond the Indus the Great King had never pretended to extend his grasp. There was a patchwork of independent states along the borders of the Five Rivers down to the sea and eastward to the desert. Kingdoms and republics vied in making a turmoil of political divisions.

Alexander had practically finished his military expedition, when he reached the limits of the Persian Empire. But several things, added to his restless ambition, combined to carry him onward. His reasons are not usually given in the authorities; the event tells the story. The king of Taxila, who was at war with Porus, lord of the region beyond the Hydaspes, had invited Alexander to come to his help. And Sisicottus, king of a land near the Indus, had joined Alexander after the fall of Bessus, and had since been faithful to him. From such persons as these Alexander not only received much information concerning India, but from intercourse with them had drunk in a deep longing to invade it.

Alexander's force at this moment is hard to calculate. Plutarch gives it as one hundred and thirty-five thousand men in the campaign down the Indus. It is probable that despite his losses, the large accessions of recruits from Macedonia, probably those classes owing military service whose turn had come for active duty, soldiers of fortune from Greece, Thrace, Agriania and other sources — about one hundred and fifty thousand men in all reached him from home — had at the present moment more than doubled the small army of thirty-five thousand men with which he crossed the Hellespont. Added to these, were large numbers of Oriental recruits embodied in the cavalry and phalanx. Many troops were drawn from the satrapies in the rear, which, in their turn, drew fresh men from home to replace the lost. Thus were repaired the enormous losses in battle, by severity of climate and the heavy marching of six long years. But there must be taken into consideration the very heavy garrisons Alexander was obliged to leave behind. In Bactria alone, as a sample, ten thousand foot and thirty-five hundred horse had been stationed. We know that he replaced these garrisons largely by levies from the warlike tribes he had just conquered; that Phœnicia, Cyprus,

Egypt each furnished its contingent; and Curtius says that his total effective, a year later, on the Indus, was one hundred and twenty thousand under the colors. In this army were all manner of soldiers, horse and foot from Arachotia, the Parapamisus, Bactria, Sogdiana, Scythians and Daäns, all showing a marked fealty to the conqueror, if furnishing elements perhaps difficult to control.

The force was no longer an Hellenic army. It was an army of Orientals with but a leaven of the old Macedonian element, moulded into the Macedonian organization and curbed by the Macedonian discipline. That Alexander was able to weld these diverse elements into a shape which gave the results he thereafter obtained from it; that he dared to trust himself and his work to a body so largely alien ; that he was able to fight such a battle as the one against Porus and win it, speaks more than volumes for this wonderful man's organizing ability and self-confidence. But Alexander never for a moment doubted his ability to do anything to which he put his hand. If his vanity was overstrained, he possessed the complementary virtue of self-reliance as perhaps no other man has ever had it.

The force left with Amyntas in Bactria, was, in the present condition of the land, abundantly able to hold the restless tribes north of the Caucasus in subjection. Alexander himself set out from Zariaspa at the end of spring, with perhaps something over one hundred thousand men. The roads were now better than when the army toiled over the mountains two years back, and provisions had been accumulated in abundance. A ten days' march, it is probable by the shorter pass of Kushan, took him across the mountains to Alexandria ad Caucasum. Here he found good cause to be disappointed at the management of affairs, and deemed it essential to make sundry changes in government. Neiloxinus, the commander of the garrison, as well as Proëxes, the satrap of the region, were both removed. The king left a number of invalided Macedonians as colonists, settled some of the native tribes in the place, and appointed Tyriaspes viceroy of Parapamisus, and Nicanor military governor of the city. He then marched to Nicea, where he offered sacrifice to Athena as was his wont at the beginning of every new campaign, and began his advance towards the Indus, down the Cophen and through the gate of rock at the easterly boundary of the Parapamisus level.

On the south side of the Cophen (modern Cabul) River lie the outpost ranges of the Sufeid-Kuh, which make one side of a narrow valley two hundred and fifty miles long, as the crow flies, from Nicea to the Indus, and dwindling to a defile forty miles long from Dhaka to Peshawur. To the north bank, mountains come down in huge scallops from Kafiristan. The Choës or Choaspes, the Euaspla and the Guræus with numerous tributaries here descend in narrow valleys from the Caucasus or western Himalayas. The whole course of the Cophen is through a huge but well defined gorge, with immense masses of mountains on either hand.

Alexander sent heralds ahead to the chiefs of the Indian tribes living along the Cophen, ordering them to report to him with hostages in proof of their submission. The king of Taxila, whom Curtius calls Omphis, and a number of native princes came to headquarters in royal state, accompanied by elephants, which they placed at the king's disposal, and bearing splendid and unusual presents in token of their readiness to serve him. Alexander informed these princes that he expected to exhaust the summer and autumn months in reducing the country between him and the Indus, to winter on that river, and the next year to cross over and chastise the nations beyond, enemies of his new associates. As it turned out, the following winter was consumed in mountain campaigning along the Cophen. He had illy gauged the size of his task in this alpine region.

At Nicea Alexander divided his army into two columns. He detached Hephæstion and Perdiccas along the right bank of the Cophen, through the land of Gandara, towards Peucelaotis on the direct road to the Indus, with the three brigades

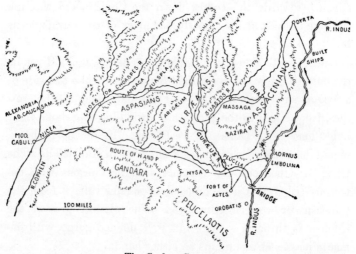

The Cophen Campaign.

of Gorgias, Clitus (the white one) and Meleager, half the Companion and all the Greek mercenary cavalry. They had orders to reduce the towns on the route, and when they reached the Indus to make preparations for bridging it. The king of Taxila and some other chiefs were to be their guides. This corps was to be a flying wing, as it were, of the army of the king, who, taking a more northerly route, proposed to reduce all the strongholds in the mountain passes on the north bank of the Cophen, which region was full of warlike native tribes, marching from pass to pass, and completing his work thoroughly as he advanced. The two columns would prevent the tribes north and south of the river from combining to assist each other, and either column could retire upon the other in case of disaster.

On the way Hephæstion and Perdiccas were delayed a month by the so-called revolt of Astes, king of Peucelaotis, who retired into his fortified city. This it became necessary to besiege, but the place was captured and Astes was killed during the hostilities. Sangæus, who had deserted Astes, was left as viceroy. Beyond this Hephæstion and Perdiccas had little trouble. They easily pacified the country, whose inhabitants were evidently far from warlike, marched to the Indus, which they reached while the king was still struggling through the mountains, and made all due preparation against his arrival, by collecting provision and materials for a bridge. The land they protected by garrisoning the fortress of Astes and Orobatis.

The king meanwhile led the bulk of the army over the much more difficult northerly route on the other side of the Cophen. His task was to reduce such of the mountain tribes there dwelling as would be necessary to secure and make permanent his control of the valley of this river. He had with him the shield-bearing guards, the other half of the Companion cavalry, the phalanx, except what marched with Hephæstion and Perdiccas, the foot-agema, the archers, Agrianians, and horse lancers. With these he first marched into the land of the Aspasians, next to which was that of the Guræans and beyond them the domain of the Assacenians. On the river Choës or Choaspes (probably the modern Kama) — some geographers make these separate streams — which rises from the glaciers of the Caucasus, and flows through an almost inaccessible valley with towering mountain masses on either hand, Alexander learned that most of the neighboring barbarians had fled for refuge into the cities of that country,

which were situated well up the valley. Their capital lay
some days' march up stream. The Aspasians were herders,
and very rich in flocks. From the upper end of the valley
was a pass to the head waters of the Oxus, by way of which
constant intercourse was kept up between these tribes and the
Sogdianians. It was highly important to gain control of this
capital, as the key of this section of country.

Anxious to settle the question quickly, Alexander crossed the
river, and advanced along the farther bank with a van consisting of the cavalry and eight hundred Macedonian infantry
mounted on horses, towards these strongholds. The chronology of Curtius is apt to be inaccurate, but he says that Alexander used pontoons in this campaign. "Now, as there were
several rivers to pass, they so contrived the boats that they
might be taken to pieces and carried in wagons, and put together again as occasion required." Other authors mention
this first on the farther side of the Indus. In any event, the
invention was made about this time. At the first town,
whose name is not given us, the barbarians drew up outside
the walls to oppose him; but without waiting to rest or for
the balance of the troops to come up, Alexander attacked,
quickly routed them, and drove them into the gates. He
himself received a shot through the breastplate in the shoulder, and Ptolemy and Leonnatus were also wounded. This
arrested further operations for that day. The army went into
camp near the place where an assault seemed to promise the
best results.

From the nature of Alexander's wounds, we can, after a
fashion, judge what the usual wounds of the Macedonians in
combat with the barbarians were apt to be. No doubt Alexander's armor was of finer make, and protected him better
than that of the ordinary soldier. As a rule, his wounds
were such as to heal readily; and, with his inflexible will and

wonderful good health, he was not wont to be long laid up. The same rule will apply to the average of the soldiers. There were probably many wounded who scarcely went off duty; who certainly kept with their commands or with the train, even if relegated to easy work or none for a shorter or longer period.

The town in question had a double wall, and was stoutly defended. The next morning the rest of the troops arrived. An attack was made. The barbarians could not resist the Macedonian onset. The outer wall, not being very substantial, was at once taken. The inner wall was more difficult, but was defended only a few hours after the ladders were brought into use. As usual, the better weapons and good defensive armor of the Macedonian heavy troops gave the barbarians no chance. The Macedonians were comparatively safe from wounds, as well as under the best of discipline. The barbarians were wise enough to make their exit while they might by the rear gates, and fled to the mountains. Here they were followed up, and many of their number overtaken and slain. Alexander's men, in revenge for their leader's wound, razed the city to the ground. Marching to the next town, named Andaca, Alexander gained possession of it by capitulation, the inhabitants being appalled by the summary fate of their neighbor.

Alexander saw that by holding with suitable forts the outlets of these valleys, he could readily control the valleys themselves, and by carefully blockading them, reduce their inhabitants to terms in his own good time. He therefore left Craterus with an ample heavy infantry force to continue the reduction of the minor towns, place garrisons in them, and arrange the affairs of the country as best might seem to him, and then, by a lower pass over the mountains nearer the Cophen River, to join him in the valley of the Guræus (modern Pandj Kora).

Two marches then brought Alexander to Euaspla on the river of the same name, where dwelt the chief of the Aspasians. Learning of his approach, the Aspasians set fire to their city, and fled into the highlands. The king and his bodyguard led the flight, full of terror. Alexander followed sharply, and slew a great number of the fugitives. Hotly pushing the pursuit, and recognizing the Aspasian king a short distance ahead on an eminence, surrounded by his bodyguard, Ptolemy, the ground being steep, dismounted his men, rushed after with a few hypaspists, and brought him to bay. A hand to hand fight took place. The Indian king thrust his spear through Ptolemy's breastplate, but the weapon stopped there; Ptolemy's pike transfixed the Indian king through both thighs, inflicting a mortal wound. The others fled; but when Ptolemy was despoiling the Indian of his arms, the bodyguard, ashamed to desert their king, turned upon him. Alexander, having seized the hill on which the barbarians had stood, came to the rescue with his agema, and here Ptolemy and Alexander engaged in individual combat with the barbarians over the corpse of their leader in true Homeric fashion. The advantage remained with Alexander and Ptolemy. The barbarians beat a hasty retreat. Events such as this have perhaps no bearing on the military question, but they serve to show the individual nature of combats in that age, and in so far explain some of those characteristics of both soldier and leader which are otherwise difficult to understand. We cannot but regret that instead of these personal recollections, Ptolemy has not told us more about how this campaign was really conducted. Alexander was leading a large army; the narration of some of the operations sounds like the work of a bare brigade. What he accomplished was wonderful; all we can do is to trace his itinerary.

From this place Alexander advanced over the mountain

passes to Arigæum, which he found burned. Here Craterus joined him by the more southerly route mentioned, having left the region of Andaca well provided for. Him again Alexander put in charge of Arigæum, which was a convenient and promising place for a settlement, instructing him to rebuild and colonize the town afresh with some of the invalided Macedonians and with well-disposed natives, and to fortify it strongly. For this city and Andaca commanded the valley heads of the Choës, Guræus and many intervening rivers and streams; and the possession of strong places at these two points gave Alexander substantial control of nearly all the passes in the uplands, and thus left no opposition or danger between him and Sogdiana. But the thoroughness of this method of working consumed much time.

Some tribes north of Arigæum had rendezvoused with the fugitives from this vicinity at a point farther up the mountains, and threatened trouble to the new city. Alexander saw that he must leave the garrison he proposed to place in Arigæum free from risk of attack for some time, and took up his march against them. While on the way, Ptolemy, having preceded the army on a foraging and reconnoitring expedition, returned with news that a very large force of barbarians was near at hand, lying on a mountain side, with camp fires vastly outnumbering Alexander's. The barbarians of the whole adjoining territory had, it seems, joined forces, their spirits by no means cowed by the loss of their town. A part of his army Alexander left in reserve, encamped at the foot of the mountain, and marched with a force which he judged sufficient towards the barbarians.

When he had reached their vicinity, he divided his forces into three parts: under Ptolemy, who took a third of the hypaspists, the brigades of Philip and Philotas, two squadrons of horse-archers, the Agrianians and half the other cavalry;

Leonnatus, with his own, Attalus' and Balacrus' brigades;
and himself, leading the phalanx and the cavalry Companions. Alexander advanced on what seemed to be the strongest part of the barbarians' line, sending Ptolemy and Leonnatus each by a hidden circuit, to take post where they could

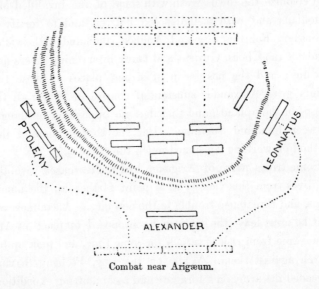

Combat near Arigæum.

attack on either flank when the barbarians should have placed
themselves at a disadvantage; for the king designed to lure
them into an ambush. Perceiving the small force of Macedonians under Alexander, and not aware of the flank detachments, the barbarians came down from their stronghold to
the plain, expecting an easy victory over such a meagre body.
But they had never yet encountered Macedonian discipline,
and reaching Alexander's steady handful while in loose order
from their hasty advance, they broke to pieces on the sarissas
of the phalanx.

Ptolemy and Leonnatus now attacked opportunely on the
flanks. Ptolemy was placed opposite a rugged ascent, and

encountered heavy resistance. The barbarians perceived his advance, and met him with unusual vigor. The natives here, whom Arrian calls Indians because dwelling near the Indus, were strong, bold and active, and made a stanch defense. But Ptolemy formed column of assault, and, though checked, finally carried the hill by storm. Leonnatus won an easier success. Thus closed in on both their flanks, and sharply thrown back from their front attack, the Indians lost heart, threw down their arms, and were surrounded and captured to the number of forty thousand. This number is the one given by Ptolemy, though it seems exaggerated. The country, however, was thickly populated. All their cattle, said to be two hundred and thirty thousand in number, were also corralled. These were of such excellent quality for size, strength, activity and for easy fattening, that Alexander picked out the best, and sent them to Macedonia to breed from. This is the origin of the hump still seen on the cattle in parts of Greece.

Craterus now joined with the forces under his command and the military engines, after settling the affair of Arigæum, and, with the whole army, Alexander advanced down the Guræus, intending to move into the territory of the Assacenians, who, in the next adjoining valley of the Suastos, were said to have assembled twenty thousand cavalry, thirty thousand infantry and thirty elephants. Alexander hurried forward with the van, Craterus followed more slowly with the heavy train and engines.

The army had been campaigning in an alpine region. The entire route of the king's column from Alexandria ad Caucasum thus far towards the Indus had been through a mountainous and difficult country, entailing much exertion on the men, excessive hardships and frequent lack of rations. The present descent to the smiling lowlands must have been an agreeable change. The route lay along the right bank of the Guræus. The barbarians attempted to defend this river at a point where they might have given Alexander much trouble, for it is swift and with a rocky bed, which afforded a poor footing to troops crossing under fire; but overawed by the firm front of the Macedonians, they retired, each party to its own city, and decided to defend their homes in lieu of risking a general battle in the open field.

It is curious that savage or semi-civilized nations so often commit the mistake of standing a siege, or of delivering a battle, in lieu of resorting to small war. In the latter, especially on their own soil, they are not unapt to be on a par with the best troops; in the former, with equal bravery, they uniformly fail against the better weapons and discipline, or the greater technical skill, of the civilized armies.

Massaga.

Alexander now marched on Massaga, the largest town and capital of the Assacenians. The barbarians had hired a force of seven thousand Indian mercenaries, and emboldened by their presence, — for apparently these professional soldiers were held in high repute, and deservedly, — they undertook to make a sudden attack on Alexander's force when it had reached their vicinity and was about to go into camp. In order to throw them off their guard, and draw them away from the town into the open, Alexander simulated retreat, and retired to a hill nearly a mile distant. The enemy followed. But when the barbarians were within arrow-flight a signal was given, and the Macedonians turned upon the Massagans and Indians, who were in loose order in anticipation of an easy victory. Their battle-shout and fierce front, as the light troops advanced, fired a volley, and opened right and left to uncover the heavy troops behind, surprised the barbarians beyond measure, and when the line, headed by Alexander, charged down in phalanx at a run, the enemy was utterly overthrown so soon as they came hand to hand. Some two hundred were killed, and the rest fled headlong to the city. Alexander at once pushed on to the wall, hoping to take the town by a *coup de main*. But he found this impracticable. The wall was well defended, and he himself, in reconnoitring for the morrow's attack, was slightly wounded in the calf of the leg. He drew out the arrow himself, ordered his horse to be brought, and went on with his work without stanching the blood. But by and by he was compelled to stop. " They may call me son of Jupiter," said he, laughing, " but I suffer none the less like a mortal. This is blood, not ichor ! "

This wound stopped proceedings for the moment. Next day Alexander, whose activity no wounds could abate, brought up his engines, and in a short while battered down a piece of the wall ; but the Indians proved themselves stanch and brave, and the Macedonians could not, despite their best efforts, on that day force an entrance through the gaps. As speedily as possible, a tower and terrace were built, — Curtius says it took nine days to build the terrace, — and on the day after their completion the tower was advanced to the wall. From this, missiles could be hurled by engines and shot by the archers and slingers, to keep the defenders at a distance ; but even this fire did not enable the Macedonians to force an entrance through the breach. Alexander had met with the stanchest troops he encountered in this region. The night was spent in preparation. These backsets would not do. The king was on his mettle. By the next morning he had got ready a bridge to throw from the tower to the wall, and had selected the shield-bearing guards, who had in similar fashion captured Tyre, to charge over it and drive the defenders from the breaches.

The preparations were duly completed; the bridge was thrown; the gallant hypaspists made the assault with all their usual dash, and with the confidence bred of a hundred victories thus snatched. But the bridge, hastily built and being overcharged by the ardor of the men, who crowded upon each other in their efforts to outdo themselves, broke, and a number of Macedonians were dumped pell-mell into the ditch. Perceiving their advantage, the eager barbarians not only showered stones, beams, fire-balls, and all manner of missiles upon the luckless wounded men below, but with a great shout of triumph made an immediate sortie from the side gates between the towers of the town, and inflicted much loss on the mass of struggling humanity in the ditch. Alexander was fain to sound the recall. He immediately ordered in fresh troops, and it was by the heroic efforts of Alcestas' taxis alone that the wounded and dead were rescued without still greater loss. Several detachments had got isolated in the general attack, had not heard the trumpet signal, and had to be withdrawn by the advance of other troops, which was done with some difficulty.

On the succeeding day another bridge was thrown in the like manner; but the Indians defended themselves with the utmost gallantry; Alexander still made no greater progress. It must have been a novelty to the Macedonians to find themselves thus matched. Nor, indeed, would the town have

yielded at all until the last extreme, had not the leader of
the Indian mercenaries haply been killed by a missile from
a catapult. Many of the body had already been killed, and
nearly all were wounded. Thus deprived of leadership, the
gallant fellows sent a message to Alexander, who agreed to
receive their capitulation if they (the Indian mercenaries)
would enlist as a body in his service, and surrender as hostages the family of the king of Massaga. To this they
agreed, marched out, and encamped on an adjoining hill. It
is claimed that they refused to carry out their promise, lest
they should, in Alexander's advance across the Indus, be
obliged to fight against their fellow-citizens, and that they
made an attempt to retreat at night. This may or may not
be true; but Alexander surrounded the hill on which they
were, intercepted their flight, if any was intended, and on
one or other pretext the Macedonians got beyond control,
attacked them, and cut them all to pieces.

Massaga was easily captured by storm after the Indians
had withdrawn. The garrison was put to the sword as if
there had been no capitulation, — apparently a quite indefen-
sible act, if these are all the facts. It is alleged that an example was necessary in order to appall the adjoining tribes,
and to prevent more Indian mercenaries from coming hither;
but this is scarcely a palliation. Alexander's loss had been
twenty-five killed, and an exceptionally large number
wounded.

Alexander now sent a force under Attalus, Alcestas, and
Demetrius, the cavalry leader, to Ora, with orders to blockade it until his arrival, which was done. He also dispatched
another, under Cœnus, to Bazira (probably modern Bajour),
hoping it would surrender on hearing of the fate of Massaga.
This, however, was not the case. Bazira was situated on a
lofty hill, and well fortified. Bad news soon came from both

places. Alexander saw that he must undertake the task in person. He had intended to march first on Bazira, but from the reports he deemed it wise to make his earlier move on Ora, where Alcestas had with difficulty defeated a sortie of the garrison. He meanwhile instructed Cœnus to fortify a strong position near by to use in besieging the town of Bazira, and to cut off its supplies ; then to leave a garrison in the works sufficient to keep the Bazirans within walls, and join him at Ora. For Abisares, king of Cashmir, northwest of this locality, was said to have sent large reinforcements to Ora.

All these orders were duly executed, but when the Bazirans saw Cœnus marching off with the bulk of his force, they imagined that they would now have matters their own way, and, emerging from their city, they attacked the garrison of the newly-built fort from the plain. In a sharp battle, however, they were worsted, with five hundred killed. This defeat had the effect to narrow the lines about Bazira, and all the more securely to coop up the inhabitants in the city. Ora proved an easy prey to Alexander, who took it on the first assault and there captured a number of elephants. And when the men of Bazira learned this, they evacuated their city in the night, and retreated to the rock of Aornus. All the barbarians were deserting their cities for this last refuge.

Hephæstion and Perdiccas had fully secured the south bank of the Cophen ; had pacified all the tribes in the mountains which hug this bank all along its course ; and had insured the land against revolt by garrisoning the forts of Astes and Orobatis. This duty had occupied but a fraction of the time consumed by the king's larger task. Alexander, on the north of the river, with everlasting snows always in sight, had successively reduced the valleys of the Choaspes, Guræus and Suastos ; had subdued the territory of the tribes living on

these rivers ; had driven the barbarians back into the mountains, and held the more important passes, as well as controlled the valleys at Andaca and Arigæum ; had fortified
Massaga, Ora, Bazira, which controlled the land of the Assacenians, and shortly after took Peucela, which commanded
the west bank of the Indus.   The whole cis-Indus land was
under Macedonian control.   The Gates to India were firmly
grasped.   But one place still held out.   The Macedonians
called it Aornus — "a spot higher than the flight of birds."

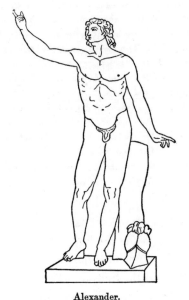

Alexander.
[From a Statue in Dresden.)

XXXIX.

AORNUS. LATE WINTER, B. C. 326.

THIS rock, the last stronghold of the Cophen barbarians, was said to have resisted Hercules. It contained arable land sufficient to sustain the garrison. Situated not far from the Indus, it was much larger than Gibraltar. Having garrisoned the strong places of the country, Alexander moved on Aornus. By promise of great rewards he procured native guides who showed him paths by which to gain a position commanding the fortress. To this he sent Ptolemy, and later with great exertion led the whole army. Between him and the fort was a deep ravine, as at the rock of Chorienes. Having tried escalade and failed, Alexander began to build a mound across the ravine, and in six days had so nearly reached the fort that the enemy asked for terms. These Alexander granted, but on their violation seized the place and slew most of the garrison. He then moved north to Dyrta, where there was an uprising; having subdued which he made his way to the Indus and descended on boats, which he built on the spot, to the mouth of the Cophen, and joined his second column. Alexander's self-imposed duty to Greece had ended when he had reduced to possession the kingdom of Darius. His right to invade India was mere lust of conquest. His *casus belli* against Porus, whom he first attacked, was enmity between Porus and the king of Taxila, with which latter prince Alexander had made an alliance.

THIS remarkable rock was the last stronghold of the barbarians between Zariaspa and the Indus, and was said to have resisted Hercules. It commanded the whole country between the Cophen, the Indus and the Suastos. From it a vast stretch of country could be observed. The more difficult of access this fortress, the more essential that Alexander should take it, not only on account of the moral effect, but in order to leave his rear secure. Such a threat to his communications, as this fort in the enemy's hands, could not be left behind, if he was to cross the Indus. No man ever looked more carefully to his communications. This was the military side of the question.

But the other aspect of the case was equally important. If Alexander could but do what Hercules had been unable to accomplish, was not his divine origin more surely made manifest to his Eastern subjects? And though this was always one of the strongest of motives with Alexander, it is very noteworthy that it was uniformly secondary to military common sense. This fact alone, and it is indisputable, silences much of the unreasoning criticism of Alexander's weaknesses.

Situated, as identified by Major Abbot (though its whereabouts cannot be surely determined), on the Indus about sixty miles from the Cophen, the last outpost of the mountain ranges, the rock of Aornus (Mount Mahabun) was some twenty-three miles

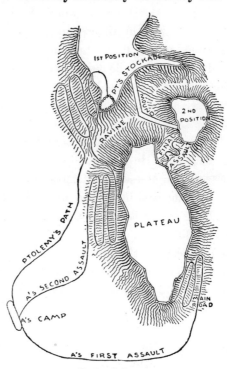

Rock of Aornus.

in circumference at the base, and stood up, it is said, five thousand feet at its summit above the plain. This made this fastness much larger and more formidable than Gibraltar, which is about six miles around the base, and but fourteen hundred feet high. According to General Cunningham, Aornus is the rock of Rani-gat, which is but twelve hun-

dred feet in height, and some five miles round at the base.
The exact spot is perhaps not material, though it would be
highly interesting to know the locality.   At the lowest place
it was said to be a mile and a quarter in the ascent, which
was artificially constructed, and very difficult.   At the top of
the rock was table-land well watered by an abundant spring ;
and there was timber and arable land enough to sustain one
thousand men by tillage ; or, as Arrian puts it, "for one
thousand men to till," which means even more.   There seems
to be no reason to doubt the accuracy of this description.   A
large army could hold this rock year in year out, and the
barbarians felt that they were entirely secure from the Macedonians.

Alexander saw that he could not avoid besieging this
stronghold.   He accordingly transformed Ora, Massaga and
Bazira into Macedonian fortresses for the purpose of helping
to keep the land in subjection, and Hephæstion and Perdiccas
did the same with Orobatis, which controlled the land near
the Indus.   A number of such fortresses were essential to the
full security of the army.   Nicanor, one of the Companions,
was made viceroy of the cis-Indus territory.   Continuing his
march towards the Cophen, Alexander, having taken Peucela,
near by, garrisoned it under Philip.   He also took possession
of some other small towns, with the help of friendly chiefs,
prominent among whom were Cophæus and Assagetes.
Thence he marched to Embolina, near the rock of Aornus,
where he left Craterus to establish an immediate base of
operations and to gather victuals for a long siege of the rock,
should it prove to be necessary.   Then taking the bowmen,
the Agrianians and the brigade of Cœnus, the lightest and
best armed of the phalanx, two hundred Companion cavalry
and one hundred horse-bowmen, he marched to the rock and
camped.   On the next day he reconnoitred the ground and
shifted his camp nearer the rock.

Some of the natives now came to Alexander, no doubt attracted by his reputation for giving princely recompense, — the king had probably made inquiries and promises on all hands, — and offered to lead him to a part of the rock which they pointed out from below, and from which the citadel could be assailed, if at all. Particularly an old shepherd and his two sons were selected as guides, and the king offered a prize of eighty talents for success in this enterprise. Alexander sent Ptolemy, son of Lagus, with some of the Agrianians and other light troops, added to a body of picked hypaspists, with directions to occupy the place and signal to him when he had done so. Ptolemy, after a long and difficult march over narrow and dangerous footpaths, in conduct of the guides, reached the position undiscovered by the barbarians, and after fortifying it by a stockade and ditch, he fired a beacon where Alexander could see it.

Next morning at dawn the king led his men to assault the hill from the main approach, expecting that Ptolemy would be able to help him from his new position. But the main approach was so well defended by the Aornians that the king could make no headway, even with the aid of a well-meant but not vigorous diversion by Ptolemy on their rear. Finding that Alexander could be easily held in check by limited numbers, the barbarians fiercely turned on Ptolemy in force, and drove him back to his stockade; but, though with the utmost difficulty, this officer managed to hold his position there, and the enemy withdrew his troops at nightfall, having lost heavily by the fire of the Agrianians and archers. The next night Alexander managed, through a deserter familiar with the locality, to convey to Ptolemy the information that he would assault early next day from a point more nearly in his direction than at the main approach, and gave him orders, instead of holding his position, to move down the mountain, and attack the barbarians in the rear, whenever he saw them emerge from their defenses to repel the assault he should make. In this way Alexander would try to reunite the forces, whose division at this moment had proven to be unwise, for it had not resulted in surrender, as the ruse of the "winged soldiers" at the rock of Oxyartes had done. At the same time he hoped that the barbarians might afford him an opening by which he could surprise the fort.

At daybreak Alexander began the ascent of the mountain, prepared for an assault. The barbarians soon perceived his movement, and began to harass his men as they climbed one by one along the steep paths, with darts and arrows, to roll stones down upon them, and to embarrass them in every manner. But the Macedonians persevered, and by sharp persistent fighting and the protection of good armor made some headway. Ptolemy now fell upon the flank and rear of the barbarians, who had advanced between the two bodies, and threw them off their guard; and towards afternoon Alexander managed to make a junction with Ptolemy. At the same time the flying Indians led him to believe that he could capture the fort, and he endeavored to follow the enemy into their defenses, but was not speedy enough to do so. The gates were closed upon him, and the place was too narrow for an assault to promise success.

The army with Alexander now reached the eminence where Ptolemy had built his stockade, — a place lower than, and separated from, the top of the rock by a precipitous ravine. This he tried the same day to cross by escalading the rocks, but found that the task was an impossible one.

On this occasion he gave the pages a chance to distinguish themselves. He called for volunteers, and thirty of these royal youths presented themselves. Under two of their number, Charus and Alexander, this forlorn hope, suitably sustained by the Agrianians and archers, started on its mission to fray a path to the fortress. The Companions had prevailed on the king not to accompany them. But the gallant pages had not gone more than quarter way, when Alexander, impatient of any one gathering glory he might share, turned towards his body-guard, and inviting them to follow, sallied out after the pages. The barbarians were prepared. Huge blocks of stone were rolled down on the assailants; many fell. But still the pages pushed on. One by one they reached the crest but only to fall pierced by many missiles. The king and his guards were still too far to hope to assist them in season to be of any avail. The assault had failed. Another promised a like result.

Alexander, after due study of the problem, determined to build a mound across the ravine so as to bring his engines into a position from which he could use them against the walls. The whole army set to work with a will. The day's stint of each man was to collect and bring one hundred stakes. There was abundance of timber. Hurdles were made of the smaller wood. Stones, earth, stumps, every available thing was put to use to help the filling of the mound. On the first day, the work was so rapidly pushed, that the Macedonians had built the mound forward from their side, where the ravine was not so deep as farther on, nearly three hundred paces. The Indians at first contented themselves with collecting on the walls beyond bowshot, and deriding these efforts; but when their astonishment and alarm grew with the progress of the mound, they sought to harass the Macedonians in their work by a fire of arrows across the ravine. But the engines and archers and slingers with their better fire held them steadily in check.

It has already been noticed that only the more necessary parts of the catapults and ballistas were carried along.

Wherever there was timber, the rough frame-work could be put together in a few hours. It is evident that Alexander had mountain-batteries, so to speak, which could be carried even on the backs of men where pack animals could not go. And it is also evident that these engines were as effective against the defenses of that time as our modern guns are against those of to-day. Their utility was abundantly demonstrated in the passage of rivers as well as in sieges.

For three days Alexander continued this work, and made considerable progress in the mound. As usual the king was everywhere and harder at work than any of his men, direct-ing, encouraging, reproving and lending a hand. On the fourth day a small party of Macedonians made their way over the mound and the rest of the ravine to an eminence which was on a level with the fortress, and drove the defend-ers from it. Some of the authorities state that the fight here was bitter, and that Alexander headed the agema in order to secure the eminence. Having done so, he now aimed the mound towards this height, which was for him the key point; for its elevation would enable him to use his fire to advantage. The height was reached on the sixth day from the start, after great effort and continuous labor.

The Indians, astonished before, were now dazed at the audacity and skill of the Macedonians and the manner in which they made vain all the natural obstacles of the moun-tains, driven on by the never-flagging energy and matchless skill of Alexander. They sent to the king, and asked for a truce, agreeing to surrender on stated terms. Their honesty Alexander mistrusted, but he accepted the terms. He soon discovered, however, that the barbarians proposed, by delay-ing the ratification, to gain time to scatter and escape in squads to the plain, and to their several cities, instead of sur-rendering themselves as agreed. He proposed to checkmate this scheme. He gave no sign of suspecting the treachery, but allowed the barbarians to begin their retreat, which they did at night. He then took seven hundred of his best men from the agema and hypaspists, and making his way across the ravine, himself was the first to scale the rock at a point where the rear-guard of the enemy had deserted it. By pulling each other up and by the use of ropes and poles, the force was, without great delay, and undiscovered by the barbarians, who were intent on collecting their valuables for flight, got upon the upper level of the rock, from whence, falling on the enemy at a concerted signal as they were just flying, they slew many; while others, in their panic-stricken endeavors to escape, threw themselves down the precipices right and left. A large number undoubtedly escaped, and made their way into the mountains; but the force was quite dispersed. Thus Alexander captured the inexpugnable rock of Aornus, against which, according to the legend, even Hercules had recoiled. Sacrifices were offered on the highest point of the rock, the works were strengthened, and a Macedonian garrison was left to defend it. Sissicottus, who had obtained Alexander's favor by his faithful and intelligent assistance, was made viceroy of the district.

Alexander now heard of a body of barbarians which had assembled in the northern country, and immediately made a retrograde movement to Dyrta, a fortified place in the land of the Assacenians. Here had been gathered, by the brother of the chief who died at Massaga, an army of twenty thousand men and fifteen elephants. This new chief hoped that the inaccessibility of Dyrta, which was well back in the recesses of the mountains, would deter Alexander from moving against him; and that when the Macedonians left, he might be able to reassert his authority, and by falling on Alexander's rear, accomplish something of importance.

Alexander was not slow in setting out to put an end to this scheme; but on reaching Dyrta after a long and arduous march, he found it deserted by the barbarians, who had been astonished and had their superstitious notions aroused by the extraordinary capture of Aornus. Alexander sent out parties in various directions under Nearchus and Antiochus, the two chiefs of the hypaspists, the former with the Agrianians and light troops, the latter with his own brigade and two others, to reconnoitre the country, and especially to search for the elephants; for the barbarians had conveyed away all these animals, of which Alexander desired to accumulate a number, either from motives of curiosity, or to be able to test for himself their value in war. He was enabled to get on their track by some natives whom he captured, and who showed him the way to the place where, near the Indus, these creatures had been sent to pasture in a spot deemed secure from discovery. The barbarians' army had fled into the pathless wilderness across the Indus, to seek the protection of Abisares, king of Cashmir; but some of the lesser chiefs had assassinated their leader, and brought his head to Alexander. This practically disorganized the force; and seeing no use in following the body into the thickets where roads had to be cut, Alexander determined to begin his move down the Indus. Of the elephants he captured all but two, which, in the pursuit, fell over precipices and were killed.

A part of the army had some time before been sent ahead to cut roads to reach the Indus. From the place to which Alexander had penetrated towards the Indus was a stretch of wilderness. On arriving at this river, Alexander discovered a supply of timber suitable for shipbuilding. He stayed here time sufficient to enable him to build a number of boats. This was a work at which many of his men were experts, and could be done rapidly; and on these, with the aid of native pilots, he carried the army down the river to the spot where Hephæstion and Perdiccas had long been busy in making preparations for a bridge. The last part of the way, near modern Attock, the men probably had to disembark and march, for the current there is very swift and dangerous. Attock is at the confluence of the Caboul and Indus.

Before crossing the Indus with his army, Alexander made a march to ivy-clad Nysa, a city said to have been founded by Bacchus, which, finding it well governed and friendly, he left in possession of its ancient freedom; and sacrificing to the god with feasts upon Mount Meros, he returned towards the Indus. Here he found that a substantial bridge of boats had been thrown, and a large number of vessels constructed; and here he gave his army a thirty days' — or perhaps longer — rest, much needed, for a large part of the men had undergone the fatigues of a most harassing winter campaign, and required not only recuperation, but some reorganization.

It was late in the winter when he broke up. On leaving Zariaspa, Alexander had expected to be able to finish the Cophen campaign before the arrival of winter, so as to rest his army in winter-quarters; but he was so long delayed that, before he actually got to work on this region, winter had overtaken him. His anxiety to cross the Indus was so great, however, that he had carried through this winter campaign rather than defer the Indian matter to another season.

The Taxiles, or king of this region, had, as we know, long ago solicited Alexander's protection; had guided the column of Hephæstion and Perdiccas to the Indus, and now came to headquarters with a present of two hundred talents of silver, three thousand beeves, ten thousand sheep, and thirty war elephants. He brought, moreover, seven hundred Indian horsemen as a reinforcement, and agreed to surrender to Alexander his flourishing and beautiful capital city of Taxila, the largest between the Indus and the Hydaspes, whose ruins to-day cover six square miles, on consideration that Alexander would help him against his enemy Porus, king of the region beyond that river.

Alexander had always placed the limit of his intended conquests and wanderings at the river Indus. His claim as Hegemōn of the Greeks was a right to the kingdom of Darius, and this only in revenge for wrongs done by Persia to Greece. But now came in this new alliance with Taxiles which gave him a pretext for crossing the boundary he had set, and of venturing into the unknown land of India. His place of crossing was probably at modern Attock near the mouth of the Cophen or Caboul River, which he had been descending from Bactriana. His bridge, according to Diodorus, was made of boats. This, and numerous craft of all sizes and kinds built or found in the neighborhood, together with what he had brought down the Indus, made the crossing a simple matter, as he was advancing into the land of friends. The king and his suite crossed on two thirty-oared galleys, with suitable ceremony. The movement was not only propitiated by the usual numerous sacrifices, but also celebrated, when accomplished, by games and feasts. The pomp and circumstance of these splendid pageants finds its proper place in the pages of many authors. It does not belong here.

On the farther side he was joined by an army of native troops twenty thousand strong, and with fifteen elephants. This force had murdered its king, Aphrices, and now joined Alexander, with a request that it might serve under his banner. At Taxila he was received with befitting splendor. Here friendly embassies came to him from many adjoining tribes, among them Doxaris, a neighboring potentate, and one from Abisares of Cashmir, headed by his brother, who strenuously denied having afforded aid to the Assace-

nians. As had now become all the more the custom with
Alexander, during the remainder of the season which he
spent here, he made his sojourn a series of festivities in the
Macedonian manner, but without neglecting the demands of
the army, whose mixture of nationalities called for much
time in discipline and organization. Then leaving a garrison,
mostly of invalided men, under Philip, son of Machatas, as a
sort of viceroy, but clothing Taxiles with practical authority,
he advanced towards the line of the Hydaspes, which he was
informed was held by Porus, king of the region beyond the
river.

No doubt the readiness with which Taxiles placed himself
under Alexander's command was due to the enmity existing
between himself and this Porus, whose kingdom was too
strong to attack single-handed, and of whom he stood in constant dread. For Porus was certainly the most able chieftain
of this country, possessed a rich and flourishing kingdom,
said to contain one hundred large cities, and had Cashmir as
an ally. Porus was not only at odds with Taxiles and the
Himalayan tribes, but also with the " kingless " peoples of
the Five Rivers.

In order to be able to bridge the Hydaspes, Alexander
sent Cœnus back to the Indus to bring forward the boats
which had been used there. This Cœnus did by cutting them
in two, or, in case of the thirty-oared galleys, in three parts,
and conveying them on wagons. This is probably the first
instance of anything resembling a pontoon bridge being trans-
ported, though, as above stated, this is alleged to have been
done in the Cophen campaign. The army then moved forward towards the Hydaspes. Alexander had from Taxila
sent his herald Cleochares to Porus, commanding him to bring
in his submission. To this high-handed call Porus replied
that he himself owned his country, owed allegiance to no

man, and that he would come to the river which was his
boundary with his whole force, and there dispute Alexander's
right or power to enter his domains.   Alexander therefore
moved against him, and, in addition to his own troops, took
with him some five thousand Indian auxiliaries.   But the elephants he left in Taxila.   The Macedonian horses had not
become used to these beasts, nor were the tactics of the Macedonians suited to their employment.

Alexander.
(From a Statue in the Louvre.)

XL.

PORUS. MARCH TO MAY, B. C. 326.

IT was the rainy season when Alexander advanced to the Hydaspes. Reaching the river, he found it half a mile wide, swollen and rapid. He could see Porus with his splendid army and many elephants on the farther side. He could not force a passage in his teeth; he must steal one. He went into camp and by ostensible preparations, rumors and other means, induced Porus to believe that he would not try to cross till the dry season. To further confuse and tire out Porus, he made constant feints at partial crossings by night and day. Porus began to meet these feints by keeping his troops under arms, but when they got exhausted from overmuch toil, and Alexander never actually attempted a passage, Porus grew careless and paid less heed to what the Macedonians were doing. Then came Alexander's time. He selected a point some miles up stream and made all his preparations for a real crossing, leaving Craterus in camp and posting many other parties at convenient stations along the bank. Finally, at night and with great care and skill, he put over fourteen thousand men to the south side. Porus was quite deceived. He could see Craterus and the other troops on the right bank, and did not know what this force of Alexander's was. He sent his son with a small . body to oppose it. This Alexander defeated, and then advanced towards Porus' main army. The latter came to meet him. This passage of the Hydaspes is the pattern of all that is best in the crossing of rivers in the face of the enemy.

THE rainy season had just set in. To-day it is said to begin in July. Unless the ancient chronology is at fault, it began earlier two thousand years ago. Thunder-storms and hurricanes were frequent. The men suffered much from the weather. Marching was hard and progress was slow on account of the roads, often cut by swollen streams, and everywhere deep and heavy. As the army passed the southern boundary of Taxila and neared the Hydaspes, it was obliged to march through a narrow pass in the kingdom of Spitakes, a relative and ally of Porus. This pass was held in force.

The hills on either side were occupied and much delay was threatened. But Alexander, by a brilliant cavalry manoeuvre under his own leadership, the details of which we do not possess, surprised and drove Spitakes out of his position, crowded him back into the recesses of the defile where he had hard work to find an exit, and obliged him after considerable loss to fly to Porus for safety. The army thence moved in two marches to the river and camped.

In summer the Hydaspes is nowhere fordable, though it is so at many places during the dry season of winter, when the frosts seal up the ice and snow in the mountain ranges. On the other side of the stream, now over half a mile wide, owing to the rains, though in the dry season relatively small and clear, could be seen Porus with his superbly accoutred army drawn up in battle array before his camp and with his three hundred elephants ranged in front, ready to dispute the passage. According to Diodorus, Porus had more than fifty thousand infantry, three thousand cavalry, one thousand chariots and one hundred and thirty elephants; according to Curtius, he had thirty thousand foot, three hundred chariots and eighty-five elephants. The Indians

were tall, athletic and agile. The infantry were armed with bows five feet long, shot arrows of three feet, and bore a long two-handed sword. Their shields were raw hide. The horsemen had two javelins and a shield, presumably also a sword. Porus, like other Eastern leaders, relied mainly on his elephants; then

War Elephant.

on his chariots; next on camels when he had them; last on cavalry. Such was the value placed on these several arms. Porus' infantry did not accomplish much in the coming battle,

though the Indian mercenaries in the Cophen region had
fought more desperately than any troops Alexander encountered east of Babylon.   Alexander's tactics made it useless.

Porus had sent strong detachments under experienced captains to guard every fordable part of the river and keep a line

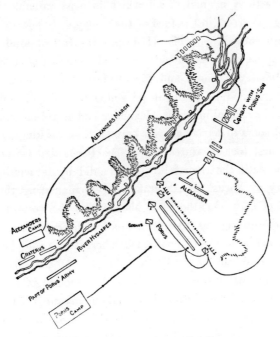

General Plan of Operations against Porus.

of posts along it up and down from his camp.   The possession
by Porus of war chariots and elephants, and of so large and
apparently well disciplined an army made Alexander cau-
tious about attempting to force a passage in the teeth of
the enemy, and induced him to manœuvre for a chance to
cross in safety.   Here was the most splendid force which had
faced him since Arbela.   From mountain fighting he was
getting back to level plains and pitched battles.   He had

gained much respect for the fighting qualities of the Indians from what he had seen of them at Massaga, and had been given to understand that Porus was a man of no common order. He was reduced to stratagem, and, happily for us, his masterly manœuvres on this occasion have furnished the world with a manual of all which is most valuable in the passage of rivers in the face of the enemy.

It was now May. The Hydaspes was full of sand banks and rapids, and was turbid and swollen with the melting of the Himalayan snows and the rainfall of the season. Diligently guarded by Porus, it presented the most difficult natural and artificial obstacle Alexander had as yet encountered. It had come to a trial of wits between the two kings. Alexander first took measures to convince Porus that he intended to wait until the river fell. This he did by devastating the country of Porus' ally, Spitakes, by accumulating the vast stores of corn so gathered in his camp on the western bank, and by settling his troops in comfortable quarters, all of which operations were conducted where they could be overseen or were sure to reach Porus' ears. At the same time, perceiving that Porus remained active in scouting the river so as to prevent himself from being taken unawares, Alexander sought to tire him out by constant activity on his own part. He desired to confuse Porus as well as exhaust his troops. He kept part of his army afoot in numberless detachments moving to and fro along the bank, began the preparation of rafts by stuffing skins with hay and accumulating beams and boards on the river bank, and sent his boats, which had been joined and launched again, up and down the river so as to distract the attention of the enemy. Parties were sent over to the islands in the river where they had many skirmishes with the Indian patrols — and thus learned to know their new enemy. He made feint after feint, often by night and with great clamor. He got his phalanx under arms in the light of the camp-fires; the signal to move was blown in the camp; the horse trotted rapidly and with much noise up and down; the boats were got ready and loaded as if to cross. All this was done *en évidence.* The troops worked incessantly, though it took comparatively few of the Macedonians to make a very lively feint. To offset these apparently threatening attacks, Porus would bring out his elephants and march them down to the bank where he heard the most noise; place his whole force under arms and wait till daylight at the spot where he supposed Alexander was attempting to make a crossing.

After some time Porus began to weary his troops by marching them to and fro, in answer to anticipated attempts to cross, and finding that the attempts were never actually made, he grew more careless. He disliked to expose his troops to the bad weather of the season. Alexander could make a deal of commotion with a small part of his forces; Porus felt safe with no less than his whole army in line. He was exhausting his men faster than Alexander his. He evidently came to believe that Alexander would wait for a low state of water, and that all these attempts argued a fear to cross. For Alexander had purposely spread a report to this effect which had reached Porus. Yet he had kept his troops well in hand, and proposed to steal a passage whenever it was possible, despite the bad condition of weather and water.

Alexander of course saw how inexpedient it would be to attempt a passage opposite the enemy's camp. His horse could probably not be made to face the elephants if these beasts were brought near the shore. To the unusual smell of the huge animals as well as their aspect they had as yet not become accustomed; and they showed the utmost dread of the trumpeting of the creatures. Alexander feared that the horses would not remain quiet on the rafts during the passage if they saw the elephants on the farther bank; and he knew that he could never get them to land. Even his infantry was unused to them. Alexander had also ascertained that Abisares, king of Cashmir, far from remaining faithful to his promises, was preparing to send his entire force to the assistance of Porus. This made it all the more important to cross the river before the junction of these armies. But he could not force, he must seize a passage by stealth.

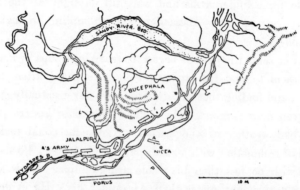

Topography of the Hydaspes, after Cunningham.

The right bank of the river, where Alexander had his camp, for a distance of many miles up and down, was high and hilly. The bank on which Porus stood was a wide fertile plain. This afforded Alexander the marked advantage of hiding his own movements while those of Porus were easily observable.

When Alexander saw that he had confused Porus as to his intentions, and that the Indian king had ceased to march out to meet his feigned crossings, but remained in camp, merely occupying the places where crossings were most likely to be attempted, he made his preparations for a real crossing, meanwhile keeping up his feints with intermittent regularity. He selected for his crossing a spot in the river seventeen miles up the stream from his camp, where there was a headland formed by a considerable bend in the river and a small affluent. This headland was wooded, and was ample to conceal a large force. It was itself curtained by a wooded and uninhabited island in its front. This place Alexander connected with the camp by a line of posts along the river bank, which was the nearest road. These were so close together that orders could be quickly signaled or conveyed from one end of the line to the other. These posts, moreover, with the sentinels calling from one to the other, the many camp-fires and the bustle and stir could be used as feints to harass the enemy, who had lost all belief in any present attempt to cross, but was still alive to the possibility of such a movement. For many nights the Macedonians made noisy demonstrations at every place between camp and island, and lighted fires at intervals in open places as if considerable bodies of troops were present.

Having made all his secret preparations, and these were particularly hastened, because Abisares was reported within three marches, Alexander openly planned a feint at crossing in force on boats in Porus' front, where there was a dry-season ford. Craterus was left here in the main camp, with instructions not actually to cross, unless Porus was beaten, or unless he moved away the bulk of his army, and especially the elephants, towards the island up the river. In no case was Craterus to attempt to face the elephants; but if they were moved off, he was to cross in reality. The king left with Craterus the latter's own division of cavalry and some Arachotian and Parapamisadian horse, the brigades of Alcestas and Polysperchon and five thousand Indians. Attalus, who resembled the king, was arrayed in armor much like his, and instructed to counterfeit his presence.

Between the main camp and island, where was another dry-season ford, Alexander posted in one body the brigades of Meleager, Attalus and Gorgias, supported by the Greek mercenaries, cavalry and infantry, with instructions to cross in successive columns when the expected battle should have been engaged. He himself took the agema of Companion cavalry and the regiments of Hephæstion, Perdiccas and Demetrius, the horse from Bactria, Sogdiana and Scythia, and the Daän horse-archers, the shield-bearing guards, the taxes of Clitus and Cœnus, and the archers and Agrianians, and marched by a route well back from the river, so as not to be seen by the enemy — and happily, there was no dust to betray him — to the selected place. His route is thought to have been along the streams, now dry, known as the Kandar-Nullah and Kasi. Hither the hay wherewith to fill the tent skins had been brought; these were speedily stuffed, and everything made ready for the crossing which at the chosen place was perhaps more difficult, but had the great advantage of being hidden.

The night was tempestuous, and the thunder and rain, usual during the southwest monsoon, drowned the noise of the workmen unavoidable in such preparations, while the woods and ravines concealed the Macedonian camp-fires. Most of the boats, including the thirty-oared galleys, had again been cut apart and conveyed hither, and lay concealed in the woods after being put together. Beams and plank had been carefully prepared. Everything was made ready for use at a moment's warning. At the approach of daylight the storm abated, and the army crossed to the island unobserved by Porus' sentinels; nor were they detected until they had passed the island, when the scouts of Porus observed the movement, and gave the alarm. The infantry crossed in the boats, Alexander leading in a thirty-oared galley accompanied by Perdiccas, Lysimachus and Seleucus, " the cavalry mounting upon the skins," which by some is held to mean that the cavalrymen, while swimming beside their horses, used these skins, as boys learning to swim use bladders, so as not to burden their horses; but which, to judge from the context and other passages, more probably means that the skins were used to help float rafts, and on these latter the horses were conveyed. Perhaps the stream was too swollen and rapid and wide to make it safe to swim the horses, especially as severe duty was to be expected from them immediately on landing.

So soon as the enemy's guards made up their minds that this crossing was real and not a feint, they galloped off at full speed to Porus to convey the news. The cavalry was ordered to land first; and as they reached the bank, they were ranged in column of march by Alexander and his officers. Two or three taxes of the phalanx were left on the right bank to observe the road from Cashmir, which comes in here to the crossing of the river. Three of the taxes mentioned in Bactriana and Sogdiana fail of mention at the Hydaspes — Philotas', Balacrus', Philip's. It may have been these which were detached on this duty.

It soon appeared that Alexander, from ignorance of the locality, had not landed on the south shore, but on another large island separated from the mainland by water generally so low as to be easily passed over, but now grown quite high and rapid from the great storm just past, which had fairly dug out the bend in the river. Here was a serious dilemma. There was no time to bring the boats around, but the troops must be got over at once, lest the enemy should gain opportunity to bring up a heavy column and perhaps some elephants, and oppose the crossing. The great advantage already won was threatened to be lost; but after some delay and a good many accidents, the most fordable place was found, and the troops, wading to their breasts, were safely got over.

As the cavalry emerged from the water, Alexander brought the agema and the best of the other horse forward into line for the right wing, throwing out the horse-archers in their front, ard placing the royal shield-bearing guards, under Seleucus, in front of the other infantry. Next the agema came the other hypaspists, and on each side of the phalanx he stationed the archers, Agrianians, and javelin-throwers.

The body of infantry which he had with him, some six thousand strong, he ordered to follow slowly and in regular order; with his five thousand cavalry, which he knew to be his right arm, he set out towards Porus, ordering Tauron to follow with the archers, — there may have been three or four thousand light troops, — and keep up with the cavalry as best he might. Alexander was confident that, even if Porus should attack with his whole force, he would be able to hold him till the infantry came up, if not worst him with the cavalry force in hand; and he knew that if Porus retired, he ought to be on hand with his cavalry to follow him up and harass his retreat. He therefore started in the direction of the Indian camp at a sharp trot, hazardous though an advance with so small a force undoubtedly was.

Porus, who had been watching Craterus' feints, at first imagined that the troops which his scouts reported as crossing above might be those of Abisares, his ally; but he was speedily undeceived. As he could see the large body of Macedonians under Craterus, and the detachments under Meleager and the others still on the farther side, he must have known that the body in his front was but a part of Alexander's army, and he ought unquestionably to have gone in person with a substantial part of his force to cut it out, particularly as some elephants, backed by infantry, could readily protect the fords for the time being. But Porus seems to have wished to put off a decisive battle until Abisares joined him, and contented himself with sending a small body to meet Alexander's advance, whose force he probably quite underestimated, or may have looked upon as a venturesome patrol. He imagined the king himself to be still on the other side.

Not long after Alexander had landed, therefore, the son of Porus put in an appearance, with two thousand horse and one hundred and twenty chariots. He had been put in command of the force and sent by his father to hold the approaching Macedonians in check. The king shortly ran across him. He at first thought that Porus was upon him with his entire army, of which this was but the van, and sent the horse-archers forward to skirmish with the Indians, while he paused to give instructions for hurrying up the other troops. But when, on reconnoitring, he could see no troops coming up behind the Indian column, he recognized that he had to do merely with a small force, and at once rode in upon them at the head of his Companions, and while the light horse skirmished about their flanks, the Macedonian cavalry charged home. It was rather a combat than a battle. The Macedonians charged in on the enemy "squadron by squadron," a term not unfrequently used by Arrian, whose meaning has already been discussed.

The charge at once broke the enemy's formation, and in the *mêlée* the son of Porus was killed and four hundred men were cut to pieces. The chariots were captured; for, being very heavy, — they contained each six men, — their movements were hampered by the deep mud in this agricultural lowland. The survivors fled; the Macedonians followed hard upon. Porus soon learned the presence of Alexander. He saw that the enemy had outwitted him, had crossed a river he ought to have been able to hold, or, at least, in the passage of which he could have inflicted heavy losses on the enemy. He must now fight on the plain instead of at the river fords.

The Indian king was much taken aback, and uncertain what to do. Alexander's manœuvre had been intended to deceive, and had completely deceived him. He could see Craterus actually preparing to cross, and could count a large body of troops with him. Yet he knew Alexander to be by far the more dangerous foe, though he had no idea of which had the bulk of the troops. He very clearly recognized his error in sending only two thousand men against Alexander, and determined now to repair it by crushing him by numbers before he could be joined by reinforcements from across the river. He therefore marched directly towards the king, leaving a few elephants and an adequate force opposite the camp to prevent Craterus from crossing.

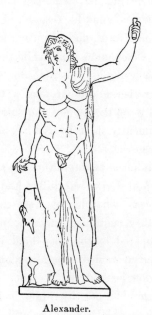

Alexander.
(From a Statue in the Louvre.)

XLI.

BATTLE OF THE HYDASPES. MAY, B. C. 326.

PORUS had set up his two hundred elephants in one line, one hundred feet apart, sustained by his thirty thousand infantry; one hundred and fifty chariots and two thousand cavalry were on each flank. His ideas were limited to a parallel order, and he chose a defensive battle. Alexander had his phalanx of six thousand men; some three thousand light troops, and, above all, five thousand splendid cavalry. Eliminating the elephants and the chariots, Alexander had a good chance to win. But could these be neutralized? The Macedonian horse could not be got to approach the elephants; nor was the infantry steady in their vicinity. Alexander saw that he could not advance direct on Porus. He chose rather to attack his left flank; and sending Cœnus with part of his cavalry by a hidden circuit to turn and demoralize the Indian right, he moved his phalanx, left somewhat refused, up towards the Indian left wing, while with his cavalry he rode around the left flank and attacked it smartly. Porus, though brave and with brave men, knew nothing of grand tactics, and was unequal to opposing this oblique attack, except by detaching the cavalry of his right over to his left to meet Alexander. This enabled Cœnus to throw the right into vast confusion by a sharp attack, and then to ride, in rear of Porus' line, over to the Indian left, and take in rear the cavalry opposing Alexander. Between them, Alexander and Cœnus used up the Indian cavalry; the chariots proved useless; the elephants, at first effective, were courageously met by the Macedonians and driven back on Porus' line; the infantry, having nothing in its front and unused to manœuvring, proved useless. After eight hours of hard fighting and the heaviest loss he ever incurred in battle, — one man in every fifteen was killed, and the majority were wounded, — Alexander was completely victorious — a result he owed to splendid management and the very best of fighting. Porus, captured, was every inch a king. Alexander made him his friend and viceroy.

PORUS had with him all his cavalry, four thousand strong, three hundred chariots, two hundred elephants, each with a tower filled with well-armed men, and some thirty thousand infantry. When he came to a place back of the river lowlands, where the ground was level, harder than near the river, and fit for manœuvring elephants, chariots and cavalry, he halted, and drew up his army in line of battle.

In this he showed considerable skill. In first line were the elephants, one hundred feet apart, covering the entire infantry body, which thus presented a front of about four miles. Porus expected by means of these animals to intimidate the horses of Alexander's cavalry, and prevent them from attacking with any kind of *vim ;* while the elephant-drivers could wheel their animals right and left and trample down the Macedonian infantry which might push into the intervals. The Indian infantry was in second line close behind the line of elephants, in companies of one hundred and fifty strong supporting each one, ready to fill the gaps between them when necessary, and to attack the Macedonian foot if it should advance so far. Small columns of foot flanked the elephants. Two thousand Indian cavalry was on each extreme flank, and in the front of the cavalry of each flank one hundred and fifty chariots. This was the Indian fashion, as it was much the usual habit elsewhere in the East. The chariots were drawn by four horses, and contained each two mailed drivers, two heavily armed men, and two archers carrying the long bows of the country. The infantry carried this long bow as well, and shot three-foot arrows ; but having to rest the end of the bow on the ground as they shot, they were not rapid in their fire.

When Alexander arrived near the place where Porus' army was drawn up in line, he found that he must hold himself by manœuvring with his cavalry while he waited for his infantry to come up. His position was precarious in the extreme. An immediate advance by Porus might have seriously compromised him, with only his cavalry and no supports. It was Alexander's good luck that Porus declined to attack, and the phalanx came on at a rapid gait. Alexander gave it a breathing spell while he inspected the line, reconnoitred the position of the enemy, and continued to keep him busy by small demonstrations, pushing a few squadrons at a time up towards the Indian front, but not so far as to provoke attack. He could not help admiring the ability which Porus had exhibited in drawing up his army, under the conditions presented. His strength lay in his line of elephants, which the Macedonian horse would not face, and Porus knew it; and knew, moreover, that this horse was the body on which Alexander chiefly relied. The elephants were the unknown quantity of the problem. Of the chariots Alexander had less fear. He had met them at Arbela.

Alexander had advanced so as to be able to lean his right flank constantly upon the river or the river bottom-lands. He did not propose to lose touch with his lieutenants on the other side. He saw that he must mould his own tactics to correspond to Porus' dispositions. He was stronger in cavalry than the enemy, but vastly weaker in infantry. He could not attack in front, for it was certain that his cavalry would not face the elephants. The horses could not be driven or coaxed up to them. Nor could he resist the onset of these and the chariots, if made in a parallel order. But as Porus was evidently bent on fighting a defensive battle, Alexander had the choice of when and where he should attack, and how he should attack. The enemy promised to be a more or less stationary mass compared with his own rapidly moving Macedonians. This was a first and great gain.

With the rapidity of clear conceptions, Alexander determined to attack the Indian flanks, the left flank in force, and to seek to grasp some advantage before any tactical manœuvre could be undertaken or change of formation made by the enemy. He knew full well that his army could work with thrice the rapidity of the enemy; and he was as always conscious that he himself could think and act more quickly. He therefore sent Cœnus with his own — the agema — and Demetrius' cavalry by a circuit, and hidden by the rolling ground, against the enemy's right, with instructions, should the horse on Porus' right attempt to ride to the assistance of the horse on his left,

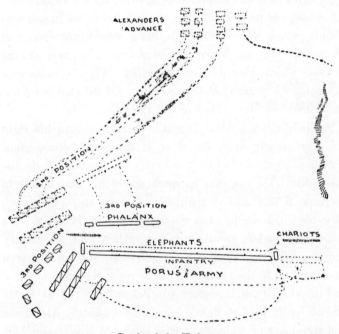

Battle of the Hydaspes.

to fall, if possible, upon the rear of the infantry. Alexander himself, with the bulk of the cavalry, followed at sustaining distance by the infantry, made an oblique movement against the enemy's left where Porus had but two thousand cavalry and the chariots — these latter a doubtful support. He chose this flank for his own attack, partly because he had been hugging the river and the protection of his forces on the other side, and partly from his usual habit of himself leading his own right wing, where he felt the most at home. He made this movement in such a way as to lead Porus to suppose that he was merely uncovering his infantry, so that this might then advance to a front attack, the very thing Porus desired.

Porus' attention was first called to the movement of the king; he failed to perceive Cœnus' flanking march; and as Alexander had shrewdly guessed, sent his two thousand cavalry of the right wing by the rear of his line to join the cavalry on the left, where he saw that he must oppose Alexander's attack.

Seleucus with the pages and hypaspists was on the right of the infantry, Antigenes with the phalangites was in the centre, and Tauron with the light troops was on the left. This whole body was ordered by Alexander to follow his own movement at a proper interval, and advance on the enemy, but not to engage until it saw that the enemy's wings had been thrown into confusion by the proposed cavalry charges. This Alexander thought would neutralize the value of the Indian elephants and chariots, and so far demoralize the infantry line as to lay it open to a fatal assault. It would appear that the phalanx had been formed in open order, so as to cover more ground, as well as better resist the elephants.

With his overwhelming force, and outflanking the Macedonians as he did with his greater length of line, Porus should by all means and at once have advanced to the attack with his elephants, which were protected by infantry much as our modern batteries are. Had he done this without giving Alexander time to manœuvre, pushing forward the elephants so as to render Alexander's cavalry ineffective, and ordering the chariots to charge from each wing and by an inward half wheel take the phalanx in flank, it would seem as if such action must have been fatal to Alexander. And Porus had sufficient horse for pursuit, and excellent for such purpose, though some part of it had been demoralized by the defeat under Porus' son. But Porus awaited the attack which Alexander was always glad to make, for no one more than he knew the advantage of the offensive. This defensive attitude of Porus was not only a piece of good luck; it was Alexander's salvation.

Thus Alexander's decision to strike the enemy in one place, the left flank, with substantially his whole force, brought him again into the oblique order of Epaminondas — this time clearly by design.

Riding forward then towards the right, Alexander opened the battle at bow-shot distance by sending the Daän horse-archers upon the Indian left to engage them in front, while he, by a wheel to the right into column and marching in their rear, could get round to the enemy's flank with Hephæstion's and Perdiccas' heavy horse, and haply strike it before it could make dispositions to meet him. The Indian cavalry leaders do not appear to have comprehended this manœuvre — as Alexander did not intend they should — for they did not hold their men well in hand, and advanced far out of support of their infantry line. Cœnus had now finished his circuit to the Indian right, and in the absence of the cavalry of that wing, fell smartly upon the right and rear of Porus' infantry, which he threw into grave confusion, and rendered useless for the day. It is evident that he struck a hearty blow, for Porus' right rendered absolutely no service during the battle. Then, completing his gallant ride, with the true instinct of the *beau sabreur*, Cœnus galloped along the Indian rear, and rode up to join in the cavalry battle already engaged on the enemy's left.

To oppose this new danger as well as Alexander's attack,

the Indian cavalry was obliged to make a double front, but the largest body remained facing Alexander. It was while they were wheeling into this front and rear formation, that Alexander drove his own stoutest charge home upon the Indian horse. The latter at once gave ground, and retired upon the elephants, " as to a friendly wall, for refuge," says Arrian. A number of these monsters were made to wheel about to the left to sustain the cavalry by charging upon Alexander's body of horse. As anticipated, Alexander's horse could by no means be made to approach them. But the elephants, by facing Alexander, were exposing themselves, and the Macedonian infantry, by now advancing, was enabled to take in flank those elephants which had wheeled to sustain the Indian horse. This they did with a will, wounded many, and slew a number of the drivers, so that the animals were without control, and rushed purposeless to and fro, equally dangerous to friend and foe. But some of them again wheeled about to the right, and urged forward by their drivers threatened to tread the phalangites under foot. Luckily the men stood in open order, so that they could the more readily avoid these creatures, and drive them back with wounds.

The Indian cavalry rallied somewhat under the diversion thus created by the movements of the elephants, and advanced again to oppose the Macedonian horse; but another charge by Alexander's stronger and better disciplined men broke their formation, huddled them up under the heels of the elephants, and increased the confusion tenfold. What the one hundred and fifty chariots on the left were doing all this while does not appear. There is no mention of them in the authorities beyond their place in line. There may be an error in this, or perhaps the confused mixture of elephants, cavalry and foot had prevented their making any charge whatever, as they needed space to do efficient work. Perhaps

Alexander's charge on the right dispersed them. They appear to have been of no use whatever in the battle, and the fact that no further mention is made of them looks as if there had been some change in their position prior to Alexander's attack.

Alexander's cavalry had by this time become so much disorganized by its repeated assaults and by the turmoil created by the elephants that he could no longer carry on his systematic charges; but as Cœnus had been able to join him, the united body of cavalry considerably outweighed the enemy's, not to speak of quality; and Alexander kept pressing home, though irregularly yet with extraordinary vehemence, upon the Indians and elephants. These creatures, now unmanageable, rushed again against the Macedonian phalanx, creating some considerable confusion and loss; but being driven back, for the phalangians bore themselves admirably under these novel conditions, and though much broken up, always rallied again at trumpet-call, they retired through the lines of the enemy, doing vastly more damage to their friends than they had inflicted on their foes.

The situation was most curious. Alexander and Cœnus continued their pressure on the enemy's right front, flank and rear, and though themselves much unstrung, they maintained their purpose, and their repeated charges became very fatal. The Macedonian horse showed that peculiar effect of discipline which results in the capacity to rally and reform, however serious the disaster, so soon as the immediate pressure is removed. The elephants were again and again urged forward on the phalanx; but they were received with wounds, and driven back, doing vast damage to the Indian line. The light troops under Tauron were peculiarly effective against them. The Macedonian infantry had plenty of elbow room, and could open ranks or retire from the elephants, and again close up or advance into hand to hand conflict; but the mass of the Indians was so huddled together that the men trod one upon another, and were at the mercy of the elephants when these brutes fled from the weapons of the phalanx. Finally the unwieldy creatures, unwilling longer to fight, as it were, between two fires, as with one accord retired out of action "like ships backing water" with trunks uplifted to the front, and trumpeting in terror. They were quite beyond control.

Alexander now saw that the victory was his. Keeping the phalanx in reserve but active, he continued with his horse to charge home upon the flank of the infantry line of the enemy, which was fast being hammered together into mere unwieldy masses, and gave it no chance to reform. Porus had been conspicuous for his bravery and his efforts to remedy a lost cause. But he had never fought in anything but parallel order, and had no conception of grand tactics. He could not have manœuvred his own right wing, even had he known how, because he was kept so busy by Alexander's tremendous blows upon his left. As a last effort the Indian king gathered forty yet unwounded elephants in a column, and essayed a charge on the victorious Macedonians, himself leading the van on his own huge war elephant. But Alexander met this charge with his archers and javelin-throwers, who skirmished about the column on every side, slaying the drivers and cutting the hamstrings of the elephants from behind. The effort utterly failed.

Alexander now ordered his phalanx to close ranks, link shields, and advance with pikes protended, and shouting their battle-cry, while the cavalry worked round to the rear, and charged in from the other side. The whole Indian army was a paralyzed, inert mass; it hung together from a mere habit of obedience; and out of it none but isolated individuals managed to escape through the intervals between Alexander's cavalry squadrons, or away towards the right flank.

The battle had lasted eight hours, and had been won by clean, crisp, tactical skill and wonderful use of the cavalry-arm. Perhaps no parallel can be found to such able, persistent and effective handling of horse. Alexander is above all others the pattern of a cavalry general. The conception of Cœnus' ride around the enemy's right and rear was bold, and in execution most brilliant. No cavalry officer, on the field of battle, ever performed a more dashing, clear-headed and splendid feat of arms. All Alexander's dispositions in this battle were masterly. He had left in his camp so large and excellent a force that his retreat was fully protected in case of disaster to the force in hand; he had abundant reserves in the brigades of Meleager, Attalus and Gorgias, though these indeed seem to have been tardy in crossing; and his appreciation of what himself and Cœnus could do on the level plain in which Porus had drawn up his army was full of the intellectual strength which wins the world's great victories. It may perhaps be said that Alexander's crossing with but fourteen thousand men to attack an army of nearly thrice the number savored of foolhardiness. It was certainly the reason why the battle lasted so long, and cost so heavily in killed and wounded. But this habit of taking risks was part of Alexander's nature, and success has always been held to justify risk in all but the exceptional cases.

Craterus now came up, having, though in face of the enemy, crossed the river successfully; and the other troops left on the farther side under Meleager, Attalus and Gorgias also put in an appearance, and not only made the victory a certain one, but undertook the pursuit instead of Alexander's tired men. Of Porus' army nearly twenty thousand infantry and three thousand cavalry were lost; or according to Diodorus, twelve thousand were killed and nine thousand captured. Their chariots were all broken to pieces, having been a hindrance instead of a help. The ground had probably been too deep for their evolutions. Two of Porus' sons, Spitakes, and nearly all of his prominent chieftains were killed, and all the elephants destroyed or captured. The Macedonians lost two hundred and thirty cavalry and seven hundred infantry in killed. This (over six and a half per cent.) is the heaviest loss in killed on record for an army of its size, and effectually disposes of the idea sometimes advanced that Alexander did not have to fight for his victories. It shows clearly that he was ready to fight until he won or was destroyed. To take the usual number of wounded would give us the extraordinary loss of seventy-three per cent. in killed and wounded. Still, this is credible. The wounded were numerous. "There returned to the camp scarcely a single person who was not wounded," says Curtius of another action, and it may have been the same in this case.

Porus himself was captured. Him Alexander had seen and admired during the entire battle. Conspicuously seated on his huge elephant, he led on his men with consummate bravery. After all was over, Porus, though wounded (Curtius says he had nine wounds), endeavored to make his escape. Alexander in person galloped after on Bucephalus. But the noble old animal fell in his tracks and died from overexertion, at the age, generally stated, of thirty years. As the legend goes, Bucephalus was wont to kneel down for Alexander to mount and dismount. This habit was not uncommon, for without stirrups, and with heavy armor and weapons, it would be a welcome aid. And now, rather than throw his rider in his fall, the gallant steed stopped, gently knelt for Alexander to dismount, and then rolled over dead. It is generally related that Bucephalus could be ridden, when naked, only by the king and his groom. But so soon as his trappings were on him, not even his groom could approach to mount, but only Alexander.

"When Porus, who exhibited great talent in the battle, performing the deeds not only of a general, but also of a valiant soldier, observed the slaughter of his cavalry, and some of his elephants lying dead, others, destitute of keepers, straying about in a forlorn condition, while most of his infantry had perished, he did not depart as Darius the Great King did, setting an example of flight to his men; but as long as any body of Indians remained compact in the battle, he kept up the struggle. But at last, having received a wound on the right shoulder, which part of his body alone was unprotected during the battle, he wheeled round. His coat of mail warded off the missiles from the rest of his body, being extraordinary both for its strength and the close fitting of its joints, as it was afterwards possible for those who saw him to observe. Then, indeed, he turned his elephant round and began to retire. Alexander, having seen that he was a great man and valiant in the battle, was very desirous of saving his life. He accordingly sent first to him Taxiles, the Indian, who rode up as near to the elephant which was carrying Porus as seemed to him safe, and bade him stop the beast, assuring him that it was no longer possible for him to flee, and bidding him listen to Alexander's message. But when he saw his old foe Taxiles, he wheeled round and was preparing to strike him with a javelin; and he would probably have killed him, if he had not quickly driven his horse forward out of the reach of Porus before he could strike him. But not even on this account was Alexander angry with Porus; but he kept on sending others in succession; and last of all, Meroës, an Indian, because he ascertained that he was an old friend of Porus. As soon as the latter heard the message brought to him by Meroës, being at the same time overcome by thirst, he stopped his elephant and dismounted from it. After he had drunk some water and felt refreshed, he ordered Meroës to lead him without delay to Alexander, and Meroës led him thither.

"When Alexander heard that Meroës was bringing Porus to him, he rode in front of the line, with a few of the Companions, to meet Porus; and stopping his horse, he admired his handsome figure and his stature, which reached somewhat above five cubits. He was also surprised that he did not seem to be cowed in spirit, but advanced to meet him as one brave man would meet another brave man, after having gallantly struggled in defense of his own kingdom against another king. Then, indeed, Alexander was the first to speak, bidding him say what treatment he would like to receive. The report goes that Porus replied: 'Treat me, O Alexander, in a kingly way!' Alexander, being pleased at the expression, said, 'For my own sake, O Porus, thou shalt be thus treated; but for thy own sake do thou demand what is pleasing to thee!' But Porus said that everything was included in that. Alexander, being still more pleased at this remark, not only granted him the rule over his own Indians, but also added another country to that which he had before, of larger extent than the former. Thus he treated the brave man in a kingly way, and from that time found him faithful in all things." (Arrian.)

Alexander.
'From a Phœnician Coin.)

XLII.

THE FIVE RIVERS. MAY TO JULY, B. C. 326.

ALEXANDER'S policy towards the Indians was not to conquer but make allies of them; not to subdue peoples but to control rulers. He ceased ownership at the confines of the kingdom of the Great King. He reconciled Taxiles and Porus and to them committed all the territory he subdued in the Five Rivers country. He then moved into the foothills of the Caucasus, where he cut shipbuilding timber and floated it down to Craterus at Nicæa and Bucephala, new cities founded near the late battlefield. Crossing the Acesines and Hydraotis he found a number of republics. These free peoples joined hands to oppose him at Sangala, their principal city, which Alexander captured only after a stoutly contested battle and sharp siege. Wherever he advanced he subdued the country or received its submission. He then marched to the Hyphasis, purposing to cross and move as far as the Ganges. But his Macedonians had grown tired of wandering.

ALEXANDER founded two cities at the most important crossings of the Hydaspes; Nicæa near the place where the battle was fought, in commemoration of the victory, and Bucephala ten miles farther up, where he crossed the river, on the main road, in memory of his gallant horse.

"This Bucephalus," says Arrian, "had shared many hardships and incurred many dangers with Alexander during many years, being ridden by none but the king, because he rejected all other riders. He was both of unusual size and generous in mettle. The head of an ox had been engraved upon him as a distinguishing mark, and according to some this was the reason that he bore that name; but others say that though he was black he had a white mark upon his head which bore a great resemblance to the head of an ox. In the land of the Uxians this horse vanished from Alexander, who thereupon sent a proclamation throughout the country that he would kill all the inhabitants unless they brought the horse back to him. As a result of this proclamation it was immediately brought back. So great was Alexander's attachment to the horse and so great was the fear of Alexander entertained by the barbarians. Let so much honor be paid by me to this Bucephalus for the sake of his master." In this wish all good friends of the noblest of animals will join.

Alexander's mixture of the generous and the firm in his policy with the Indians was admirable. He had gained a distinct but not a fundamental control of this part of India which abutted on his Persian possessions. He had seen enough of the country to understand that he could not conquer this people out of hand. Nor had he any intention of so doing. He had control of all the territory from the Hellespont to the Indus, and could pretend to mould this into his long dreamed Græco-Persian empire. But with India it was different. All he could pretend to do here was to make adherents and allies of the princes; not to conquer the peoples, but to control their rulers, and his acts to this end were well gauged.

Porus had in earlier days endeavored to extend his rule to the whole country between the Indus and the Hydaspes and had nearly succeeded, when the king of Taxila, fearful for the balance of power, had sought to put a limit to his advances, and the two had become active enemies. Alexander did not wish to depend on one prince alone. It was better that the power of the Five Rivers should lie between at least two; and he was wise enough to make these two princes equal in power and expert enough to reconcile them. He increased the territory and power of each, by merging the smaller principalities into theirs, and made each one content with what he held. In this manner Alexander maintained a marked control of this country.

At this time Alexander learned from Sisicottus, whom he had made viceroy of a part of the cis-Indian district and whose headquarters were at Aornus, of the revolt in his rear of the Assacenians, who had murdered their governor and joined hands to expel their new masters. This revolt was probably

The Five River Country.

instigated by Abisares of Cashmir, who we remember had been playing a double part, and after sundry embassies of friendship and submission to Alexander had been on the point of joining Porus, and now that Porus was Alexander's vassal, was again ready enough to surrender. This revolt made a disagreeable breach in Alexander's communications which must be at once repaired. He gave Philip, satrap of India, and Tyriaspes, satrap of Parapamisus, orders to join forces and suppress the revolt, instructing the other satraps in his rear to aid them. This course speedily checked a trouble which might have grown to be alarming.

Alexander remained a month in the vicinity of the Hydaspes to celebrate his victory and the funerals of the brave men who had fallen, by sacrifices and games. He then committed the building and fortifying of the cities he had projected to Craterus, and himself set out in a northeasterly direction against the Indians beyond the dominions of Porus in the foothills of the Caucasus, who were called Glaucians. Both Porus and Taxiles accompanied him. He led one half of the Companion cavalry, some picked phalangians, the horse and foot archers and Agrianians. This campaign was a direct threat at Abisares, for the conquest of this land opened the road to Cashmir, and the latter made haste to crave peace, sending another embassy and a present of forty elephants. From superabundance of work to do, Alexander was fain to overlook the past. Throughout the territory of the Glaucians all the towns and villages capitulated. Of these no fewer than thirty-seven had over five thousand population each, and some over ten thousand, a fact which shows a wonderfully prosperous condition of the country. This land he also gave over to Porus to rule, as he had previously added a large stretch to the territory of Taxiles.

In the mountain district through which this campaign led, Alexander found a fine supply of wood suitable for shipbuilding, cut a great deal of timber and floated it down to Craterus as material for the fleet he intended to make, and on which, after conquering India, he proposed to sail down to the Indus and the sea. Many deputations from other neighboring nations came to him here. These ambassadors must have been as much astonished to know Porus vanquished as to see him now held in high honor by Alexander. He was joined here by the Thracian cavalry which had been with Phrata-phernes, viceroy of Parthia and Hyrcania. He did not deem it wise to be without a sufficiency of cavalry from home, which might leaven the huge lump of Oriental horse now serving under his colors.

He next moved southerly towards the Acesines, a river flowing with the rapidity of a mountain torrent, and over two miles wide. Alexander selected the widest part of the river for his passage, because here the current was less strong. The bed was full of rocks, and the stream was a succession of eddies and rapids. There was much difficulty and loss in putting the troops over. Those who crossed with skins for floats or used them for the rafts did well enough, but the boats and some of the rafts were not so fortunate; many of them were dashed to pieces on the rocks, and a considerable number of men perished.

From beyond this river, Alexander sent Porus home to col-lect the most warlike of his troops, and all his elephants, and rejoin him. He left Cœnus with that part of the phalanx he now commanded — just how large a division is not stated — on the left bank of the Acesines River, to see to putting over the details which had been sent out on foraging expeditions, when they should return, and to hold, as it were, a bridge-head on the road along which the Macedonians were oper-ating.

There was another Porus, a cousin, says Strabo, of the Hydaspes king (the "cowardly Porus," the Macedonians dubbed him, because he deserted his relative in a season of distress), who was king of one of the tribes in the foothills. He had offered to surrender when he thought that subservi-ence to Alexander would rid him of his uncle's influence, but had again taken up arms and retired into the farther confines of his land when he found that the elder Porus was again in favor. Him Alexander set out to pursue with his light troops, leaving posts along his line of advance, at suitable intervals, so that Craterus and Cœnus might be protected in coming up, and in the foraging they were ordered to do for the army. But on reaching the Hydraotis, up which river he proposed to operate, and finding that the pursuit would be long and tedious, he detailed Hephæstion, with his own and Demetrius' hipparchies, one half of the archers, and two brigades of the phalanx, to finish the subjection of the land of this Porus, which was a district of Gandaritis, as is called the territory between the Hydaspes and Hydraotis rivers. Hephæstion was given orders to subdue other Indian tribes in this district, and to found a city on the left bank of the Acesines, at the main-road fords. Hephæstion was then to turn this territory over to the faithful Porus to govern in addition to his own.

Alexander himself then advanced on and crossed the Hydraotis, an operation which was more easily managed than the Acesines. Beyond this river he was in the land of the free Indians, the Cathæans being one of their tribes. Curiously for this tyrant-ridden part of the world, there has always been here, from time immemorial, a set of republics, or "kingless" peoples, as they were called. They were looked down upon by the subjects of the neighboring kings, but could no doubt afford to be so. Their largest city and capital, Sangala (modern Lahore), was strongly walled, and here the near-by allied tribes had met to arrest Alexander's advance in their direction. These free tribes were very warlike, and had never been subdued. Porus told Alexander that he had tried his hand against them more than once in vain, and that he would find them very obstinate in battle. Some of the qualities of the true republic appear to have been prominent among them. This report whetted Alexander's ambition to subdue them.

Turning back upon his course, Alexander marched against these confederates, and on the way, two days from the Hydraotis crossing, he passed through the city of the Adraisteans, Pimprama by name, which surrendered to him at his approach. Having in three days more, by recrossing the Hydraotis, reached Sangala, he found the barbarians drawn up on a hill in front of the city, with their wagons forming a triple line of defenses around them. The hill appears to have been precipitous on two sides, but approachable on the front, which commanded the entire surrounding country. The city was also on a hill standing sharply up out of the plain, and on its rear was protected by a lake or piece of low wet ground of some extent but no great depth.

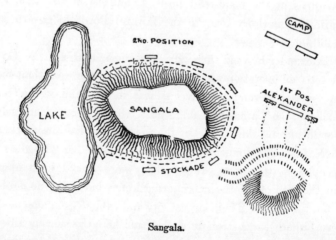

Sangala.

Alexander at once recognized that a difficult problem lay before him, and that he had not been misinformed as to the warlike qualities of these freedom-loving Indians. But he also recognized that he must not hesitate, but impose on the Indians by immediate attack, if he expected respectful submission when he had beaten them. He sent out the horse-archers as skirmishers, to protect his advance and to allow him to form at his leisure and without interference from the Sangalians. He drew up his army in much the usual formation, with the cavalry and archers on the wings and the phalanx in the centre. The royal horse-guards, led by Alexander, and Clitus' ilē (still so called) were on the right; then came the hypaspists and Agrianians; then the phalanx and Perdiccas' horse. Presently the rear-guard came up, and its horse was placed on the right and left, and the infantry troops mixed in with the phalanx in the centre.

Alexander first threw forward the cavalry of his right wing on the Indians' left, as this seemed the least strong part of their line, the wagons being placed less closely together. He hoped to demoralize the enemy by a sudden onset, or perhaps get them to make a sortie, and thus secure a chance at open field fighting. But he quickly found that cavalry was not the arm to operate against the Indian wagon-fort. These warriors were too shrewd to come out from their improvised defenses. They knew the value of their position, and stood on and among the wagons and hurled their weapons with skill and excellent effect. So stanch was their defense that the cavalry and light troops both recoiled from the assault. Dismounting, Alexander headed the phalanx and led it with its fierce battle-cry and gallant rush against them. The first row of wagons was speedily taken; but in the confined space between the first and second rows the phalangites were unable to act to advantage; the sarissa was unadapted to such work; a short sword or thrusting pike would have been far more effective. They were more than once repulsed by the Indians, who swarmed about in vast numbers; concealed themselves under both the first and second rows of wagons; shot their arrows and cast their javelins from all sides and with fatal aim upon the Macedonians. They showed not the least sign of wavering, but fought with the utmost gallantry and steadiness, as if certain of and used to victory. The phalangites were not so good at this sort of fighting as at contests in the open field. Alexander rarely came so near to failure in his task. But after a long and bloody tussle, the barbarians were finally ousted from the second row of wagons. And as if despairing of success in contending against such foes, they attempted no stand at the third row, but retired into the city and closed the gates.

The walls were of such extent that Alexander could not fully surround the city, but he posted cavalry pickets on the sides he could not blockade, for he expected that the Indians would make an attempt to escape in the night. This expectation proved true, but the sortie was unsuccessful; the foremost Indians were at once cut down by the Macedonian videttes, who were alert and active, and the rest gave up the attempt and returned within walls. Alexander was now driven to something like a siege. He began by surrounding three sides of the city with a stockade which he could hold with fewer men. But the side farthest from his main camp, where lay the lake, he picketed carefully with cavalry. He prepared also to build towers and engines to override and batter down the walls. But he learned from some deserters that the enemy would try again on one of the succeeding nights to escape from the city by way of the lake, where they saw that there was no stockade, and through which, the water being shallow, they could wade. Alexander accordingly stationed Ptolemy, son of Lagus, at this point, with three chiliarchias of shield-bearing guards, the Agrianians, and one taxis of archers, giving him orders, in case the Indians made a sortie, to hold them in check at all hazards, and sound the alarm. And he instructed the rest of the forces to remain under arms and ready, upon hearing this signal, to march at an instant's notice to the spot thus indicated.

As Alexander anticipated, so the event occurred. Ptolemy had put to use many of the old wagons, and had interlocked them as an obstruction near the lake; and at night his men blocked the roads and paths leading from the city, and threw up a mound in advance of the lake, in lieu of parts of the stockade which had been knocked down. Towards morning, in the third watch, the Indians made the expected sortie, but Ptolemy caught them as they came forth, vigorously attacked them, and, on sounding the alarm, Alexander promptly put in an appearance with the other troops. The Indians were stopped by the wagons and obstructions, and were driven back into the town, with a loss of five hundred killed.

Porus now arrived with five thousand Indian troops and a number of elephants; sheds, towers, and rams had been built, and these military engines were being gradually advanced to the city wall, which was of brick, well constructed. A double intrenchment had now been built by the Macedonians all around the city. The walls were also gradually undermined at a number of places. Everything savored of success. But Alexander became impatient at the delays of a siege, and concluded to order a fresh assault. Preparations were carefully made, ladders were supplied in abundance to the men, and, undertaken in a moment when the Indians expected nothing less, the assault was entirely successful. The city was taken, and, under Alexander's orders to cut down all found with arms in their hands, seventeen thousand men were killed, and seventy thousand captured, with three hundred of the wagons. There is some reason to doubt these figures. The ruins of Sangala do not appear to show a city large enough to harbor so many people. Still, many may have been outside the walls. Alexander had one hundred killed and twelve hundred wounded, among them Lysimachus, the somatophylax. Sangala was razed to the ground, and the territory added to the dominion of Porus, and garrisoned by his troops.

Eumenes, Alexander's secretary, was one of the most valuable and expert officers in the army. But being a Greek, the jealousy of the Macedonians had prevented his rising to a rank for which he was eminently qualified. His name occurs rarely in Alexander's exploits. On this occasion Alexander sent him, with a guard of three hundred horse, to two cities which had joined Sangala in its opposition to Alexander, to inform them that if they at once surrendered they would receive fair treatment. But Eumenes found the cities deserted, and the tribes in abject flight. The news of the horrible butchery at Sangala belied the peaceful message which Eumenes brought; the people had a fearful dread of the Macedonians; and they could not be turned back. Alexander set out to pursue them, but they had too great a start, and the pursuit had to be given up. Those who had been left behind, however, — probably invalided, decrepit, and aged persons, — were slain by the soldiers to the number of five hundred. Such usages of war strike one as equally awful and unnecessary. But they were of every-day occurrence. The management of this land also was confided to Porus. The rest of the free Indians, now treated with a generosity by Alexander, in great contrast to the severity at Sangala, gave in their submission.

From here the army made a march to the capitals of King Sopeithes whose territory extended beyond the foothills of the Imaus and towards the sources of the Hyphasis, and of King Phegeus who reigned over neighboring peoples, at each of which places the Macedonians were received with great hospitality and rich gifts. Their dislike of the "kingless" tribes no doubt influenced their actions.

Thence Alexander descended to a suitable place on the

Hyphasis, intending to cross and subjugate the tribes beyond. For there seemed to be no limit to the king's desire to conquer, so long as any land or city or tribe remained within reach to be conquered. And the territory beyond the Hyphasis was said to be fertile and to be inhabited by a fine people, tall in stature and gallant in war, who possessed larger and fiercer elephants than were to be found anywhere else in India. Their government was a liberal aristocracy. With these people Alexander wished to become acquainted, and add them to the population owing fealty to his sceptre. He had the feeling, too, that so long as he did not reach a natural barrier, such as the sea or a desert or great mountain range, he ran danger from nations he did not subdue. He had also conceived the desire of reaching the Ganges, and of moving down this river to the Indian Ocean. Alexander himself was tireless, insatiable. But the spirit of his Macedonians had begun to flag.

Alexander.

(From a Statue in the Smith-Barry Collection.)

XLIII.

TURNING BACK. JULY TO OCTOBER, B. C. 326.

THE Macedonian soldiers had determined to proceed no farther. They had, through their officers, certain rights of protest. These they concluded to enforce. For three months, rain had incessantly fallen, and with it the moral tone of the troops. They were ragged; their arms were worn out; of armor there was scarcely any. They were not only unwilling, they were unfit, to march farther in advance — to the Ganges and the sea, as Alexander wished them to do. Alexander's eloquence on this occasion failed. The men did nothing mutinous; they simply declined to advance. Alexander recognized the conditions. The sacrifices proved inauspicious. He agreed to return. It was well that he turned back. Much longer absence from Babylon would have seen his empire crumble into anarchy for lack of the controlling hand. Returning to the Hydaspes, he built a fleet, sacrificed, formally invested Taxiles and Porus with viceregal authority over their respective territories, and began his descent to the Indus with a pomp and ceremony and splendor never before seen. A column marched on either bank; another followed at two days' interval; the king and eight thousand men, and the baggage and camp-followers, floated down the river on a fleet of one thousand boats.

ALEXANDER had had much to contend with in the jealousies of his Macedonians. He could scarcely do a favor to an Asiatic without provoking the selfish protests of his countrymen. He had presented one thousand talents to Taxiles, whose land had furnished his army ten times as much. Said Meleager: "Must we come so far as India to find a man worthy of such a gift?" To accomplish his end, the king had grown to overlook these things, — to control his ancient temper. "Let them grumble," said he, "so long as they obey." And their obedience was marked. Near by or far away, Alexander's lieutenants acted as if they were under his eye. Of Cæsar's or Napoleon's lieutenants one could not say so much. It was with his satraps, not his generals, that Alexander had trouble. Whatever orders he issued were carried out. Marches were doubled, the most difficult mountains and rivers and deserts were crossed, toil of the most grievous undergone, the all but impossible accomplished, but Alexander's lieutenants were always on time as ordered. Perhaps no captain ever got from his subordinates such unequivocal obedience. But for all that, the army exercised its rights and wagged its tongue.

There had been growing for many months a spirit of unusual restlessness under Alexander's hungry schemes of territorial acquisition. This sort of dissatisfaction had really been at the bottom of the several conspiracies of Philotas, the pages, and Callisthenes, but now it had expanded into a different phase. There was a manifest determination among all concerned, not to disobey or mutiny or conspire, but to exert their free-born right to check the king in his ceaseless forward marches by a refusal to be led farther from home. There is nothing to prove that the Macedonian common soldier had rights anything like those which our own republican volunteers possessed as citizens; but there is a great deal which looks as if the chiefs of the Macedonians and Greek allies had much to say with regard to what they should do or where they should be led. These rights, whatever they were, now came to be exerted.

The feeling against further advance existed in the whole army, even to the warmest friends of Alexander, and the expression of it had taken the form of many meetings at which the matter had been openly discussed. The army, under the Macedonian unwritten law, may be said to have constituted, in its commanding officers, a sort of popular assembly, with undefined powers, to be sure, but none the less wielding something like a right of decision. We have repeatedly seen

Alexander appeal to it; and this was now used as a lever to enable the men and officers to so shape the movements of the army as to be able to look, at some distant period, to a return home and the enjoyment of their hardly-won riches, rather than to indefinite absence and the encountering of still greater dangers; for the rumor ran that near the head waters of the Ganges, Xandrames, an Indian prince, had blocked the way with two hundred thousand foot, twenty thousand horse, two thousand chariots, and three thousand trained elephants. No doubt all this was vastly exaggerated, but the effect remained the same. Further meetings were held, and the subject was fully ventilated. The conclusion come to by the more moderate was that they did not wish to advance farther, while the more radical declared openly that they would not advance beyond the Hyphasis. The criticisms of the soldiers often had their origin in idleness, which Alexander knew full well how to control by active work, but here it was a very different matter.

Alexander at once grasped the situation. He well understood the limitations of his own authority as well as the limitations of human endurance. He recognized that so far his Macedonians had faithfully followed him, not only from native loyalty and courage, from admiration of his military achievements, from love of war, and from the desire of sharing the wealth which had been pouring in upon them, but also from genuine affection for his person quite apart from their sense of fealty. But he also recognized that they held the constitutional right of veto, as it were, upon his decision, and that this might not be recklessly tampered with; and he further recognized that there was a point beyond which human toleration refuses to be taxed, and that his army had reached that point.

Before the danger grew into a form in which it could not

be handled, Alexander called the usual council of commanding officers and explained to them his position. The head
waters of the Ganges were not far off, said he, and on reaching that river, the sea would put a positive boundary to his
conquests, whereas a less certain boundary must always remain a provocation to revolt or to invasion from beyond.
He invoked their ardor, patriotism and love of glory, and
showed them that it was they who really ruled the land, and
won its wealth, not he. But he said that he would abide
by their decision and called for an expression of opinion.
" Either I desire to persuade you to advance," said the king,
" or to have you give me reasons for returning." After some
hesitation — for Alexander was equally loved and feared and
in the past more than one man had suffered for having spoken
freely — Cœnus rose and expressed the feeling of all the
others, or as he said, what he thought would be best for both
Alexander and the army.

Of the original Macedonians, who had left Hellas, said he,
few indeed were left, most having perished by disease and
wounds or been left — perhaps unwillingly — in garrisons in
various parts of Asia. Those "few out of many " who
remained, naturally enough desired to return home to their
parents, their wives and children, where they could enjoy the
honors and fruits of their courage and labors. He advised
Alexander, if he desired to make further conquests, to head
homeward, consolidate his enormous possessions, and, waiting
till times were ripe, take a fresh start with younger troops.
" Self-control in the midst of success is the noblest of all
virtues, O King! For thou hast nothing to fear from enemies, while thou art commanding and leading such an army
as this; but the visitations of the deity are unexpected, and
consequently men can take no precautions against them."
Cœnus' speech was received with cheers by all, as it reflected

the feelings of all.   Others are said by Curtius to have spoken to the same effect.

The above is the reason generally assigned by the historians for Alexander's turning back from the Hyphasis.   But Strabo and Diodorus hint at a deeper reason, namely, that the troops were exhausted, physically, mentally, and morally, by the incessant rain of the season.   Says Diodorus, probably quoting Clitarchus, an inaccurate writer but full of a species of local color: " Few Macedonians were left and these were near desperation ; the horses were footsore by the long marches ; the weapons of the soldiers dulled and broken by the number of battles ; no one had Greek clothes left : rags of barbaric and Indian booty, miserably patched together, covered the scarred bodies of these conquerors of the world ; for seventy days the most terrible rainfall had streamed from heaven, in the midst of storms and thunders."

Whoever has served through a campaign during a period of unusual storms can well picture to himself the hopeless, desperate condition of the Macedonian soldiery, and understand their refusal to proceed.   No consequences of refusal could be worse than the actual conditions.   The same low but determined pitch of mood was occasionally to be observed after the terrible slaughter of the Virginia campaign of 1864.   And that Alexander, in lieu of punishing the refusal of his Macedonians to obey his intended orders of march, — as he later punished their mutiny at Opis, — should have given way to them, well shows not only that he recognized their rights, but understood their pitiable condition, their fidelity and affection, and knew that there was abundant excuse for their want of discipline, if such indeed it was.

Alexander was much disturbed at Cœnus' voicing of the opinion of the army.   He called another meeting the next day at which he announced his intention to discharge those who desired to return home and to advance with the faithful remainder. The rest might go back to Macedon and tell their friends that they had deserted their king in the midst of his enemies. But the Macedonian army well understood its powers; the men were saddened, but remained unmoved in their determination, though their king withdrew himself from their sight and remained in his tent for three days, nursing his wrath in private. He imagined that he could once more alter their mood by this means.

But Alexander finally recognized that he must submit to a state of things which he could not control, and sought a means of gracefully doing so. The sacrificial victims proved or were ordered to be declared unpropitious to further advance, and thus having the excuse of bowing to the fiat of the gods and not to men, the king deemed it well for his own dignity to follow the indication of the sacrifices. For he was certain that his army would no longer follow him and he must decide to turn his face in the direction of home. This decision he announced to the army; and it was received with shouts and exultation. The men crowded around the king's tent and prayed blessings upon him, " because by them alone he suffered himself to be conquered."

According to Curtius and Diodorus, Alexander had endeavored to wheedle the army into a further advance. He allowed the men to indulge in a looting raid into the land of the adjoining friendly King Phegeus; while absent, made their wives and children, vast numbers of whom were always with the army, presents of all manner of valuables, amounting to fully a month's pay ; and on the return of the men, laden with booty, endeavored to persuade them, not in a conference with leaders, but in open meeting, to continue on the course he had cut out. But this has not the smack of reality. Arrian's relation is much more probable, as it comes from a better source.

It was time Alexander did turn back; for the term of his absence, and the distance he had come (from his base at Tyre to this point he had marched over nine thousand miles), not only had demoralized his soldiers, but had utterly unstrung the fidelity of many of the satraps he had left behind. When he returned to the heart of his new kingdom, he found that he must visit heavy punishments on a great number of his viceroys, and had he been gone much longer, the whole system he had so carefully established would probably have fallen to the ground for mere lack of the controlling hand. Had Alexander actually marched to the Ganges, he would have found no kingdom when he returned, if indeed that return had ever taken place. This indeed was improbable, for, when one considers the enormous stretch of desert he would have to cross to reach the Ganges, the present condition of his army and all the factors in the case, it is doubtful indeed if even his almost superhuman energy would have sufficed to put such a campaign through. Moreover, it may be suggested, in view of the entirely different manner in which he had been organizing the government of this Five River territory, whether his intention was more than a passing fancy.

Porus and Taxiles, Sopeithes and Phegeus were left all but independent; the former two in charge of enormous territories, the latter as a sort of balance of power between them. The Caucasus and the mountains on the western bank of the Indus were a far better boundary to his possessions than any which India could afford, and it is probable that Alexander had the same object in view in his political dispositions in the Five River country that he had in those made with the Bactrians and Sogdianians who were to keep in control the Scythians beyond the Jaxartes. He may perhaps have proposed a sort of raid towards the Ganges with a select small force;

but had he not in reality already determined to leave these allies to guard the real eastern boundary of his kingdom, the Indus, and turn back? The incident of the Macedonian protest was alone enough to impel his natural obstinacy to make a point of a march farther on into the bowels of India.

It was the end of August. To commemorate the event and to mark the spot where the hero arrested his conquering hand, as a thank-offering to the gods who had smiled upon his efforts and as a monument to the labors of the king and of the army, twelve altars of the shape of very high towers, but much wider, were erected and inaugurated with the greatest pomp, sacrifices, feasts and games. Alexander then gave to Porus charge also of this territory and marched back over the Hydraotis and to the Acessines, where he found the city Hephæstion was to build all but completed. This, as usual, he populated with Indians who volunteered to settle there and invalided Greek mercenaries, whom he left with abundant resources. The denizens of these new towns were no doubt given marked privileges to compensate for their change of home.

The rain had now ceased, the land began to dry, and the rice covered the lately flooded fields with a mantle of green. The soldiers rejoiced at their once more facing homeward as well as at the smiling aspect of the country.

It was here that Abisares' brother reached Alexander. He came with gifts and thirty elephants, and brought excuses from Abisares that he did not personally report to the king, for he was sick. Alexander chose to accept the excuses, and appointed Abisares satrap of the country lately his kingdom. He had no time for an expedition to chastise him; nor was he of any great moment. Taxiles and Porus sufficed to keep him in check. Arsaces, king of the adjoining territory, likewise concluded to send in a capitulation and was placed under Abisares' authority. The proper arrangements were made for the payment of tribute by both.

Alexander then returned to the Hydaspes, where some time was spent in repairing the damage done by the floods to Bucephala and Nicæa, whose new and hastily built walls had been unable to resist the overflow and rapid current of the river. They were now made more solid and substantial. Here too he found reinforcements from Greece, consisting of six thousand cavalry and thirty thousand infantry, brought by Harpalus. There were also twenty-five thousand panoplies of complete armor, and many medicines, the latter extremely necessary. Had he sooner received these reinforcements and supplies he might, it is thought, have persuaded the army to advance across the Hyphasis.

But though Alexander, as the historians allege, had in this retreat suffered the most cruel disappointment which ever befell him, when he had accepted the inevitable, he turned his mind to utilizing the conquests he had already made, and to consolidating his empire with as much energy as he could possibly have put into the conquest of the rest of India. He now proposed to carry out his original scheme of moving down to the Indus and to reduce the people along the lower course of this river, and head back to Babylon along the coast. He had heard that some tribes near the Indus, especially the Mallians and Oxydracians, were ready to resist him; and unless the rivers, of which he held the head waters, were made absolutely his so far as the sea, his conquests at their source would be held on slight tenure. And, as always, part of his plan was to found other cities and carry with him the Hellenizing influences which he had already spread so far.

Alexander concluded to return by descending the Hydaspes, which empties into the Acesines, and thence through the

Indus to the sea. For this purpose he ordered a number of vessels to be got ready, many of them thirty-oared galleys, and others with one and a half banks of oars; flat-bottomed, deckless boats for horses, and others suitable for the men, artillery, and baggage. The Phœnicians, Cyprians, Carians and Egyptians, multitudes of whom were in the ranks, furnished plenty of shipwrights and crews.

A fact which throws into high relief the extraordinary energy and enterprise of Alexander is the unreliability of the information he was able to procure about these distant countries, in despite of which he continued to push forward. When he saw crocodiles in the Indus, and the lotus bean growing on the banks of the Acesines, he imagined and for some time believed that he had discovered the sources of the Nile, where alone he had seen or heard of these animals and plants. Among all his suite of wise men, there was none to correct this error, and it was not till some time later that he ascertained the existence of the Persian Gulf, southern Arabia, and the Red Sea.

Herodotus tells us that the vessels of Nechaus, in the seventh century B. C., left the Red Sea and made in three years a circuit of Libya; also that about 512 B. C. the vessels of Darius, son of Hystaspes, under pilotage of the Carian Scylax, floated down the Indus, sailed west, and reached the Red Sea. But this information was of the crudest. What it meant had not impressed itself on Alexander's mind.

Cœnus at this time died, and was buried with as great pomp as the circumstances allowed. It is said, however, that Alexander had not forgotten his taking up the cause of the soldiers at the Hyphasis. This scarcely accords with Alexander's character, which, though passionate, did not long harbor unkindness, and the splendid services of Cœnus, so worthily capped at the Hydaspes, must still have dwelt in his recollection.

As a last act before leaving the Five Rivers country, Alexander solemnly invested Porus with the sovereignty of all India east of the Hydaspes, so far as he had overcome it, embracing seven nations and lands containing more than two thousand cities; and clothed Taxiles with equal authority over the territory he had assigned to him. He prescribed the relations which the smaller independent princes — Sopeithes, Phegeus, Abisares — should bear to them, and the tribute all should pay.

He then got his vessels together, some eighty thirty-oared war vessels, two hundred horse transports, and seven hundred of all other kinds, river-craft, old and new, — the number is given by Arrian, on the authority of Ptolemy, as not far short of two thousand, — and gave the command of thirty-three of the war vessels, as honorable distinction, to thirty-three of his best subordinates. Of these, twenty-four were Macedonians, — the seven somatophylaxes and Peucestas, shortly to be an eighth, Craterus, the phalanx-strategos, Attalus, Nearchus of the hypaspists, a civilian Laomedon, Androsthenes, who later sailed around Arabia, and others, many of whom were probably staff officers. Among the Greeks were Eumenes, the secretary, and the king's intimate Medius. Among the foreigners, Bagoas, the Persian, and two Cyprians, sons of kings. The rest are not well-known names, or prominent. Having thus, with great ceremony and magnificence, settled the preliminaries of his departure, he himself embarked with the shield-bearing guards, the Agrianians, and the body-guard of cavalry, — some eight thousand men, all told. It is probable that the baggage and camp-followers monopolized the greater part of the small craft.

The start was made in early November. Craterus, with part of the cavalry and infantry, marched along the right bank of the river; and along the left Hephæstion led the better part, including two hundred elephants. Each of these bodies was in light marching order, and, like the modern army corps, some forty to fifty thousand strong; while Alexander's force in the river was so placed as readily to sustain either one at need, or to enable a crossing to be made. These generals were ordered to march rapidly on the capital of Sopeithes, three days down stream, — this must have been a second potentate of the same name, — and Philip, viceroy of the region between Bactria and the Indus, was to follow as rear-guard, at an interval of three marches. The Nysæan cavalry was sent back to Nysa well rewarded. The whole fleet was placed under Nearchus as admiral. The pilot of Alexander's ship was Onesicritus. Arrian's description of the progress of this fleet is very picturesque : —

" When he· had made all the necessary preparations, the army began to embark at the approach of the dawn ; while, according to custom, he offered sacrifice to the gods and to the river Hydaspes, as the prophets directed. When he had embarked he poured a libation into the river from the prow of the ship, out of a golden goblet, invoking the Acesines as well as the Hydaspes, because he had ascertained that it is the largest of all the rivers which unite with the Hydaspes, and that their confluence was not far off. He also invoked the Indus, into which the Acesines flows, after its junction with the Hydaspes. Moreover, he poured out libations to his forefather Heracles, to Ammon, and the other gods to whom he was in the habit of sacrificing, and then he ordered the signal for starting seawards to be given with the trumpet. As soon as the signal was given, they commenced the voyage in regular order ; for directions had been given at what distance apart it was necessary for the baggage vessels to be arranged, as also for the vessels conveying the horses, and for the ships of war ; so that they might not fall foul of each other by sailing down the channel at random. He did not allow even the fast-sailing ships to get out of rank by outstripping the rest. The noise of the rowing was never equaled on any other occasion, inasmuch as it proceeded from so many ships rowed at the same time; also the shouting of the boatswains giving the time for beginning and stopping the stroke of the oars, and the clamor of the rowers, when keeping time all together, with the dashing of the oars, made a noise like a battle-cry. The banks of the river, also, being in many places higher than the ships, and collecting the sound into a narrow space, sent back to each other an echo which was very much increased by its very compression. In some parts, too, the groves of trees on each side of the river helped to swell the sound, both from the solitude and the reverberation of the noise. The horses which were visible on the decks of the transports struck the barbarians who saw them with such surprise that those of them who were present at the starting of the fleet accompanied it a long way from the place of embarkation. For horses had never before been seen on board ships in the country of India; and the natives did not call to mind that the expedition of Dionysus into India was a naval one. The shouting of the rowers and the noise of the rowing were heard by the Indians who had already submitted to Alexander, and these came running down to the river's bank, and accompanied him, singing their native songs. For the Indians have been eminently fond of singing and dancing since the time of Dionysus and those who under his bacchic inspiration traversed the land of the Indians with him."

Three days after embarking, Alexander reached the rendezvous with Hephæstion and Craterus, and remained two days for Philip to come up. His force here is stated by Curtius at one hundred and twenty thousand men; by Plutarch, at the same number of foot and fifteen thousand horse; almost the only definite statement on the subject since Arbela. The following taxes are named : Cœnus, Polysperchon, Meleager, Craterus, Philotas, Alcestas, Attalus, Gorgias, Clitus, Balacrus, Philip, Peithon, Antigenes. Philip he then directed to march across to the Acesines and down that river, to assure himself of the possession of its western bank.   Hephæstion and Craterus were given fresh orders as to their march, which were to sweep farther inland; and as they proceeded down the Hydaspes they reduced by force or surrender the tribes through whose land they passed. "But he himself continued his voyage down the river Hydaspes, the channel of which is nowhere less than twenty stades broad.   Mooring his vessels near the banks wherever he could, he received some of the Indians dwelling near into allegiance by their voluntary surrender, while he reduced by force those who came into a trial of strength with him."   (Arrian.)

Modern Statue of Alexander in the Tuileries Garden.

XLIV.

THE MALLIANS. NOVEMBER, B. C. 326, TO FEBRUARY, B. C. 325.

At the confluence of the Hydaspes with the Acesines were dangerous rapids. In these a number of ships were lost and damaged. From here Alexander undertook a campaign against the Mallians. This tribe was about to be joined by the Oxydracians, but Alexander anticipated them. He divided his army into three columns. One he himself headed, to march across a desert tract against the Mallians, for the reason that they did not expect him from that direction; on his left, Ptolemy, three marches up river, was to intercept the Mallians if they fled thither; on his right, Hephæstion, five marches down river, was to perform the like office; Nearchus and Craterus remained with the baggage and fleet. Marching across the desert with much toil, Alexander surprised the Mallians and captured Agallassa, their capital. Thence moving restlessly to and fro, he wasted the country and slew all with arms in their hands. He was too busy to subdue; he exterminated. In a number of places he found stanch opposition — and in the attack on the chief city of the Mallians (modern Multan) after a deed of personal valor worthy of Achilles, he was grievously wounded and nearly lost his life. While disabled there was great fear among the Macedonians; for who but Alexander could lead them back to their homes? The Mallian campaign was however ended. The whole country handed in its fealty.

Alexander now learned that the Mallians and Oxydracians, who were the most numerous and reputed most warlike of all the Indian tribes, had put their families and treasures in the strongest cities and made vast preparations for disputing his passage over their land. Curtius gives their joint forces as ninety thousand foot, ten thousand horse and nine hundred chariots. Alexander made haste to attack this problem before these preparations were completed. In five days from his second start down river he reached a point below the confluence of the Hydaspes and Acesines where the double volume of these two rivers is suddenly driven into a narrow gorge with high banks, and flows with great rapidity. A number of his vessels were here damaged by the whirlpools and eddies in the stream, and the rapids and bad bottom came close to wrecking the entire fleet. The round ships, as the transports from their unwieldly structure were called, got through fairly well. But the long ships or war galleys suffered greatly from the oars of the lower tiers getting caught, and a number of men perished. Even Alexander's ship scarcely escaped being engulfed and the king is related to have already cast aside his mantle and upper raiment in expectation of having to swim for his life. He was forced to halt some days to repair damages. On the right bank below these rapids, in a bend of the river to the west, there was a jutting promontory which made a sort of roadstead. Here he was able to pick up much wreckage and many of the corpses.

Alexander was on the confines of the territory of the Mallians, which extends northerly of the confluence of the Acesines and Hydraotis. This tribe expected that Alexander would continue his route down river to this confluence and thence move up stream to attack them; because the stretch of land north of the confluence and between the two rivers was a desert region entirely without water and difficult to cross. But Alexander determined to do what they least expected and to march across the desert.

While repairs were being made Alexander headed an incursion some thirty miles westward into the land of some tribes known as the Sibæ, on the right bank, they being said to be about to reinforce the Mallians by crossing the river. They were some forty thousand in number, but he easily defeated them, destroyed their capital and wasted their territory as an example. He then joined the fleet and his lieutenants. Craterus he found in camp. Hephæstion and Philip were between the rivers at the confluence.

In order that the Mallians should find opposition wherever they might turn, he divided his army into several detachments. Philip's corps, the brigade of Polysperchon, the horse-bowmen and the elephants, which had been marching down the river, were now transferred to the right bank of the Acesines, as the united stream is still called, and the whole added to Craterus' force. Nearchus with the fleet was first started down the river. Craterus followed Nearchus three days later. This joint naval and military force was to form a base for future operations on the westerly side of the river. Nearchus was to land on the right bank below the point where the Acesines receives the Hydraotis, and hold the vicinity to prevent reinforcements being sent to the Mallians south of the desert, as well as to intercept any barbarian forces which attempted escape that way. The rest of the army was then divided into three parts. Alexander commanded the body which marched directly against the Mallians across the desert. It consisted of the hypaspists, archers, Agrianians, Peithon's brigade of the phalanx, the horse-archers and half of the Companion cavalry. By this march he proposed to surprise them and cut them off from Gandiritis and the Cathæan country, and drive them down towards the mouth of the Hydraotis and there have them run foul of the Macedonian forces ordered to that point. Hephæstion was sent along the left bank southerly, five marches ahead of the king, so that if the Mallians or part of them fled down stream when Alexander attacked them he could be in a position to intercept them even before they reached Craterus and Nearchus. Ptolemy followed three marches behind Alexander, so that if the Mallians or part of them fled up stream when Alexander attacked they would meet a like reception.

A rendezvous was given to all the detachments at the junction of the Hydraotis and Acesines.

These bodies thus marched in such a manner as to be able to coöperate in working against the Mallians; Nearchus and Craterus were to look after the western bank, and keep an eye on the barbarians opposite. Alexander was to march directly against the Mallians as was his wont, while Hephæstion would be within sustaining distance of his right and Ptolemy of his left flank. It should be noted that the present confluence of the Acesines (Chenab) and the Hydraotis (Ravi) is thirty miles above Multan. In Alexander's time it was just below Multan, with a branch inclosing the town and citadel. There has always been a tendency in these Indian rivers to seek channels farther west. The course of the Indus has greatly changed.

It is said that the Mallians and Oxydracians had laid aside their usual quarrels to meet the overwhelming danger and agreed to work together to resist the threatened invasion. The forces they had raised were sixty thousand foot, ten thousand horse and seven hundred chariots, and they had given mutual hostages. As the Mallian territory was the one primarily threatened, the Oxydracians would have been obliged to leave their own to join the Mallians. The joint army proposed to manœuvre under cover of the desert. But as the tribes could not agree on a common leader (being among the free Indians and, says Arrian, jealous of each other to the last degree) the confederate scheme fell through. While not vouched for on good authority this statement seems to agree with subsequent facts.

The first half day's march brought Alexander to a small water a dozen miles (one hundred stades) from the Acesines (perhaps the small river Ayek, midway between Jungh and Shorkot, eleven miles from the Chenab). Informed that this

was the last water to be had till the army reached the city to
which the largest force of the Mallians had fled, — for on the
failure of the scheme of confederation all the barbarians had
retired to their respective strongholds, — Alexander rested the

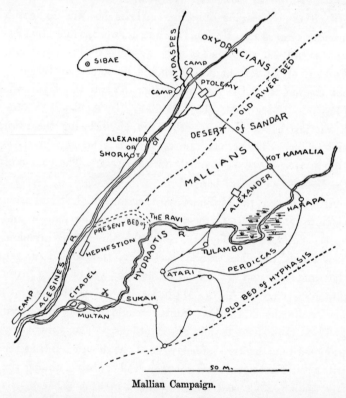

Mallian Campaign.

army and gave each man orders to fill whatever vessels he had
on hand with water to last him across the desert tract before
them.   From this water on, the march occupied the balance
of this day and the succeeding night, no stop being made and
about forty-five miles (four hundred stades) being covered in
this time, a remarkable march for the twenty-four hours.
Alexander had calculated well in choosing this route so as to

surprise the Indians. They did not in the least expect him from this direction. When nearing the end of the journey, he advanced ahead of the phalanx with the cavalry and soon came in sight of the Mallian city of Agallassa (modern Kot-Kamalia) on the edge of the desert of the Sandar.

There have been numerous attempts to identify and locate the places thus made the objectives of Alexander's marches. Some have resulted happily ; many cannot be reconciled with the various statements of the ancient historians. General Alexander Cunningham, R. E., in his Ancient Geography of India, seems to be the most reliable guide ; and in all Alexander's campaigns, from the head waters of the Cophen to the delta of the Indus, much heed has been paid to his very intelligent and painstaking work. Still there are difficulties, as he himself acknowledges, in the way of many of his identifications. The route he traces, in difficult and conflicting passages, is, however, as reliable as any can be. He has largely made use of the records of the Chinese pilgrim Hwen Thsang, whose travels in India in the seventh century give the then condition of Alexander's towns, and aid materially in the process of identification.

So utterly disconcerted was the enemy at Alexander's sudden appearance that he found most of them outside the city, which was too small readily to shelter the multitude, and unarmed. Entirely unprepared for resistance, they were at the mercy of the Macedonians, who slew a vast number and drove the rest into the city, around which Alexander at once posted a cordon of cavalry, so as to hold it until the infantry could come up to begin operations against it.

On the arrival of the infantry, Alexander detached Perdiccas, with his own and Clitus' cavalry ilēs and the Agrianians, to blockade another city of the Mallians in this vicinity (Harapa, sixteen miles southeast of Kot-Kamalia, according to

Cunningham) until he himself could come to attack it. But he bade him by no means to undertake an assault, lest the rumor of its fall should too soon alarm the country. Alexander then attacked the wall of Agallassa. The enemy did not defend it to any purpose, but after a number had been killed and wounded by missiles, some retired into the citadel of the town, while the majority took to the woods. The citadel they defended gallantly for some hours against repeated partial assaults, though these were handsomely made; for this burg was situated on a height difficult of access. But Alexander ordered a final assault in force. This was so vigorously renewed, himself heading the storming party, that, under the influence of his example, who was everywhere, instinct with words of cheer and deeds of valor, the citadel was captured and its garrison of two thousand men put to the sword.

Perdiccas reached the city to which he was sent only to find it deserted by its inhabitants a short time before. Giving chase, he overtook and slew a great number of the stragglers; but most of them got away and fled to the marshes of the river Hydraotis.

Alexander, giving his men a short rest after taking Agallassa, marched with the cavalry in pursuit of the rest of the Mallians who had fled from the second city and from Agallassa. By a rapid night march he reached the Hydraotis. Here he came up with a number of stragglers of the column of fugitives, who suffered the usual fate. Crossing by the same ford to the south or left bank, he pursued in such haste that he overtook the rear-guard of the Mallians, broke it up, and slew and captured a great number. The rest made good their escape to a fortified town near by, a strong place by nature and by art (modern Tulambo). Waiting for the infantry to come up, Alexander sent Peithon, with his taxis and two ilēs of cavalry, against the latter place. Peithon captured it, and brought back all who were not slain for sale as slaves.

It is common and very natural for historians to question the propriety of waging such wars of extermination. And according to our views they are not justifiable. But it must be remembered that Alexander lived in an era when human life, as such, was not the sacred thing which the civilization of our century has made it. Even the life of a Hellene was of small consequence; these barbarians were not even considered. It is not probable that Alexander ever debated the question of cruelty; that it ever occurred to him that he was trenching on the everlasting laws of common humanity. Such a law was not at that day recognized. The extermination of a people or the devastation of a region, as a means of protecting boundaries from invasion, was then and has always been, down to this generation, within certain limits, a well recognized military scheme. And when we look at the ruthless cruelties of modern nations, practised after the Christian religion had been preached for fifteen centuries, it is less hard to palliate Alexander's acts, which proceeded by no means from a cruel nature, or lust of blood, or drunken fury, as has so often been said, but which were in pursuance of a clear and defined military policy. Nothing short of fearful examples would subdue these barbarians and semi-barbarous tribes, or deter them from rising in rebellion so soon as the conqueror turned his back. Alexander's course was now in retreat, as it were. He had not always time for careful systematic conquests. He must exterminate when he could not readily subdue. And it may perhaps be said that the influence of the trades and arts and civilization of the Greeks, which remained behind, to a greater or less extent, in every territory over which Alexander left a satrap, was of more

eventual good than the slaughter of many thousands of barbarians did harm. Perhaps Alexander had no right whatever
of conquest. That proposition is certainly capable of being
ably advocated. But he did go abroad to conquer ; and once
he set forth, he was wise, in a military sense, to take the
means he did to carry through his conquests, however much
we may shudder at the awful array of figures which computes
the human souls his conquering progress swept from before
him.

While Peithon was capturing the second city, Alexander
headed an expedition against a town of the Brahmins, whither
some of the Mallians had fled (probably modern Atari,
twenty miles southwest of Tulambo, thirty-three miles northeast of Multan). No sooner had he reached the place and
marched the phalanx to the wall, in order to undermine it,
than the Indians, divining his purpose and believing that the
city wall would not long resist the Macedonians, and being,
moreover, harassed with the missiles of the light troops, retired into the citadel, thinking here to be able to make a
better defense. The Macedonians followed hard upon, and
some of them penetrated the citadel with the barbarians, but
could not hold themselves there. But they were expert sap-
pers and miners. They went to work with a will, and soon
one of the towers and a part of the wall near by were undermined and thrown down. An assault was then ordered.
When the Macedonians reached the breach, where the opposition was stoutly maintained, and were seen to hesitate in the
assault, Alexander rushed to the front, — as he could never
refrain from doing, — headed them in person, mounted the
wall first of all, carried the works, and at once captured the
citadel. The gallant defenders themselves set their habita-
tions on fire, and, standing on the roofs, hurled their missiles
or firebrands upon the foe until they fell engulfed by the

burning walls. Here five thousand brave men perished. Sad and strange that civilization, as well as Christianity, has always needed so much blood to propagate its benignant doctrines. And yet, as Voltaire said, Alexander founded many more cities than other conquerors have destroyed.

Scarcely pausing to give his men one day's rest, though they had marched and fought almost continuously for five, Alexander moved with fresh ardor against the other tribes of the Mallians. He knew that exertion now meant quiet by and by. He found that the barbarians had all fled into the desert from their several cities, all of which he destroyed. The army was given one day more rest. He then dispatched Peithon with his infantry brigade, and Demetrius with his ilē of cavalry and some light-armed men, back to the river Hydraotis to follow it up and down, and capture all who had fled for safety into the woods and marshes which lined the banks. For many had taken refuge in these places. This work was done thoroughly; all who did not surrender were captured and killed.

While this diversion to keep his rear cleared of enemies was going on, Alexander himself led the rest of the troops against what was reputed the largest city of the Mallians, where he heard that many had taken refuge on fleeing from other towns. This was probably Multan. It was on the direct route prescribed to Hephæstion, who, however, either had no orders, or was too weak to attack it. The inhabitants had abandoned the city proper, owing to the terror inspired by the Macedonian name. For the utmost bravery appeared not to forestall defeat. They had then moved across to the north bank of the Hydraotis, had advanced up stream, and had taken up a position on the western side of the most available ford. The bank on their side was high, and they hoped to be able to arrest Alexander's crossing here, and thus protect at least a part of their territory and their capital city.

On perceiving their determination, Alexander, with his customary reckless daring, headed some squadrons of his cavalry, plunged gallantly into the current, forded the stream, and fell upon the enemy, white weapon in hand. The Indians, astonished at such a bold act by a mere handful of men, did not even wait for the foremost horsemen, of whom Alexander was always first, to reach the bank, but at once abandoned

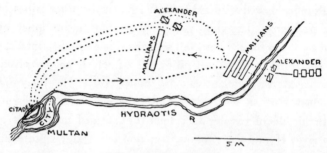

"The City of the Malli."

their position, and retired into the interior. Alexander followed upon their heels with his cavalry alone. When he had given chase some distance from the river, the Indians, recognizing the small number of their pursuers, — there were but four or five thousand Macedonian horse to fifty thousand Indians, — turned and advanced upon them in close order, presenting a very brave front. Here was a dangerous situation, but the king was used to such. The salvation of the Macedonians lay in their compact formation, their rapid manœuvring and in their being on a large plain where there was plenty of elbow-room. Instead of attempting to fight the Indians in line, Alexander quickly wheeled into column, and led his men round and round their army, coming to a front, and charging in upon their line in flank or rear wherever a chance afforded. The Macedonians could always retire in good order, reform and return to the charge. The Indians were not so active.

The light troops now arrived, and after a while the head of the phalanx was seen approaching at a rapid pace across the plain. The Indians lost courage, and fled to the citadel of their town, suffering grievous loss in the pursuit. Alexander kept close behind them, and on reaching the place, cooped them up in the citadel, first by a line of cavalry and then by the infantry as fast as it arrived. He then gave his troops a few hours' needed rest. For the infantry was exhausted by severe marching, and the cavalry equally so by marching and heavy fighting beside.

Early next day the king formed two storming columns, himself heading one and Perdiccas the other. The Indians but weakly defended the wall, and retired wholly into the citadel. This was a strong work, over a mile about, with many towers, and with the Hydraotis flowing around it. The town was separated from the citadel by a branch of the river, and all told was five miles in circumference. There is no mention in the authorities of the citadel being surrounded by the river. In this particular, Cunningham has been followed, as in all the topography of this campaign. Alexander speedily made his way into the outer circuit through a gate which he forced, but Perdiccas was unable to make much progress for want of scaling ladders. Arrived at the citadel, the Macedonians at once began to undermine the wall, and ladders were sent for hurriedly. Alexander, always impatient in his valor, seeing that the work did not advance as fast as his own desires, himself seized one of the first two scaling ladders which arrived, planted it against the wall, and ascended foremost of all, bearing his shield aloft to ward off the darts from above. He was followed on the same ladder by Peucestas, the soldier who always carried the shield brought from the temple of the Trojan Athena before him in battle, and by Leonnatus, the confidential body-guard. Up the adjoining ladder went Abreas, a soldier who received double pay for his conspicuous valor. The other ladders were delayed. Alexander, from whose fiery ardor the barbarians retired, swung himself up on the battlements, and frayed a place for himself with his sword. This was the affair of an instant. The hypaspists, anxious for his safety, crowded upon the two ladders in such number as to break them down. Alexander was left standing with only Peucestas, Abreas and Leonnatus upon the wall in the midst of his enemies; but so conspicuous was his bearing and gallantry, that none came within reach of his sword but to fall. The barbarians had recognized him by his armor and white plumes, and the multitude of darts which fell upon him threatened his life at every instant. The Macedonians below implored him to leap down into their outstretched arms. Nothing daunted, however, the descendant of the Æacidæ scorned one backward step, and calling on every man to follow who loved him, Alexander leaped down inside the wall, and with his three companions, backing up against it, held his own with wonderful countenance. In a brief moment he had killed a number of Indians, and had slain their leader who ventured against him. But Abreas fell dead beside him with an arrow in his forehead, and Alexander was at the same instant pierced through the corselet by an arrow whose point penetrated the lung. Yet he bravely defended himself till he fell exhausted by loss of blood, and over him, like lions at bay, but glowing with the halo which only crowns the brave, stood Peucestas defending him with the sacred shield, and Leonnatus with his sword, both dropping blood from countless wounds. It seemed that the days of all three were numbered.

The Macedonians, meanwhile, some with the ladders now arriving, some on the backs of the rest and some by means of pegs inserted in the earth or between the bricks of the wall, had begun to get to the top, and one by one leaped within, and surrounded the now lifeless body of Alexander. Others forced an entrance through one of the gates, and flew to the rescue. Their valor was as irresistible as their number was small. The Indians could in no wise resist their terrible onset, their war-cry doubly fierce from rage at the fate of their beloved king, to them in truth a demi-god. They were driven from the spot, and Alexander was borne back to the camp. So enraged were the Macedonians at the wounding of their king, whom they believed to be mortally struck, that they spared neither man, woman nor child in the town.

Alexander's wound was indeed grave, but his good constitution and robust health helped him, and, under the care of Critodemus of Cos he recovered, much to the joy of his army. While his life was despaired of, a great deal of uncertainty and fear as to their situation must have prevailed, for Alexander was the centre-point, the motive power, the balance wheel of the entire body. Without him what could they do? How ever again reach their homes? Every man felt that no one except the king could lead them, and how much less in retreat than in advance!

At the upper camp at the confluence of the Hydaspes and Acesines, from which Alexander had started, says Arrian, it was thought for some days that Alexander was really dead, and that his captains were concealing the fact. Bad news spreads fast. The lower camp caught alarm. This threatened to give rise to lack of discipline from very fear. And here again I cannot refrain from quoting from Arrian: —

"When Alexander became acquainted with this, for fear some attempt at a revolution might be made in the army, he had himself conveyed, as soon as it could be done with safety, to the bank of the river Hydraotis, and placed in a boat to sail down the river. For the camp was at the confluence of the Hydraotis and Acesines, where Hephæstion was at the head of the army, and Nearchus of the fleet. When the ship bearing the king approached the camp, he ordered the tent covering to be removed from the stern, that he might be visible to all. But they were still incredulous, thinking, forsooth, that Alexander's corpse was being conveyed in the vessel; until at length he stretched out his hand to the multitude when the ship was nearing the bank. Then the men raised a cheer, lifting their hands, some towards the sky, and others to the king himself. Many even shed involuntary tears at the unexpected sight. Some of the shield-bearing guards brought a litter for him when he was conveyed out of the ship; but he ordered them to fetch his horse. When he was seen again mounting his horse, the whole army reëchoed with loud clapping of hands, so that the banks of the river and the groves near them reverberated with the sound. On approaching his tent, he dismounted from his horse, so that he might be seen walking. Then the men came near, some on one side, others on the other, some touching his hands, others his knees, others only his clothes. Some only came close to get a sight of him, and went away having chanted his praise, while others threw garlands upon him, or the flowers which the country of India supplied at that season of the year."

It cannot be denied that there is a difficulty in accepting Multan as the "City of the Malli," where Alexander was wounded. The main camp was at the confluence, less than a dozen miles below Multan, and yet the troops were apparently unable to ascertain whether the king was really dead, as rumored, or only wounded. The whole paragraph just quoted looks as if the city in question were farther up the river. Moreover, Hephæstion was at the camp, in joint command with Nearchus. His route had been close to Multan from the upper camp down the left bank. Yet he had neither captured nor attacked nor masked it, nor placed his column at Alexander's disposal; nor yet ascertained the king's condition. This fact alone looks as if the city in question were far up stream. But General Cunningham has been on the ground, and has diligently compared authorities with localities. No better series of towns can be ventured on with less knowledge than his.

Alexander's officers were now emboldened to make a loyal protest against his exposing his person in battle as recklessly as had been his wont, the consequences of which had in the last battle threatened to be so fatal. With Craterus as spokesman they begged that he would leave such feats of daring to them and to the privates, though indeed none of them could vie with him in strength or skill or valor. Alexander listened to their protest, but is said secretly to have been displeased at what they said, " for," says Arrian, " he had not sufficient self-control to keep aloof from danger, through his impetuosity in battle and his passion for glory."

On this occasion a certain old Bœotian came near to him, and, quoting a line from one of the lost tragedies of Æschylus to the effect that the man who performs great deeds must also suffer, said, " O Alexander, it is the part of heroes to perform great deeds," a word which gave the king vast satisfaction, and for which he rewarded the Bœotian with his intimacy.

To this camp at the confluence of the Hydraotis and Acesines came envoys bringing the submission of the Mallians, who were thoroughly subdued by the terrible campaign just ended. Though much of their land remained unconquered, they despaired of preserving their independence. The Oxydracians, equally demoralized, though passing for the bravest of all the Indians, also came bearing the same message. Alexander demanded as hostages, to serve in his army till he had finished the war, the one thousand best men of the Oxy-dracians. These they sent with five hundred chariots, each fitted for two warriors. This brave and interesting people claimed that they had been free ever since Bacchus had passed through their land; but that Alexander, who claimed descent from the gods and as his deeds showed, rightly, was entitled to their submission; and they were glad to bring it.

Alexander appointed Philip viceroy over the Oxydracians and the surviving Mallians, his satrapy extending to the con-fines of Porus and Taxiles. Many vessels had been built here and others were brought by the Xathrians on Alexan-der's order, and a much larger part of the army — seventeen hundred cavalry Companions, ten thousand foot and the ar-chers and Agrianians — was now transferred by water down stream to the mouth of the Acesines where the Indus takes up all the waters of the Five Rivers country. Here Alexander awaited the arrival of Perdiccas with the rest of the army. This had marched by land and on the way had received the submission of many tribes, the Abastanians alone needing reduction by force.

Other nations, among them the Ossadians, likewise brought in their submission and here too Alexander founded one more Alexandria and began the construction of a dockyard. The junction of the Indus and the other great rivers seemed to him to be a promising place for a great mart. This city was to be the limit of Philip's satrapy. And he left with him all the Thracians and such other troops as seemed to him sufficient to hold the land and foster commerce and Hellenism. Oxy-artes, the father of Roxana, also came hither, and to him Al-exander gave the viceroyalty over the Parapamisans in lieu of the former satrap Tyriaspes, who had been exercising his authority with cruelty and injustice.

XLV.

GEDROSIA. FEBRUARY, B. C. 325, TO FEBRUARY, B. C. 324.

ALEXANDER reached the delta of the Indus after subduing the land of Oxycanus, Sambus, and Musicanus, and chastising the Brahmins who had on several occasions instigated revolt. Here, at Patala, he established a city and
dockyard; and from here he sailed down both branches of the delta to the sea.
Then he began preparations for moving back to Babylon along the coast, for he
had conceived the idea that ships could sail from the mouth of the Indus to the
mouth of the Euphrates, and proposed to send a fleet, and himself march that
way. He dispatched Craterus, with half the army, invalids and trains, by
way of Arachotia and Drangiana; and with the stronger part of the army, after
subduing the border tribes, he started across the desert of Gedrosia. Nearchus, somewhat later, sailed with the fleet along the coast. No body of men
had ever crossed this desert; and the provisions Alexander ordered to be sent
to meet him never came to hand. The king was gravely at fault in not being
sure of his supplies. On the march he dug wells at places on the coast, and
left stores of provisions for Nearchus. After sixty days' march over burning
sands, in which nearly all the beasts and three fourths of the men are said to
have perished, Alexander reached Paura, and after a rest, returned to Pasar-
gadæ and Susa. He found his kingdom all but falling to pieces for lack of the
hand of the master.

CRATERUS was now put over the Acesines to the left bank
of the Indus, with the elephants, and the army was collected
in one body. On this bank the marching was easier, there
being no mountain range, and there were more unsubdued
tribes. Alexander was now entering the province of modern
Sindh. Cultivation existed some distance inland, along this
part of the Indus. The king headed down stream to the
country of the Sogdians or Sodrians, whose capital city
(modern Faxilpur) he transformed into another Alexandria,
built shops and a dockyard, and made necessary repairs to
the fleet. The character of the river, the people and the

country here began to change. The high mountain chain on the west bent away from the river, leaving a more moderate

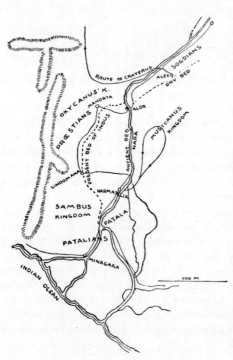

range in places, and the Indus widened into many channels. Fruitful lowlands lined its banks. To-day, as then, this district is thickly peopled and thrifty. The main change is in the river itself, which has shifted its course to a new and western channel. In the times we are speaking of the Indus ran in the bed now called Nara.

Alexander made Oxyartes, who had reported at head-

Campaign on the Lower Indus.

quarters, in addition to what he already controlled, the viceroy of all India from the confluence of the Acesines and Indus to the coast line, and associated with him Peithon as general, with ten thousand troops. Here, too, Craterus made preparations to march back to Persis by way of Arachotia and Drangiana, with the invalids and heavy trains. But he appears to have been delayed, perhaps by the threatened revolt of Musicanus. He apparently started later, but it was from here that led the road he followed.

Below the land of the Sogdians there had been no offer of

submission. Alexander felt that he still had much work to do,
He continued down the river to the kingdom of Musicanus,
who had made no tender of fealty, and who was said to be
king of the most prosperous part of India, as was, to judge
from the condition of to-day, a fact. To any one having the
Anglo-Saxon feeling for independence, this assumption of
Alexander that all kings should volunteer submission at his
mere approach is grating; but the idea itself was well carried out. So rapid was his progress that he reached the borders of Musicanus before this potentate was aware that he
had started from the land of the Mallians. Thus surprised,
Musicanus deemed it wise to accept the inevitable, and came
to meet the Macedonians with gifts and apologies. Alexander, always open to abject submission as well as flattery,
forgave him his opposition, built a fortress at his capital,
modern Alor, in which he placed a Macedonian garrison, and
left Musicanus in possession of his ancient kingdom as satrap.
This extended, in all probability, as far as modern Brahmanabad.

Thence, with the seventeen hundred horse which had been
with him on the fleet, the archers and Agrianians, Alexander
struck inland to the west, on a campaign against the Præs-
tians and Oxycanus (or Portikanus), a king who had also
failed to tender his submission. This territory ran as far as
the foothills, and about a hundred miles north and south.
The first of his two cities Alexander took at the first onset,
and distributed the booty among the soldiers. The second
city was the capital, Mahorta (ten miles from modern Lark-
hana, and forty from Alor), a place of much importance,
which controlled the high road from this Indus country *via*
the Gandara and Bolan passes to the plateau of Iran. Alexander was obliged to besiege this town three days, and then
to storm the citadel. In the assault the barbarian king was

killed.   There were some elephants here, which were added
to the already large herd.   The other towns, numerous and
mostly large and wealthy, submitted, for the Indians were
cowed by Alexander's apparently superhuman successes.   It
is difficult to identify these cities.   They are all in ruins, and
there have been few to investigate the contents of the ruined
mounds.   In this locality, General Cunningham is still followed as the most reliable guide.

From this place Alexander was compelled to hasten against
Sambus, a king who had come far up stream to tender fealty,
whom he had made viceroy of the mountaineer Indians, and
sent back home with favor.   Sambus had long been at war
with Musicanus, which fact had induced him to submit to
Alexander in the hope that he would thus gain the upperhand,
but when Musicanus was pardoned and received into the king's
confidence, under the idea that he himself would now be the
sufferer on account of the enmity of his ancient foe, he concluded to revolt from his newly-acknowledged master.   On
Alexander's approach, however, Sambus fled across the Indus,
and his people opened the gates of his capital city, Sindomana (modern Sehwan), now on the Indus, but then sixty-
five miles from the river.   Sindomana was situated on a high
rock, near a large lake, and in the midst of plenty ; and was
a city of the first importance.   Alexander now returned to
his fleet, left on the Indus below Alor.

He next moved against Harmatelia, a city of the Brahmins (modern Brahmanabad), near by the Indus.   This was
captured by the digging of a subterranean passage by which
the soldiers entered the town under the walls.   A number of
citizens were punished with utmost severity for instigating
this revolt.   It was while he was conducting this campaign
that Alexander learned to his surprise that Musicanus had
likewise revolted and put the Macedonian garrison to the

sword. When Alexander had disappeared from immediate view, Musicanus imagined he had gone for good. The Brahmins had roused the religious frenzy of this people also. Arrian calls these Brahmins the philosophers of India. They appear to have been hard to reconcile to the new régime, and excessively bitter in their antagonism. Alexander, incensed that this barbarian king should thus reward his favors, countermarched sharply against him, captured many of the cities in the southern part of his domains, razed some to the ground and sold the inhabitants into slavery, and garrisoned others; while Peithon was sent to Alor and beyond after Musicanus, who had imitated Sambus and fled into the regions east of the Indus. Having captured him, Peithon brought him to Harmatelia. Alexander ordered him to be crucified in the public roads, with a number of Brahmins who had been the prime movers in the revolt.

To offset this treachery, the ruler of the Patalians, Moëris by name, now came from the apex of the delta of the Indus and tendered submission, offering to do whatever Alexander should prescribe. This practically put an end to all opposition along the Indus. Alexander could fairly call this great river, with its mighty affluents, his own. How strong the ties which bound to him the vassals he had made might have remained, had Alexander lived to consolidate his conquests, it is hard to say; how lax they actually were was shown immediately after his death.

However uncertain or limited the information on which Alexander conceived his gigantic schemes, he none the less had a very definite general idea of what he desired to accomplish. He always looked ahead, gauged the outcome of his ventures correctly, and, after using due care, left the details to be met as they came up. From the delta of the Indus, which he next proposed to visit, Alexander's homeward march was to be across the desert of Gedrosia. This was an unknown route, never successfully traversed by an army, and never attempted, except, tradition said, by Semiramis, whose entire army perished in the passage.

To avoid having too great a force to feed in crossing this desert, and because it was not now necessary to keep so large a body for further military operations, which would probably be limited in extent, Craterus, who had been kept in command of the army during Alexander's western campaign, was now ordered to start on his overland trip with a large part of the troops and the elephants. His route lay through Arachotia and Drangiana, and with him went a number of invalided Macedonians and Companions who were to return to

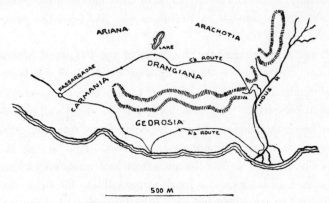

Routes of Craterus and Alexander.

Hellas, the phalanxes of Attalus, Antigenes and Meleager, and part of the archers. This column crossed the mountain range which runs down the west bank of the Indus from the Cophen, separating the luxuriant tropical vegetation of India from the barren table-lands of Persia, probably through the pass now called Bolan.

There was an additional motive for Craterus' march, in

that many troubles and quarrels among the satraps on the Arianian uplands made the appearance of an army among them essential to restore order. Craterus had at least one third of the force which started down the Indus. On the way through Arachotia and Drangiana he was given authority to settle controversies and punish delinquents, and was especially instructed to order the satraps of the adjoining territories to send provisions to the desert of Gedrosia, through which the king was himself to march.

Alexander for the present continued down the river in his fleet, while Hephæstion, with the bulk of the army, marched down the right bank, and Peithon, having first swept the defiles in the mountains clear of hostile tribes, to protect the flanks of the army, crossed and marched, with horse-archers and Agrianians, down the left bank. The rendezvous was to be Patala, and each on his way was to provide for the future security of the country through which he passed. The delta of the Indus has so much altered the course of its waters in two thousand years that the position of Patala cannot now be identified. It may be modern Haiderabad.

Before arriving at Patala, which he reached about midsummer, Alexander learned that it was deserted. The inhabitants had fled to a man from very terror at what they heard of Alexander. But the king sent after them, captured a few prisoners, and made the latter his messengers to their fellow-citizens, and thus persuaded them to return; whom, when they did so, he treated with the utmost generosity and helpfulness. At Patala the delta of the Indus began. Here the king transformed the city into a new Alexandria, which he left Hephæstion to fortify, built a dockyard, and sent out many days' journey into the desert to teach the inhabitants how to sink wells and thus increase their limited supply of water. These well-digging parties had many brushes with nomads, but nevertheless persevered and carried out their plan.

Alexander now determined to explore the delta of the Indus. It required as true courage and enterprise to sail down the Indus delta with Alexander's small craft, propelled alone by oars, quite ignorant of what lay beyond, and with crews which had never yet been out of the eastern Mediterranean, as it has ever required of the great discoverers to venture forth on unknown seas in search of unknown lands. There is some confusion as to which branch the king first attempted; but judging by the measures he adopted it seems probable that he began with the east branch, though Arrian calls it the right one. He detailed Leonnatus, with eight thousand foot and one thousand horse, to explore the island of Patala between the arms of the delta.

Alexander set out with his thirty-oared galleys, and some with one and one half banks of oars. After a perilous journey — for the Indus is twenty-five miles wide and subject to heavy water — he reached the open sea. Many of his vessels had been damaged, and he had been unable to procure natives for pilots a good part of the way. He was greatly astonished at the phenomenon of the tides, with which he was not familiar. Having put some distance out to sea, so as to be sure he had reached the great ocean, he returned to Patala, where he found his plans for a new city fairly completed. He then descended the west branch of the Indus. His first stop was at a point where the river broadened out into a huge lake. Here he again laid the foundations of a city and dockyard, Minagara; and proceeding to the sea, satisfied himself that this western arm was the best adapted for navigation. The details of these trips, as of the later voyage of Nearchus, are of vast interest, but scarcely belong to Alexander's military history. He then explored the coast to the west with the cavalry for a distance of a three days' journey, dug wells for the fleet he proposed to send that way, and ordering a detachment farther along for like purpose, he returned to Patala. Finding everything in progress here, he again descended to Minagara, and spent some time in collecting food for four months. The summer was drawing to a close. Alexander had been the better part of a year moving down the great river.

There is abundant internal evidence in the stories of the ancient authors that Alexander was not alone a great soldier, but that he was a statesman whose ideas were broad and whose intelligence fully grasped the extent of what could be accomplished by commerce and the arts. It is altogether probable, familiar as he must have been with the history of Tyre, with the writings of Ctesias, which, however unreliable, still were full of suggestiveness, with the statement that Scylax had sailed from the mouth of the Indus to the Red Sea, with all that the history of the Jews and Arabs could tell, and other not altogether meagre if ill-digested information of that day, that Alexander had, even before starting on the expedition, a hope that through his conquests he might concentrate the valuable trade of the East in a direction which should bring it towards the Mediterranean by an easier route than across the uplands of Iran. In endeavoring to conquer India, probably the wealth-bringing control of trade was as much the underlying motive as the greed of territory. His care in studying out the navigable character of the Indus, and subsequently that of the Persian Gulf; his later effort to send a fleet around Arabia into the Red Sea, his founding Alexandria in Egypt, all tend to show that he had great political and commercial schemes in his head which he intended should tread in the steps of his military successes. It is rather the habit of modern writers to reduce everything Alex-

ander did, excepting military exploits, to the level of crass
luck, to deny him any skill except that of the soldier, and
even to base this on the fortune which often attends the gam-
bler. And yet the great among his contemporaries all gave
him credit for vast and true conceptions, and there were
giants in those days. The historians who had in hand the
best sources of information never doubted that his commercial sense and statecraft were as great as his power to lead
men ; and it seems as if what he accomplished is better susceptible of this construction than explainable on the hypothesis of chance. For we can no more gauge his knowledge by
the intelligence of to-day than measure our own petty conquests by the limitless extent of Alexander's.

Nearchus had been selected to command the fleet on
account of ancient amity, as well as courage and ability. In
moving from the Indus, he was to sail the fleet along the
coast; the army was to march by land. Alexander had him
wait for the season of favorable coasting winds which came
in October, now close at hand. Nearchus, one of the friends
of Alexander's youth and one of those who had been ban-
ished when he quarreled with his father, had volunteered to
perform this perilous duty. The intelligence as well as the
boldness of his voyage can scarcely be understood to-day, so
difficult is it to place one's self in the position of those who
wrought more than twenty-two centuries since. Though he
had for a while imagined the Acesines to be the head waters
of the Nile, the king no doubt had come to believe that
the Persian Gulf could be reached from the mouth of the
Indus; and it was this which Alexander desired to prove,
so as to carry out his scheme of trade between India and
Persia and the West, in other words, to connect the Indus
and the Euphrates.

But it was a leap in the dark. The army was to march

through a desert where it was doubtful whether it could render any aid to the fleet; the bold seamen might disappear into unknown seas, and never again be heard from. Both army and fleet were forlorn hopes. It is hard to say which was the more inhospitable, the shores along which Nearchus was to sail, where alone dwelt the Ichthyophagi, or the broiling sands of the Gedrosian desert, never yet crossed by a body of men. The boldness of Nearchus' voyage is extraordinary. He had, measured by his exploit, very poor vessels at command. He had naught but sun and stars to tell him his direction. He must land each night on a shore ill-conditioned by nature and dangerous perhaps from its population. His vessels could carry but small supplies. He might sail into seas and gulfs out of which he could never find his way, or whose coasts would afford him neither food nor water. Nearchus undertook this peril at Alexander's behest. This surely looks less like greed of conquest than the true discoverer's instinct.

Alexander was the first to start. It was the close of summer. He marched with the army from Patala by way of his depot at Minagara, and in nine days reached the Arabius, about one hundred miles from the Indus. Himself with Leonnatus and Ptolemy commanded the three columns of march. The troops were one half the targeteers and archers, the phalanx, except what marched with Craterus, the agema of Companion cavalry, a squadron from each cavalry regiment and the horsebowmen. These three columns kept near the coast and, on the way, dug wells in all the large coves from which the fleet might get water, when it should sail by. These wells were marked in such a manner as to be easily found. Hephæstion followed with the main army on a line farther inland. This division of forces was made in order to cover as wide a space as possible, and pick up as many of the barbarians as should

scatter towards the desert. The Arabitians dwelt on the
hither side of the river Arabius (Purali), and the Oritians
on the farther side. Neither had sent ambassadors to sue for
friendship, which neglect, in Alexander's code, at once placed
these tribes in the rank of his enemies. The Arabitians, on
learning of the approach of the Macedonians, fled towards
the desert as had been anticipated. The Oritians Alexander
reached in one night's march across a desert stretch beyond
the Arabius. He divided his cavalry into detachments by

Oritian Campaign.

squadrons, and sent these out at given distances from each
other like a huge skirmish line, in order to cover a large part
of the plain, the cavalry advance being sustained by the infantry in closer order. He thus speedily covered the entire
territory of the Oritians. This was an odd manœuvre, but
well adapted to the conditions, which, after all said, is always
the test. This was not the age of the new military art, nor
was the division of an army subject to the grave danger
against the barbarians, which it would be to-day against
civilized nations. A small force of the well-armed and perfectly disciplined Macedonians was equal to a horde of these
nomads.

The inhabitants were sold as slaves and the land was
wasted wherever he met resistance, and finding the capital

of the Oritians, named Rhambasia, situated in a large and fertile oasis, he left Hephæstion to found a final Alexandria there. Then, taking half the hypaspists, the Agrianians, the agema of cavalry and the horse-bowmen, he marched against some tribes of Oritians and Gedrosians who had assembled in the mountains between these two territories, to hold the passes against his advance. The barbarians, however, scarcely awaited his approach. Those who did not flee, surrendered. Over this territory Alexander left Apollophanes as viceroy, and gave him special instructions to accumulate and send forward provision for the army on its dangerous transit. For this there was ample time. Leonnatus, in command of all the Agrianians, some archers, and the Greek mercenaries, foot and horse, remained behind in Ora to await the arrival of Nearchus, not only to aid the latter, but to get the government of the land into running order. Having arranged these matters to his satisfaction, and Hephæstion having rejoined, Alexander set out to cross the desert of Gedrosia. Not long after his departure, the Oritians rose in rebellion, and, it is said, killed Apollophanes. But Leonnatus was equal to the occasion. He met and defeated the rebels in a great battle near the coast, between the Arabius and Tomerus rivers, and slew all their leaders. This pacified the new province.

The king's force was not large. It may be estimated thus : —

Alexander had in India		120,000 men
Garrisons left by the way, say	30,000	
Nearchus, say 100 vessels @ 150 men each . . .	15,000	
Craterus took with him some	40,000	85,000
Leaving to march with Alexander across the desert . . .		35,000 men

This march would not have involved such grievous peril and loss if the provisions which Alexander had ordered collected by Sibyrtius, satrap of part of Carmania, and by Apol-

lophanes, satrap of Gedrosia, had been promptly got together.
The latter had been especially ordered to station beeves and
corn along the route.   Alexander expected to be met on the
way by caravans of victuals.   There were none; and he must
be blamed for starting on his dangerous route without a certainty of provision.   He was so entirely in the habit of being

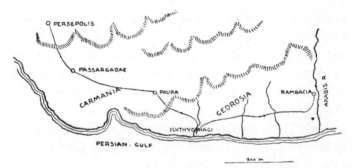

Desert of Gedrosia.

obeyed that he was wont to consider as already accomplished
whatever he ordered to be done.   But this does not excuse in
any degree the carelessness of the present occasion.   This is
the only instance in all Alexander's campaigns when he failed
to have a care to his rations.   The satrap of Carmania appears
not to have been held to blame, for Alexander afterwards
added to his dignities.   Perhaps he had received his orders
too late.

It was a matter of tradition that Semiramis returned from
her conquest of India through this desert, and that of the
hundreds of thousands of which her army consisted, but
twenty individuals came back with her to Babylon.   Cyrus
too, though incorrectly, was reputed to have crossed this
desert with like sad results.   Even the fanatic Islam considered Gedrosia as a boundary placed there by God, and refused to cross it.   It was indeed a terrible land.   Along the

coast lived only the Ichthyophagi, whose huts were built of
bones of the whale, shells and seaweed, and whose entire diet
consisted of fish. Inland to the mountain ranges some twenty
miles from the coast were sand stretches inhabited solely by
jackals and wolves and insects. Beyond the mountains lay
the still more terrible desert of Gedrosia. It has been said
that Alexander chose this passage simply because of its difficulties — because he was minded to do greater things than
Semiramis and Cyrus. This seems a partial way of looking
at the matter. Is it not easier to believe that Alexander was
really seeking to discover and establish the best outlet for
commerce between his Indian satrapies and his Persian, and
that he was willing to run a risk for this so desirable end?
Unless he were to go this route, how could he prove that his
great plan of commerce between India and Persia was feasi-
ble by way of the Indus, the sea and the Euphrates? How
could he forsake his friend Nearchus, who was sacrificing
himself to carry out the king's great schemes? How indeed
would he know the extent, boundaries and resources of this
coast land unless he passed this way? Was he not, in fact,
compelled to choose this route, in order not to have an unconquered strip full of wandering robber tribes between his
Indian satrapies and Persia? It was essential for him to
march by a route along which he could sustain his fleet by
digging wells, and leaving supplies at convenient places on
the coast. The ancient fleets were able to sail only during
the day and in fair weather; at night and in storms they were
compelled to put in shore, to find water and provision. The
crews of rowers and warriors were so numerous for the ton-
nage and the oars took up so much space, that they could
carry but a limited supply of food. If he expected him to suc-
ceed, Alexander could not send Nearchus along an unknown
coast without some aid. And while he might have dispatched

a lieutenant on this perilous mission through the desert, this was not Alexander's way. He always undertook the most difficult task himself, and saw with his own eyes what needed to be seen.

Should the voyage of Nearchus prove that the mouth of the Indus could actually be reached by sea from the mouth of the Euphrates, the coast must be explored, wells be dug, and stations built for the purpose of opening the route to travel and commerce. How could the king intelligently direct this to be done unless personally, by a march across Gedrosia, he ascertained the actual conditions? He may no doubt be accused of undertaking a great risk without adequate provision, and this is a grave accusation. But such is the sum of his lapse, and into the danger he only led the stronger and better part of his army, leaving the rest to march under Craterus through a well-known district. What had been serious dangers to others he had easily overcome. It was natural that he should underrate the perils of Gedrosia.

The expedition, twenty years later, of Seleucus Nicator to India, for the purpose of stimulating trade between that country and Syria, seems to prove Alexander's views to have been far-sighted. Seleucus went as far as the Ganges — his road had already been opened by Alexander — and his treaties with the Indian potentates, which lasted many years, resulted in an enormous trade between the two countries. Alexander's entire scheme seems much easier to explain on the hypothesis of an idea long pondered and as well digested as the existing knowledge warranted, than on that of an adventurer or knight-errant seeking vast difficulties merely for the sake of overcoming them.

In this land of Gedrosia there was an abundance of myrrh and other spices, but naught else but suffering and death. As the army marched onward, the desert grew sandier and more sterile; brooks dried up in the sand; the heat became intolerable; vegetation ceased. Not a path of any kind existed; and the marches had to be made at night. The men were scantily provided with rations, and these were finally exhausted. Supplies, so far as they could be got, or as long as they lasted, were in part taken to the coast for the fleet; wells were dug for it, and signals erected to catch Nearchus' attention when he should sail by. One of these convoys of food to the coast, even under Alexander's own seal, was broken open by the famished soldiery in disobedience of orders, little regarding what manner of death they died. With the utmost difficulty were any fresh supplies procured, and these were carefully husbanded and left along the coast under safe charge of the most trustworthy men. The army, after a few days' march, left the coast, and struck inland. Water was often sixty and eighty miles apart. The sand was like the waves of the sea for tracklessness. Discipline broke up. The men killed the cattle used as beasts of burden and even mules and horses, and ate their flesh, saying that they had died of thirst and heat. The very animals which drew the wagons on which lay the wounded men were killed for food, and the wounded left behind. All this Alexander was fain to overlook. Worse than the thirst was the terror of reaching water, followed by the agonizing death of those who too freely drank of it.

The advance of the army was headed towards Paura, the capital of Gedrosia, which was reached in sixty days from Ora. All accounts agree that the hardships of the campaigns they had undergone were as nothing compared to the sufferings of the march across this desert. The exact amount of loss is not known; it must have been very great. It is said that but a quarter of those who started from Ora reached Paura; and these in rags and without weapons. The beasts of burden almost all perished, mostly from lack of water, but many dropped from weakness and were engulfed in the sand. The marches had to be made from water to water, and are said by Strabo to have been of two hundred, four hundred and six hundred stades, — twenty-two, forty-four and sixty-six miles, — and yet the progress was no more than ten or twelve miles a day. When they could reach the next water by a night march, they did well enough; but when the march had to be by day, the suffering was indescribable. The wagons soon got broken up, and much baggage was thrown away. The sick and weak had to be abandoned. Stragglers were rarely able to regain the column. On more than one occasion, when they camped at the brooks they reached, the sudden overflows from storms in the mountains, which are usual in this country, drowned men and swept away baggage and beasts. Alexander was wont to pitch camp a couple of miles away from water, so as to prevent both this trouble and overdrinking by the men.

It was here that Alexander, in a time of great scarcity of water, when some soldiers had gathered a little supply, and brought it to him in a helmet, refused to drink, but poured it out on the ground, saying that he would not quench his thirst when his men could not. Other authorities place the incident — or a similar one — in the pursuit of Darius. It is also said that when the army had lost the way, and the guides could not find it, Alexander himself started out with but five companions, and by moving in the direction he knew the sea must be, did actually find it and water near by. Thither he brought the army, and for a week thereafter they kept along the seashore, and then again, when the guides had oriented themselves, moved inland.

Arrived at Paura, Alexander gave the relics of his army a rest. Here he found that a number of the viceroys had, of

their own motion, accumulated provisions for him on learning
that he was to march through the desert. But these came too
late to be of any use. It was little satisfaction to punish the
careless satraps who had not forwarded the required supplies.
After this the march was resumed towards Carmania, where
Craterus, who had easily marched through the upper country,
joined him. Winter had now set in.

Here Alexander rectified a number of abuses which had
grown up since he left Persepolis, by the change of officers
and the punishment of those who had proved corrupt or
cruel. He celebrated his victory over the Indians and his
march through the desert by feasts and games, and made
Peucestas one of the somatophylaxes and afterwards viceroy
of Persis. It indeed needed the arrival of supplies and the
presence of old companions-in-arms to restore to the sad relics
of the proud army which had but three months since left the
Indus the self-respect and discipline it had lost in the
march across the desert. Its terrible experiences naturally
led Alexander to fear that the brave and faithful Nearchus
with the fleet had fallen a prey to the dangers of the voyage.
But soon came the cheering intelligence that the gallant admiral had arrived on the coast at Salmus, near the river Ana-
mis. It was some time before he made his way up to the
camp. He then came and reported his voyage to Alexander,
who received him with great favor and affection, and sent
him to pursue his way as far as Susiana, where he was to
report again at the mouth of the Tigris. Hephæstion was
ordered, with the bulk of the army, elephants, and heavy baggage, to march by a southerly route into Persis, this being
warmer during the winter season, while Alexander himself,
on the way to Susa, marched to Passargadæ by the direct
mountain road, with his light infantry, archers, in part, and
Companion cavalry.

In Persis, also, Alexander found many punishments to inflict and abuses to correct. Phrasaortes, satrap of Persis, had died, and Orxines had assumed his office, but having been guilty of pillaging and cruelty, was put to death, and Peucestas made viceroy in his stead. Atropates, viceroy of Media, came, bringing Baryaxes, who had attempted to make himself king; and him, with his adherents, Alexander treated in like manner. Stasanor, viceroy of the Arians and Zarangians, and Phrataphernes, viceroy of the Parthians and Hyrcanians, came, bringing beasts of burden and camels at a time most opportune. These were distributed to the troops as required. Stasanor was sent back to Aria.

At Passargadæ Alexander found the tomb of Cyrus broken into, rifled of its treasures, and the corpse desecrated. But nothing could be elicited about the occurrence, even by the torture of the guard. The body was replaced in its resting place in greater state and security than before.

It was time, indeed, that Alexander should return. Everything was beginning to assume the aspect it wore so soon after his death. Sad prophecy of what would happen when there was no more Alexander! Nothing short of the most scrupulous and exact severity in meting out justice could restore the obedient kingdom he had left. It was on the point of falling to pieces through the greed, ambition, dishonesty, cruelty and rapacity of the satraps he had created. But the people soon learned that Alexander was no respecter of persons. They made haste to lay complaints before the king, whenever these were of a nature to attract attention. In no instance was just cause of complaint thrust aside.

In Carmania the satrap Aspastes, who, five years before, had submitted to Alexander and been continued in control of his territory, was not only removed, but executed, for malfeasance, and was replaced by Tlepolemus. The Arachotian noble Ordanes was brought in chains to Persis by Craterus, and was likewise executed for plotting revolt in that satrapy, and Arachotia was added to the satrapy of Ora and Gedrosia, under Sibyrtius, Apollophanes having been deposed for neglect of the king's orders to furnish provision in Gedrosia. From Media, Heracon with the mercenary horse, Cleander with the mercenary veterans, and Sitalces with the Thracian foot, who had been in Media with Parmenio, now reported with their respective commands; but they were also accused by the Medians of misuse of their office. The two latter were found guilty of peculation, pillage, and cruelty, and were executed with six hundred of their equally guilty soldiers, who had been their agents in oppression. Heracon was at that time acquitted, but was later executed for a repeated offense of plundering. Baryaxes of Media, and Oxyathres of Parætacenæ, suffered a like fate. Philip had been killed in a mutiny in India; but the mutiny was readily suppressed, and his satrapy was given to the king of Taxila and Eudemus. Encouraged by Alexander's evident intention to be just, the people came forward more and more freely with their troubles, and none had cause to feel that he failed to receive ample justice. Evenhandedness such as this, especially when exerted against his old and now sadly-needed Macedonians, showed the Persians that Alexander meant to be their protector as well as king, and was a well-timed lesson to all satraps. It was found, also, that Harpalus, the treasurer, had been playing fast and loose with Alexander's hoarded gold. But the thief was clever enough to make good his escape from the king's wrath, conveying with him, according to Diodorus, fifty thousand talents.

It is asserted by some that Alexander often acted on insufficient or on perjured evidence. That he made mistakes in this wholesale administration of justice is altogether prob-

able; but that his motive in punishing the delinquents was
the good of the peoples under his sceptre is shown by his uniform recognition of their rights throughout his entire reign.
Whatever his own course towards conquered nations, he held
his satraps to strict accountability in their dealings with
them.

The king now took up his march through the Persian
Gates, towards the heart of his empire. In Susa, which he
reached in February, after an absence of five years, he also
found many things to rectify. Foremost of all, Arbulites
and his son Oxathres were put to death for bad government and for despoiling the Susians. To Susa soon came
Hephæstion with the heavy column of the army, and Nearchus, from his last exploring expedition. Elated at his admiral's success, Alexander is said to have contemplated a voyage
not only around Arabia, but around the entire coast of Libya,
as Africa was then called, as far as the Pillars of Hercules,
and others to the Euxine, Scythia and the Sea of Azov. But
these projects were destined to interruption.

Alexander, from an unknown Coin.

XLVI.

MUTINY. JULY, B. C. 324.

THE Macedonians had reached their goal. They could enjoy their hard-earned wealth. Alexander paid their debts — some twenty thousand talents — and made them valuable presents. He coupled this bounty with intermarriages between his chief officers and Persian noblewomen, himself wedding daughters of Darius and Ochus, thus uniting both Persian royal families. To the soldiers who had Eastern wives he was especially generous. All this was in the line of his idea of a merger of races so as to make his kingdom homogeneous. Alexander had long had many Orientals in the army. He had thirty thousand of the best youths of the East in a special phalanx. He promoted many notable Orientals to high office — as was natural and necessary. These favors to conquered peoples galled his Macedonians. Distrust between king and soldier had been growing since the Hyphasis. Now, when, at a camp council in Opis, Alexander proposed to send home all disabled Macedonians with wealth and honor, his generosity was misunderstood and met by sullen protests, as if he were trying to get rid of the men who had helped him conquer the world. This feeling broke out into mutiny. Alexander summarily put down the outbreak with the strong hand, and dismissing his Macedonians from his service in an address of wonderful power, he placed himself in the hands of his Eastern army. This act absolutely broke up the mutinous sentiment; brought grief and repentance; and the ancient love came back in double measure. Confidence was restored. Alexander had won. He was quits with the army for its refusal to cross the Hyphasis.

AFTER many years of toil and hardship, the Macedonians now saw an end to their venturesome campaigns; and the king perceived that the time had come to distribute the anticipated rewards to his faithful soldiers. Alexander was more of a dreamer on the subject of removing national distinctions than on any other. From the time he conquered Egypt his mind was constantly bent on maturing a scheme to coalesce his vast empire into one mass of equal rights and privileges.

This end he mainly sought to accomplish by what proved to be the impracticable means of introducing Macedonian customs among peoples unused to them and wedded to their old ways, and in climates to which they were unsuited; and by the still less effectual practice of fostering intermarriages of Greeks and Orientals. This last idea Alexander now proposed to inaugurate on a gigantic scale, and couple it with an equally gigantic bounty to his men. His own present marriage with Statira, Darius' eldest daughter and widow of Mentor, and with Parysatis, youngest daughter of Ochus, by which he might graft his descendants upon the two royal families of Persia, was part of this universal scheme. To Hephæstion he gave in marriage Drypetis, another daughter of Darius; to Craterus, a niece; and to eighty of his other generals, the most prominent noblewomen of the land. The names of all soldiers, some ten thousand in number, who had wedded Asiatic women were registered, and Alexander made liberal presents to them all. The marriage feasts were celebrated in the Persian manner, and all the great and distinguished from every satrapy of the empire — the world and his wife of that day — came to the banquet. There is no space to devote to a description of this almost unparalleled feast, which lasted many days. That must be sought elsewhere. On this occasion Alexander capped his generosity to his soldiers by paying all their debts, — a gift, according to Arrian and Justin, of twenty thousand talents, or not far from twenty-five million dollars of our money; or, according to Plutarch, Diodorus, and Curtius, of ten thousand talents. Those who had done exceptional service received additional rewards. A few whom Alexander chose to distinguish for bravery and merit were crowned with golden chaplets. These were the somatophylaxes and the king's chief aides and generals. First of all, Peucestas, who had saved his life among the Mallians; then

Leonnatus, who had won a victory over the Oritians at the
river Tomerus ; Nearchus, who had become the most famous of
admirals ; Hephæstion, his bosom friend ; Lysimachus, Aris-
tonus, Perdiccas, Ptolemy and Peithon. Onesecritus, the
pilot of the king's galley, was also thus honored. But there
were some whom all this failed to satisfy.

Ever since Alexander started in pursuit of Darius, he had
incorporated in the army a great number of Asiatic soldiers.
And it seems altogether probable that they were drilled and
instructed in the Macedonian manner. Some historians
doubt the fact, but in no other way can we explain the marvelous results obtained in the five years' campaigning which
had since been conducted. Only on this hypothesis can the
essential unity of tactical action be explained. No doubt
many national peculiarities were retained among the foreigners so serving ; and there must have been kept up some decided distinguishing mark between these Asiatics and the
Macedonians. But we find no particular mention of Oriental detachments. The authorities mention the phalanx, the
light troops, the Companion or other cavalry, and only the
Daän horse-bowmen are frequently spoken of as a special
corps. What Asiatics there were seem to have been distributed among the brigades of the phalanx, or to have been
among the light troops, horse and foot. Nor does the proportion of light troops appear to have been increased. However this may be, whatever distinction there was it was now
part of Alexander's plan to obliterate. The way was already
paved. He had long ago caused to be chosen in all parts
of the empire, from the choicest of the youth of Persia just
reaching the age of manhood, a force numbering thirty thousand men. This body for five years had been assembling and
drilling. They were known as Epigoni, the "successors,"
were now under command of Seleucus, and in their entire

organization, drill, and equipment they conformed to the Macedonian fashion. A considerable extension of this system had been determined on by Alexander from the time of the refusal of the Macedonians to cross the Hyphasis, and he had sent orders to increase the number of these youths, to what extent is not determined. Some of them had already served with the army. He proposed to have fresh and submissive troops, and these had become, under so consummate an organizer, a powerful body, which added to pride in their calling and gratitude for the distinguished favors of the king the natural blind obedience of the Orient. The full importance of this body, so far as concerned their own relations to the fortunes of the great empire of Alexander, had perhaps not fully dawned upon the Macedonians until some time after they reached Susa, where they were brought face to face with the new corps. But now this became a fresh and unfortunate cause for suspicion and irritation on the part of the old Macedonian soldiers, who had for some time been fretting under the assumption by Alexander of the Median dress and manners and the promotion of Orientals.

There were probably left not more than twenty-five thousand Macedonians, if so many, of the two hundred thousand men who had come with the army of invasion or as reinforcements. Half of these had been in continuous service since 334 B. C. — ten long years. Most of them were utterly tired of war. They were, moreover, getting to be less easy to handle; no wonder they felt their own importance. But Alexander wanted no more Hyphasis troubles. It is not improbable that since the Hyphasis there had been a sort of moral wall building up between Alexander and his Macedonians, where before there had been perfect trustfulness. The king had hoped by his generosity, his feasts, and the abundant marriage gifts, to quell this bad feeling, but he had so far failed of success. In fact, when he offered to pay the debts of his soldiers, — and it was a frank piece of good will and entirely above-board, — it was at first suspected that he was trying to ascertain who had been extravagant, in order to punish such habits. Their ancient confidence in their king had weakened, as perhaps Alexander himself had changed. In this instance the suspicion had bred no evil; for the king at once convinced his old soldiers that he meant them naught but kindness, and had money-tables erected, where, without registering their names, each one could have the means of discharging his debts by a simple statement of their amount. In view of the enormous sum of these debts, this was a certain proof of sincerity.

But other things combined to complicate the situation. The mixing of Asiatic squadrons with the Companion cavalry, which was the easiest method of keeping up the old *cadres*, as well as of beginning the merger of races which Alexander contemplated, and the placing of distinguished Persians in the ranks of the Companion cavalry and foot-guard, added fuel to the flame of discontent. There were squadrons of Bactrian, Sogdianian, Arachotian, Zarangian, Arian and Parthian cavalry, as well as the Persian Evacæ, a choice cavalry corps, bodily incorporated with the Companion cavalry, and a fifth division of horse of mixed nationalities was now added to the body. The fact that the new-comers were especially fine men by no means drew the sting. Into the agema of foot were admitted: Artiboles and Hydarnes, sons of Mazæus; Cophen, son of Artabazus; Sisines and Phrasdamenes, sons of Phrataphernes; Histanes, Roxana's brother; Autobares and Mithrobæus; and last and most grievous, to Hystaspes of Bactria was given the command of the agema. A further grievance lay in the honors heaped upon Peucestas, who, on being made viceroy of Persis, adopted all the Oriental magnificence, and continued in the king's favor as of yore. That these new appointees were all men of standing, ability and worth, many of whom had earned their reward, was no palliation. It seemed to his old Macedonians that Alexander was losing his national character and growing to despise the men who had helped him conquer the world. All these were real grievances, to be sure; but beyond this, the Macedonians had lapsed into a chronic feeling that injustice was done them, and anything would serve its purpose.

When spring had fairly opened, Alexander sent Hephæstion with the army along the road up the Tigris to Opis, and himself ordering the fleet up to Susa, sailed with the hypaspists and agema and a few cavalry Companions down the Passitigris or Eulæus to the coast, and there founding another Alexandria on the seashore near by, sailed up the Tigris to Opis. He wished to become familiar with his new dominions. The Persians had erected dams or weirs in the Tigris to prevent a foreign fleet from invading the country. These Alexander removed, having no such fear of invasion, in order to facilitate free navigation up to Opis. This was part of his general scheme.

It was at Opis in July that dissatisfaction broke out into the great mutiny of the Macedonian soldiers. Alexander had announced a new march into Media, and, in the honest belief that he was doing an act of gratification to his veterans, he had called them together and told them that he would now discharge and send home all those who were incapacitated from further military service by age or wounds, and that he would give each man so much as to make him the object of envy to all at home. Instead of being received, as he expected, with approbation, Alexander's announcement was taken as another sign that he wished to discard his old brothers-in-arms and have Asiatics about him rather than Macedonians.

Alexander's notice had been given at a camp council called outside the town, and no doubt held in the usual or Macedonian style. He was addressing the assembled soldiers from a platform upon which he could be seen by all. That there had long been open discontent Alexander well knew; but he hoped to allay it by just this course, and he felt that his action was generous and would be received as such. Instead of his words producing the desired effect, however, the ringleaders of the Macedonian party began a murmur of dissent which soon grew to a loud outcry of protest. Their feelings had finally broken bounds. Once their tongues were untied, their pent-up anger got the better of them, and after some other slurring remarks, the ringleaders impudently urged the king to make a clean sweep of all the Macedonians and to prosecute his wars alone. These seditious cries speedily drowned Alexander's voice and the wordy tumult of a few soon burst out into every sign of general mutiny. Astonished beyond measure at this unexpected and ungracious outbreak, and letting his naturally quick temper get the upper-hand, Alexander, unarmed as he was, leaped down from the rostrum on which he had been standing, and immediately followed by a few of his Companions who had stood beside him, he seized with his own hands upon some and ordered all the others who were apparent ringleaders to be arrested, himself singling them out, as he had been witness of the whole affair, and probably knew each man by name. Thirteen of these he ordered away to instant execution, and then again ascending the platform, he addressed the rest, who were cowed by terror at this new rôle which their king had, at their incentive, assumed: "You may every man of you go home," said he, "for aught I care. I am and always have been independent of such as you. But before you go, you shall hear what I think of you. Who were you when my father Philip found you? Hide-

clad vagabonds, feeding a few stray sheep which you had
pains to guard from the border barbarians. What are you
now? The kings of the earth. Who gave you cloaks instead
of hides to wear? Philip. Who taught you to wield your
arms so as to become the dread of your neigbors? Philip.
Who gave you laws and good customs, spread abundance over
your country, opened your mines, and raised you from slaves
to citizens? Philip. Who made you rulers over the Thessalians and Phocians? Who humbled the Athenians and ʌ
bans at your feet and led you triumphantly through the Peloponnesus? Philip. Who raised you to the first rank among
the Hellenes? Philip. And what he did for you is little
compared to what Alexander has done. Starting from home
so poor that he had to borrow eight hundred talents to feed
and clothe and arm you, what has Alexander given you?
The dominion and wealth of Asia, Ionia, Lydia, Babylon,
Susa. Even the confines of the Scythians and the Indians
are yours. Who has made you viceroys, generals, captains?
Alexander. Who has watched and worked so that you might
sleep in security on your conquests? Alexander. And what
has Alexander to show for all this, but this paltry purple robe
and this worthless diadem? Does Alexander fare more sump-
tuously than many of you? Who among you has worked so
hard as Alexander? Who can show more wounds? Let the
bravest among you stand forth, and bare his breast, and your
king will show you wound for wound, and yet wounds more
than he. No weapon that the enemy has borne or hurled but
has left its mark upon Alexander. Spear, sword, arrow, dart,
stone and bolt have left, each one, its witness on Alexander's
person. I have celebrated your weddings with my own.* I
have paid your debts. The best among you have also golden
crowns. The brave dead have been magnificently buried.
Their statues in eternal brass adorn the temples of the gods

at home. Their parents are held in honor, and are relieved from taxes. And now I have proposed to send each one of you home loaded with spoil which will make him the envy of his native town. Ingrates! I will no more of you. Go home and tell your neighbors that you have deserted your king, Alexander, who has overcome the earth to make you powerful, to give you repute and wealth. Tell them that him, Alexander, whom no nation has yet been able to resist, ye deserted to the services of conquered foreigners. This shall be your glory and your piety to the gods. Ye are no longer my soldiers! Get you gone!"

Upon this, Alexander left the rostrum, allowing none to follow him, retired to his palace in the city, and secluded himself for three days. His orders he gave only to his Asiatic soldiers, his personal companions and the body-guard, entirely overlooking the Macedonians. The old soldiers thus discharged were utterly humbled and cast down. They were without head or counsel. Though perhaps there was some just cause of complaint, yet the magnificence of the king's anger overwhelmed them, and buried them under their own wrong.

There was for all that an element of grave danger in the situation, unless the Macedonians should decide to throw themselves on the king's mercy. For in such a body of old heroes a leader would be sure to be found, and who can say what might occur? Indeed, the body without a leader contained perhaps elements of yet greater danger. The men still had their arms, and were twenty thousand strong. But Alexander determined, as he always did, to play out the game to the end. He was ready to rely on his Orientals, and made preparations accordingly On the third day he again called in all his Persian and Asiatic officers, and to them gave his orders, entirely ignoring the Macedonians, and making appointments as for a quite new army, organizing it in the Macedonian fashion, in phalanx and hipparchies, horse and foot agema and palace guards. He is then said to have sent word to the Macedonians to leave the camp, or if they pleased, to take up arms against him. He would show them, then, that he could do without them, but that they without him were powerless. When the Macedonians ascertained that to an entire new army which had been created of Medes and Persians all the orders were being given, that they themselves were totally ignored, as if indeed, they did not exist, they lost heart, and, running in a body to the palace, they cast their weapons down at the gates, and pleaded bitterly for pardon, exclaiming that they would not withdraw day nor night from the palace gate till Alexander had restored them to his favor.

Alexander was at length mollified. He came out to meet his veterans, forgave them, and admitted them all to their ancient honors. Then one of the Macedonians, an old and worthy "hipparch of the Companions," Kallines by name, advanced and spoke for the rest: "O king! we are grieved that thou hast admitted as kinsmen many Medes and Persians, and hast not admitted us." To which Alexander replied: "Ye are all my kinsmen," and as many as desired saluted him with a kiss, the privilege of kinsmen only, according to the Persian custom which Alexander had at this time adopted. The Macedonians then retired to their camp, shouting and exulting for very joy. This reconciliation was followed by sacrifices, and by a great feast at which the Macedonians sat next the king and the Persians below them. Of this feast nine thousand men are said to have partaken at the tables of the king. This victory over his army was probably a full compensation to Alexander for the refusal of the Macedonians to cross the Hyphasis. He had conquered the Macedonian spirit of obstinacy. He now made Orientals and Macedonians equal in the army, and no longer dreaded the mutinous spirit which at times for several years had come to the surface. But however much he honored the Persians, his old Macedonians always retained the deepest hold in his affections.

The invalided were then picked out to return to Macedonia, some ten thousand in number. Each man was paid up to such time as he would reach home, and was given a talent beside. Just how much a talent represented, it is now hard to say, but it no doubt enabled a veteran to buy himself a house or farm, and to live in ease, or comparative luxury, for the remainder of his days without toil or worry. The children of the Macedonians by Asiatic wives were left in Asia in the cause of family concord, and the king promised that all such should be brought up as Macedonians and soldiers. To the children of the dead the portions of their fathers were assured. In charge of the column moving homewards, he sent Craterus, his most trusted officer, whom he appointed to rule over Macedonia, Thrace and Thessaly. For Craterus was growing old, and was weakened by the hardest service. Polysperchon was sent second in command, and Clitus, Gorgias, Polydamas and Amadas accompanied them.

Craterus is said by Diodorus to have carried with him written instructions to build a fleet in Phœnicia and the adjacent countries, with which Alexander could later move against Carthage and other nations on the Mediterranean; and to begin a system of deportation of people from Europe into Asia and vice versa in pursuance of Alexander's general scheme. But the plan was too vast for any one but Alexander; and his successors made no attempt to carry it out.

Antipater was ordered to bring to Asia in person an equal number of young men of military age to replace the veterans

who returned home.   He was so instructed to come because
the queen-mother, Olympias, and he were always at odds, the
quarrels had of late waxed hotter, and Alexander had fears
lest some harm should come of it.   The king had always held
his mother in great love and reverence, despite his recognition
of her short-comings.   In regard to Antipater's letters com-
plaining of Olympias' mixing in public affairs, Alexander
once observed: " Antipater does not know that one mother's
tear wipes out a thousand letters such as this."

Alexander, from a Statue in Dresden.

XLVII.

BABYLON. AUGUST, B. C. 324, TO JUNE, B. C. 323.

ALEXANDER planned to visit and regulate each part of his enormous empire in turn. He had been down the Euphrates to the Gulf, and up the Tigris to Opis. He now marched to Ecbatana. Here Hephæstion died, and Alexander, whose grief was extreme for this friend of his soul, made his funeralia more magnificent than any before. Ptolemy and he then undertook a midwinter campaign against the Cossæans, mountain robbers who made insecure the road from Ecbatana to Susa, and in a forty days' campaign subdued them. Thence he went to Babylon, where he built a vast dockyard, began the construction of a fleet, and made large calculations for future public improvements. The new Macedo-Oriental army was organized and its discipline begun. Eastern nobles were put in command beside his old and trusted Macedonians, and often over them. But his work was cut summarily short. In the course of his labors on the fleet, Alexander caught a fever, of which, after the lapse of a few days, he died, leaving his kingdom "to the strongest," and giving his signet-ring to Perdiccas.

IT was part of Alexander's plan to visit all parts of his kingdom in turn. From Opis he went, about the end of August, to Ecbatana, along the straight Median road. No doubt there was much to do in this treasury city, especially since the flight of Harpalus. At Ecbatana Hephæstion died. Alexander mourned greatly for this, his one friend of friends; for as Patroclus to Achilles, so was Hephæstion to Alexander. He prepared a funeral pyre in his honor at Babylon which is said to have cost ten thousand talents (twelve millions of dollars). His funeralia were celebrated by the most magnificent gymnastic and musical contests he had ever given, at a further expense of two thousand talents. Alexander is said to have crucified Glaucus, Hephæstion's doctor, for allowing him to eat a roast fowl and wash it down with a goblet of new wine.

There had been a quarrel between Eumenes, the king's secretary, and Hephæstion; but Alexander had managed to reconcile the two. Eumenes had for seven years been Philip's secretary. For the thirteen years of Alexander's reign he filled the same position to the king. History is apt to show us its heroes surrounded by their military family and lieutenants. The civil officers one more rarely hears about. And

Alexander's Last Marches.

yet, in moving such an army as Alexander's, what efficient men they must have been! Cornelius Nepos abundantly testifies to Eumenes' ability, and he showed it after Alexander's death.

After the mourning for Hephæstion had been prolonged for many days, and the year was drawing to a close, Alexander brought himself to undertake an expedition against the Cossæans. This was rather a campaign necessary to secure the road from Susa to Ecbatana than a mere "man hunt" to rouse himself from his sorrow for Hephæstion's death. The Cossæans were a tribe of marauders northeast from Susa, who, like the Uxians, had not been subdued by Persia, but kept quiet by gifts. They never came to an open fight, but would disperse in small parties to their strongholds and hiding-places whenever attacked, and then again emerge and resume their marauding expeditions. Against these Alexander and Ptolemy, son of Lagus, marched in two columns in midwinter, for at this time these people could not take refuge in the mountain heights, but must stay in the valleys; and, despite the ruggedness of the ground and the difficulties of snows, by sending small detachments up each valley to attack the forces there, they subdued the barbarians in a forty days' campaign, destroyed their fastnesses, and dispersed them utterly. No details of the campaign have survived.

From here Alexander returned towards Babylon, which he had selected as his future capital on account of its central position between India, Egypt, and the Mediterranean. On his way he received embassies from Lydia and Carthage, and from the Bruttians, Lucanians, and Tyrrhenians (Etruscans) of Italy, to salute him as king of Asia. The Ethiopians, Scythians of Europe, the Gauls, and the Iberians, nations whose names were heard for the first time by Macedonians, also came to pay tribute to the great conqueror, and some invoked his wisdom in settling disputes. Aristus and Asclepiades have stated that Rome also sent an embassy to congratulate Alexander; no others mention it, and it seems scarcely probable that the freedom-loving Romans should pay court to a man they would have considered in the light of a despot. Livy doubts that contemporary Romans knew of Alexander even by report. Their horizon did not extend beyond Italy. In fact, Rome had not conquered Italy until two generations later than this.

Alexander had always been anxious to discover the topography of the Caspian Sea, and now sent a number of shipwrights, under Heraclides, into Hyrcania, to build vessels and launch them on the Caspian, ready for this use when he should be prepared to make an expedition thither.

After crossing the Tigris, Alexander was met by some Chaldæan philosophers who entreated him not to enter Babylon, as they foresaw evil to come to him if he did so; or, if he must, at least not to enter the city by the western gate. Alexander imagined some ulterior purpose in the request of the Chaldæans. He was proposing to rebuild the temple of Belus, whose revenues the Chaldæans were now appropriating, and he thought these soothsayers desired to prevent his doing what would be a manifest loss to themselves, though he could not fathom their immediate motive. He however so far heeded their counsel as to endeavor to enter the city from the east, but the shoals and marshes on this side of the city prevented his so doing. In addition to this one, there had been sundry other prophecies concerning the death of Alexander which do not particularly concern us.

In Babylon Alexander found the fleet under Nearchus which had sailed up the Euphrates to meet him, and another fleet from Phœnicia, consisting of two quinquiremes, three quadriremes, twelves triremes, and thirty triacontors, which had been taken by wagons, in parts, overland to Thapsacus, had there been joined, and thence floated down the Euphrates. The cypresses of Babylon were devoted to the building of more ships; and a harbor was excavated in Babylon large enough to contain one thousand vessels of war, and a dockyard built beside it. Recruits were got from Phœnicia and

Syria for this fleet. Alexander proposed to colonize the shores of the Persian Sea, and also to attack Arabia, because this country had sent no embassies to him, and because he coveted their territory and spices. Alexander, in fact, sent out three expeditions, designed to sail around Arabia; but neither of the three went as far as he had commanded them to go. The trip was yet an unknown one, except from hearsay.

Not having suffered any harm from returning to Babylon, Alexander made an expedition down the Euphrates to the Pallacopas, a canal near that river running towards the sea through marshes and lowland which afford an outlet to the annual floods. Here he founded a city and established in it a number of the invalided Greek mercenaries. Thence he again returned to Babylon.

Hither Peucestas came with a force of twenty thousand Persians, Cossæans and Tarpurians, the most valiant men he could collect. Philoxenus brought an army from Caria; Menander one from Lydia; Menidas returned with the cavalry. The foreign soldiers were divided up into files, each headed by a Macedonian decurion, next to whom came a double-pay man, and next a ten-stater man, then twelve foreigners, and then another ten-stater man, making the sixteen deep file. The Macedonians were armed as usual. The foreigners had bows or javelins so as to fire over the heads of their front-rank men. The king did not live to fully carry this Macedonian-Asiatic organization into effect. At first blush such a disposition of troops appears to lack solidity. Alexander also held many reviews and sham fights with his fleet, in the nature of games, intended to exercise the men and ships in the duties and tactics of war.

Here, too, Alexander received favorable answer to his message to the oracle at Ammon, asking whether Hephæstion might not be worshiped as a hero. This worship was in consequence introduced, and so punctiliously carried out that Alexander even went to the length of forgiving Cleomenes many deeds of tyranny and rapacity in Egypt on the score of his acts of reverence to the newly canonized hero.

From the exposure to which Alexander had been subjected in overseeing the construction of his fleet, harbor and dockyard, he unhappily caught a low fever ; but relying as he always did on his great bodily strength, he paid small heed to it, but continued to attend certain feasts which were then being held. The revelries developed a more marked feverish condition, but Alexander continued them for another day and night. He was then unable to leave the house of Medius, where he had last supped. Each morning he performed his usual sacrifice, being carried out to do this, and afterwards lying still all day. He continued his orders for the approaching expedition around Arabia into the Red Sea, — a gigantic and perilous one for those days, — and insisted on attending to all matters of business. This he persisted in doing each day, though the fever kept on the increase, and finally took a fatal form. Before his death, in June, 323 B. C., most of his old soldiers passed his couch to take a last farewell. Alexander could not speak, but he knew them, and beckoned to each one with his hand. His last words were said to be an answer to the question to whom he left his kingdom : "To the strongest !" or, as Curtius puts it, 'to the most worthy,' — his last act to give his signet-ring to Perdiccas. The rumor that he was poisoned probably had no foundation.

Alexander's embalmed body was carried by Ptolemy to Egypt, and placed in Memphis. A few years later it was removed to Alexandria.

XLVIII.

THE MAN AND SOLDIER.

ALEXANDER possessed uncommon qualities of body, head and heart. His bearing was that of a king, but he was kindly and considerate. He read much, and enjoyed the society of men of brains. He was abstinent of pleasures except drinking — the national vice. Intemperance with Alexander was occasional, not habitual. His bodily strength and activity were matched only by his extraordinary courage. He courted danger, but its excitement never clouded his intellect. He was naturally excitable and superstitious. The latter quality he kept well under control; the former sometimes ran into violence, and overcame his better nature. His two vices may be characterized as hasty temper and vanity. To these, joined with overdrinking, may be ascribed all Alexander's ill deeds. But as man and monarch, there are few with so much to their credit and less to their charge. He was not a Greek, but had a strong Hellenistic flavor. His life's idea was to conquer and then Hellenize Asia. He did the one; the other he could not do. As a soldier, Alexander was the first who conducted war in what Napoleon calls a methodical manner; as a captain and conqueror, he will always stand at the head of his peers. To him is due the credit of giving the world, on a large scale, the first lessons in the art of war. His campaigns form a text-book almost complete in its scope.

ALEXANDER was possessed of uncommon beauty. Plutarch says that Lysippus made the best portrait of him, "the inclination of the head a little on one side towards the left shoulder, and his melting eye, having been expressed by this artist with great exactness." His likeness was less fortunately caught by Apelles, who made him too dark. He was fair in complexion and ruddy, of sweet odor and agreeable in person. Above the average height, though not tall, his presence was commanding, his bearing kingly. Fond of study, he read much history, poetry and general literature. His favorite book was the Iliad, a copy of which, annotated by Aristotle, with a dagger, always lay under his pillow. In his youth he was given to music, and played well, but in later life neglected the accomplishment. He enjoyed martial music, but disliked sentimental airs. He had devoted some time to medicine, and did not lack skill as a physician. He was at all times surrounded by men of brains, and enjoyed their conversation. He understood and grasped all the science of the day. An admirer of the drama, he considered comedy lacking in the inculcation of the hardier virtues. He strictly observed his duties to the gods.

While he had no code of morals beyond the usages of that day, though indeed Plutarch credits him with more than natural chastity, Alexander was moderate, respected the rights of others, was unselfish in his dealings with women, and often showed a self-denial and continence which, in one so young and naturally of a very passionate nature, calls for the highest praise. He was abstinent of pleasures except drinking. Aristobulus says Alexander did not drink much in quantity, but enjoyed being merry. Still the Macedonian *much* was more than wisdom dictates. He was fain to talk over his wine and to sit long at table chatting with his friends, rather than overdrink. His principal meal was after dark. He ate little himself, but paid much heed to his guests. When Ada, queen of Caria, sent him, daily, curious dishes and desired to send him some skillful cooks and pastrymen, he told her that his preceptor, Leonidas, had given him the best: a night march (*quære*, early morning walk) to prepare for breakfast, and a moderate breakfast to prepare for supper. His table was always open to, in fact was intended for his military family and friends. It is said, in Asia, to have cost 10,000 drachmas ($2,000) a day — no very great outlay for the owner of the world. Many of his officers were more extravagant and more given to luxurious living than he. But Alexander was undeniably fond of flattery at his meals, as at all other times. Indeed, he may be said to have fed on flattery rather than on rich meats.

Alexander was active, and able to endure heat and cold, hunger and thirst, trial and fatigue beyond even the stoutest. His strength and courage were altogether exceptional. Quintus Curtius says that he saved his father's life in a mutiny among the Triballi, when a mere lad, by his sole personal gallantry. "He was invincible to those things which terrify others." "His bravery did not only excel that of other kings, but even that of those who have no other virtue." He was never known to change countenance at wounds. The Mallian arrow which had penetrated his lung, was cut out without a motion on Alexander's part.

He was exceeding swift of foot, but when young would not enter the Olympic games, because he had not kings' sons to compete with. An athlete himself, he disliked professional athletes, saying that they ought to place their strength at the service of the country. He was always glad to incur hardship and danger in hunting, and is related to have slain a huge lion single-handed when in Bactria. He kept his body in good training. On the march he was habituated to shoot from his horse or chariot for practice, and to mount and dismount when at full speed. He was given to playing ball with the royal pages. He frequently marched on foot with his troops rather than make use of horse or chariot. Naturally disposed to sleep but little, he increased his watchfulness by habit. In an iron body dwelt both an intellect clear beyond compare, and a heart full of generous impulses. He was ambitious, but from high motives. His desire to conquer the world was coupled with the purpose of furthering Greek civilization. His courage was, both physically and morally, high-pitched. He actually enjoyed the delirium of battle, and its turmoils raised his intellect to its loftiest grade of clearness and activity.   His instincts were keen; his perception remarkable; his judgment all but infallible.   As an organizer of an army he was unapproached; as a leader, unapproachable in rousing the ambition and courage of his men, and in quelling their fears by his own fearlessness.   "That the soul of this king was fashioned on a superhuman pattern," says Polybius, " all men agree."

Alexander kept his agreements faithfully, and had wonderful generosity coupled with grace in giving.   He was a remarkable judge of men.   He had the rare gift of natural, convincing oratory, and of making men hang upon his lips as he spoke, and do deeds of heroism after.   He lavished money rather on his friends than on himself.

Alexander's chief attachment was for Hephæstion, with whom he had been brought up, and to whom he clung with never-changing devotion.   To Hephæstion he confided his every secret.   His affection for his mother, Olympias, never waned.   Hephæstion alone knew what Olympias wrote to Alexander.   One day when the king and his intimate had together read one of the queen-mother's letters, Alexander drew his seal ring from his finger and pressed it on Hephæstion's lips.   Next to Hephæstion came Craterus.   The former was Alexander's friend, the latter the king's.   Alexander had more love for Hephæstion, more admiration for Craterus; Hephæstion wore the same Persian dress which was adopted by Alexander, and was often his mouth-piece to the Orientals; Craterus retained his Greek dress, and was the spokesman to the king for his Macedonians.

While every inch a king, Alexander was friendly with his men; shared their toils and dangers; never asked an effort he himself did not make; never ordered a hardship of which he himself did not bear part.   His eagerness to brave dan-

ger was so marked that he could never stand idle by and see
another doing deeds of valor. He invariably chose the hardest task himself. No doubt he was as conscious of his own
ability to do it better than any one else, as he was of his power
to endure. During the herculean pursuit of Darius, — after
a march of four hundred miles in eleven days, at the close of
which but sixty of his men had been able to keep beside him,
— it was he who always led the van, cheered on his men, inspired all with the ambition to keep on to the very end, and
who stood the heat and thirst, the fatigue and danger best of
all. It was he who headed the weary handful in a charge on
the Persian thousands. Such things endear a leader to his
men beyond the telling.

But Alexander's temper, by inheritance quick, grew un-
governable. A naturally excitable character, coupled with a
certain superstitious tendency, was the very one to suffer from
a life which carried him to such a giddy height, and from successes which reached beyond the human limit. We condemn,
but, looking at him as a captain, may pass over those dark
hours in his life which narrate the murder of Clitus, the execution of Philotas and Parmenio, and the cruelties to Bessus
and to Batis. Alexander was distinctly subject to human
frailties. His vices were partly inherited, partly the out-
growth of his youth and wonderful career. But he repented
quickly and sincerely of his evil deeds. When all is summed
up, there are few monarchs in the world's history at whose
door is cast less reproach ; few of whom more that is great
and good is written. Until the last few years of his life,
his habits were very simple. He was not by nature fond of
dress. " A prince ought to surpass his subjects rather in the
culture of virtues than in the finery of his clothes," said he.
But like Hannibal he was a great lover of fine arms and
weapons, and of good horses. His adoption of Persian dress

and manners was so largely a political requirement, that it can be hardly ascribed to personal motives, even if we fully acknowledge his overweening vanity. His public claim to superhuman lineage was not remarkable; for the descent of the Macedonian kings from Hercules was allowed by the judges at the Olympian games when Macedon was but a small kingdom.

We can get far closer to the kernel of Alexander's character by the study of those who lived nearer to his age, than by relying on the cold, statistical criticism of to-day. Altogether too much time has been devoted to belittling Alexander. The king of Macedon had innumerable enemies in Greece; Alexander had more; many outspoken ones, many backbiters. That every scintilla of ill which could be said of him was set down in malice by some one, and by hosts believed, is as natural as that his admirers should overpraise him. Arrian draws principally from the relations of Ptolemy, son of Lagus, the very best of witnesses, and of Aristobulus, also one of Alexander's officers; from the story of Nearchus and others who saw and were part of what they narrated, and from the diary of Eumenes, the secretary, and Alexander's own letters. In some respects what Alexander's laudators have said may be overdrawn, but Arrian has from them given us the only history which yields to the military man a crisp idea of how this great captain wrought; and those things which are susceptible of exaggeration are not of the essence. Losses may be diminished to place the courage of the Macedonians in higher relief; the numbers of the enemy slain may be increased. But as to what Alexander did, all agree; how he did it, Arrian best explains, and its bare recital suffices to make him in intellect, moral force, excellence of heart, and splendor of physique incomparably the first of men.

The life work of Philip had been transcendent. That of

Alexander surpasses anything in history. Words fail to describe the attributes of this monarch as a soldier. The perfection of all he did was by no means understood by his historians. But to compare his deeds with those of other captains excites our wonder. Starting with a handful of men from Macedonia, in four years one grand achievement after another and without a failure had placed at his feet the empire of the Great King. Leaving home with an enormous debt, in fifty moons he had possessed himself of all the treasures of the earth. Thence, with marvelous courage, endurance, intelligence and skill he completed the conquest of the entire then known world, marching twenty-two thousand miles in his eleven years' campaigns. And all this before he was thirty-two. There is no other instance in the world's history, it has been observed, of a small nation overrunning the earth, and impressing itself for all ages on the countries overrun. Persia had conquered the world, had threatened Greece, had in a measure asserted her authority over the islands of the Ægean, and fully over the Greek cities of the coast, and yet she went down before Alexander's sword. His health and strength were still as great as ever; his voracity for conquest greater, as well as his ability to conquer.

It is an interesting question, had he not died, what would have become of Rome. The Roman infantry was as good as his; not so their cavalry. An annually elected consul could be no match for Alexander. But the king never met in his campaigns such an opponent as the Roman Republic, nor his phalanx such a rival as the Roman legion would have been. That was reserved for Hannibal. It is altogether probable, had Alexander lived to carry his career of conquest westward, that Rome in her then condition would have succumbed to his arms, and the history of the world have been modified. For Alexander was master of the art of war; the Romans knew nothing of it until Hannibal, by dire defeat, had taught them that hard blows alone cannot stand against hard blows well delivered.

Greek civilization, to a certain degree, followed Alexander's footsteps, but it was not solely due to him. "You are a man like all of us, Alexander," said the naked Indian, "except that you abandon your home, like a meddlesome destroyer, to invade the most distant regions, enduring hardship yourself, and inflicting it on others." Alexander could never have erected a permanent kingdom on his theory of coalescing races by intermarriages and forced migrations. His Græco-Persian empire was a mere dream. Alexander was never a Greek. He had but the Greek genius and intelligence grafted on the ruder Macedonian nature; and he became, to a marked extent, Asiaticized by his conquests. His life work, as cut out by himself, was to conquer, and then to Hellenize Asia. He did the one, he could not accomplish the other aim. He did not plant a true and permanent Hellenism in a single country of Asia. Still, what he and his successors did left a decided Hellenistic flavor throughout Persia. Few of Alexander's cities have lived. They were rather fortified posts than self-sustaining marts. As a statesman, intellectual, far-seeing and broad, he yet conceived and worked on an impossible theory, and the immediate result of all his genius did not last a generation. What he might have accomplished had he lived a longer life remains a mere subject of speculation.

What has Alexander done for the art of war? When Demosthenes was asked what were the three most important qualities in an orator, he replied, "Action, action, action!" In another sense this might well be applied to the captain. No one can become a great captain without a mental and physical activity which are almost abnormal; and so soon as this exceptional power of activity wanes, the captain has come to a term of his greatness. Genius has been described as an extraordinary capacity for hard work. But this capacity is but the human element. Genius implies the divine spark. It is the personality of the great captain which makes him what he is. The maxims of war are but a meaningless page to him who cannot apply them. They are helpful just so far as the man's brain and heart, as his individuality, can carry them. It is because a great captain must first of all be a great man, and because to the lot of but few great men belongs the peculiar ability, or falls the opportunity of being great captains, that preëminent success in war is so rarely seen.

All great soldiers are cousins-german in equipment of heart and head. No man ever was, no man can by any possibility blunder into being, a great soldier without the most generous virtues of the soul, and the most distinguished powers of the intellect. The former are independence, self-reliance, ambition within proper bounds; that sort of physical bravery which not only does not know fear, but which is not even conscious that there is such a thing as courage; that greater moral quality which can hold the lives of tens of thousands of men and the destinies of a great country or cause patiently, intelligently and unflinchingly in his grasp; powers of endurance which cannot be overtaxed; the unconscious habit of ruling men and of commanding their love and admiration, coupled with the ability to stir their enthusiasm to the yielding of their last ounce of effort. The latter comprise business capacity of the very highest order, essential to the care of his troops; keen perceptions, which even in extraordinary circumstances or sudden emergencies are not to be led astray; the ability to think as quickly and accurately in the turmoil of battle as in the quiet of the bureau; the power to foresee to its ultimate conclusion the result of a strategic or tactical manœuvre; the capacity to gauge the efforts of men and of masses of men; the many-sidedness which can respond to the demands of every detail of the battlefield, while never losing sight of the one object aimed at; the mental strength which weakens not under the tax of hours and days of unequaled strain. For in truth there is no position in which man can be placed which asks so much of his intellect in so short a space as that of the general, the failure or success, the decimation or security of whose army hangs on his instant thought and unequivocal instruction under the furious and kaleidoscopic ordeal of the field. To these qualities of heart and head add one factor more — opportunity — and you have the great soldier.

Now, Alexander was the first man, the details of whose history have been handed down to us, who possessed these qualities in the very highest measure; whose opportunities were coextensive with his powers; and who out of all these wrought a methodical system of warfare from which we may learn lessons to-day. Look at what he accomplished with such meagre means! He alone has the record of uniform success with no failure. And this was not because he had weak opponents; for while the Persians were redoubtable chiefly from their numbers, the Tyrians, the tribes beyond the Caucasus, and the Indians made a bold front and good fight.

Alexander's movements were always made on a well-conceived, maturely-digested plan; and this he kept in view to the end, putting aside all minor considerations for the main object, but never losing sight of these. His grasp was as large as his problem. His base for his advance into the then known world was the entire coast-line of the then known sea. He had not Napoleon's advantage of a complete knowledge of the theatre of operations and its resources. He was compelled to study his every step forward. But he never advanced, despite his speed, without securing flanks and rear, and properly garrisoning the country on which he based. Having done this, he marched on his objective — which was wont to be the enemy's army — with a directness which was unerring. His fertility in ruse and stratagem was unbounded. He kept well concentrated; his division of forces was always warranted by the conditions, and always with a view of again concentrating. His rapidity was unparalleled. It was this which gave him such an ascendant over all his enemies. Neither winter cold nor summer heat, mountain nor desert, the widest rivers nor the most elaborate defenses, ever arrested his course ; and yet his troops were always well fed. He was a master of logistics. He lived on the country he campaigned in, as entirely as Napoleon, but was careful to accumulate granaries in the most available places. He was remarkable in being able to keep the gaps in his army filled by recruits from home or enlistments of natives, and in transforming the latter into excellent soldiers. Starting from home with thirty-five thousand men, he had in the Indian campaigns no less than one hundred and thirty-five thousand, and their deeds proved the stuff that was in them.

It is true that we do not see every trivial detail of the school text-books illustrated in the campaigns of Alexander. And yet, had history vouchsafed us a fuller insight into the minutiæ of his work, it is scarcely to be doubted that we should have found as much skill in the minor as is shown in the larger operations. The results clearly prove it. But such details are not what make the captain. Few martinets have won any rank as soldiers. Details are essential ; no extended operations can be successful without scrupulous attention to the last detail. What, however, places a great captain far above the rank and file of generals is something greater than this. It is the broad conception of how to do the work in hand, and its execution with intelligence and boldness. In this there is scarcely a principle illustrated by Napoleon, in which Alexander is not his prototype.

We are apt to think that the art of war is constantly improving. This is at least open to doubt. There has been an extraordinary advance in the last generation in the appliances of destruction, in the devices for making war horrible. But can it be claimed that the art of war, in its leading principles, has advanced *pari passu* with the mechanics of war? To such a state of uncertainty have modern inventions reduced even the wisest of soldiers that no one can predict on what lines the next great war will be conducted. To be said to improve, an art must become more positive, more certain. To-day we are in doubt as to many almost elementary factors in our problem. We do not know whether the best formation for infantry will be an open or a close order; whether the new powder may not call for still other tactical formations; whether cavalry has succumbed to arms of precision, or will be of more service in the future than in the past; whether higher explosives than gunpowder will be availed of; whether the spade is to play a greater or lesser rôle than it has of late; and a host of other important questions are being forced on the military man by the rapid sequence of inventions. At sea matters are still more doubtful. Expensive ironclads prove unseaworthy; big guns are damaged by a few trial shots; torpedo warfare is on trial. What will the next naval war develop? There was more certainty in arms in Alexander's era than there is to-day. For the demands to be made upon it, Alexander's methods were as perfect as Napoleon's, though no doubt inadequate to our present wants. It might be said that the art of war is in a less exact and satisfactory condition to-day than ever before. Even some of the plainest requirements of strategy as taught by Bonaparte have been qualified by modern conditions and by the size of modern armies.

Alexander's battles are tactically brilliant examples of conception and execution. The wedge at Arbela was more splendid than Macdonald's column at Wagram. It was a scintillation of genius. No parallel exists to the battle of the Hydaspes. Wonderful as Alexander's intellect was, his power of execution exceeded his power of conception. It was his ability to seize openings with a rapidity perhaps never equaled which won him his battles, rather than his mere battle plan. However excellent this, he bettered it in the execution. His will sometimes overrode his sagacity, but always in such a way as to breed success. His stubbornness bore down the opposition which his limited numbers could not overcome.

In the use of cavalry Alexander stands without a peer. No one ever hurled his cavalry on the enemy with such precision, momentum or effect. Its charge was always well-timed; it always won. No one ever headed horse with such godlike boldness, or fought it to the bottom as he did. Had Alexander not been one of the world's great captains, he would have been the typical *beau sabreur* of the world's history.

Alexander always saw where his enemy's strength and weakness lay, and took prompt advantage of them. He utilized his victories to the full extent, and pursued with a vigor which no other has ever reached. He was equally great in sieges and in battles. The only thing he was never called on to show was the capacity to face disaster. He possessed every remarkable military attribute; we can discover in him no military weakness. Napoleon once, in a fit of exaggeration, is said to have characterized Alexander, *the man,* as

beginning with the soul of a Trajan to end with the heart of
a Nero and the habits of Heliogabalus.   The characterization
is not only warped, but Napoleon could not cast the first stone
at Alexander's personal bearing.   Of *the conqueror*, the great
Corsican says : " The campaigns of the son of Philip are not
like those of Jenghis Khan or Tamerlane, a simple irruption,
a sort of deluge ; all was calculated with depth, executed
with audacity, conducted with wisdom."

As a captain, Alexander accomplished more than any man
ever did.   He had no equal predecessor who left him a model
for action.   He showed the world, first of all men, and best,
how to make war.   He formulated the first principles of the
art, to be elaborated by Hannibal, Cæsar, Gustavus Adolphus,
Turenne, Prince Eugene, Marlborough, Frederick and Napoleon.   It is certain that Hannibal drew his inspiration from
the deeds of the great Macedonian ; equally certain that Napoleon, robbed of his knowledge of Alexander and Hannibal
and Cæsar, would never have been Napoleon.   Alexander's
conditions did not demand that he should approach to the
requirements of modern war.   But he was easily master of
his trade, as, perhaps, scarce any other soldier ever was.   For,
as Napoleon himself aptly says, " to guess at the intentions
of the enemy ; to divine his opinion of yourself ; to hide from
him both your own intentions and opinion ; to mislead him
by feigned manœuvres ; to invoke ruse, as well as digested
schemes, so as to fight under the best conditions, — this is,
and always was, the art of war."

XLIX.

THE SUCCESSORS OF ALEXANDER. EUMENES AND ANTIGONUS. PHILOPŒMEN.

ALEXANDER'S lieutenants divided up his kingdom, ostensibly for his heirs. But ambition and mutual jealousies soon broke up the empire, and brought on wars. Discipline declined. Corps and armies sold themselves for gold, or betrayed their generals. Courage ebbed with discipline, and Oriental devices were adopted to eke out valor. Still, the old officers trained by Alexander showed that they were good soldiers, and their campaigns and battles bear the stamp of their great master. Fortification especially grew apace, and received its highest exemplification at the siege of Rhodes. The stratagems employed by Eumenes in manœuvring against Antigonus, and the third battle of Mantinæa, won by Philopœmen over the Spartans, are good samples of the work of the successors of Alexander. But Greece had degenerated, and with her Macedon; and finally the proud nation of Philip and Alexander, forgetful of the virtues which had made her great, sank under the sway of sturdy Rome.

ALEXANDER's lieutenants divided up his kingdom, ostensibly in trust for his heirs. But ambition and jealousies led to wars, and the great empire fell to pieces. Macedon, Egypt and Syria remained the prominent divisions, and a relic of Hellenism in the East still testified to the king's broad method. Discipline in the armies declined fast; mercenary troops multiplied, and missile-throwers, chariots and elephants crept into the line of battle. The armies became Asiaticized. Despite this, however, the wars of Alexander's immediate successors show a clear following of the great master's methods. In some minor respects, these were even improved. After the battle of Ipsus the military art declined fast. Only brilliant exceptions, of which the manœuvres of Antigonus and Eumenes and the third battle of Mantinæa are fine samples, remained to testify to its having ever existed.

Greece and Macedon were no longer what they had been. Their preëminence had departed with their patriotism.

The campaigns of Alexander in Asia had not tended to keep up the admirable spirit of discipline which Philip had created in the Macedonian army. Its contact with the riches, luxury and low moral tone of the East had sapped its hardy virtues to the core. It had needed Alexander's own wonderful power as a soldier and a king to keep this evil from destroying the army, root and branch, even during his life. Only he was capable of getting from it the work it did. That Alexander's army was no longer what it had been in earlier and simpler days was manifested by the several conspiracies which occurred in Drangiana and Bactria, the refusal of the soldiers to cross the Hyphasis, and the mutiny at Opis. On Alexander's death, there was no one capable of checking the further and rapid spread of this demoralizing evil. His generals,—the Diadochi, or successors,—Perdiccas, Antipater, Craterus, Ptolemy, Antigonus, Eumenes, Cassander, Leonnatus, Lysimachus, Seleucus, divided up the empire, ostensibly as regents and lieutenants for Alexander's half-brother Philip Arrhadæus, whom the army had chosen king, and as some say also for Alexander, his posthumous son by Roxana. But ambition for absolute control and jealousies among the Diadochi soon led to wars which were continuous and bloody, which extinguished by murder the entire family of Alexander, and which were not ended until the close of the century, at the battle of Ipsus.

But out of all this turmoil there arose several monarchies, the Eastern ones of which represented the influence of Alexander's life in their marked Hellenistic character. These monarchies were: Egypt, under Ptolemy, son of Lagus, and his descendants; Syria, under Seleucus and his descendants; Pergamon under the Attalidæ; Macedonia, under the descendants of Demetrius Poliorcetes, son of Antigonus; Bithynia, Pontus, Gallacia, Bactria, Rhodes, and the Greek cantons. In these countries Greek remained as the language of the polite world and of the government. Monuments were inscribed, and records kept in Greek; coins bore Greek legends, and the educated classes made use of the language and the manners of Hellas. In some of them Grecian art, literature and learning reached a high development; but coupled with intellectual good were mixed the elements of moral decay, and from their formation to their fall these countries bore the impress of the unreal and transitory.

The successors of Alexander soon began to indulge in extensive wars among themselves. These required enormous forces, and they were unscrupulous as to their means of gathering them. Money was poured out like water to raise armies; bribery was resorted to as a means of seducing the troops of the enemy from their allegiance; and as a result the soldiers discovered that they had a money value, and acted accordingly. Discipline became a thing of the past, and into its place stepped every vice which loosening organization is apt to engender. It was this falling-off in discipline which eventually made Greece and Macedon a prey to the Roman arms.

What had been the chief strength of Alexander's army, the Companions and the select bodies of troops chosen from the best men of the nation, gradually became a danger instead of a protection to the state. Whoever could gain over these prototypes of the Prætorian guards — and as a rule, money was the open sesame — could control the government. The demand for soldiers made the profession of arms the only one worth pursuing for a livelihood; and all Greece became a vast recruiting ground. Gold could not only buy armies of any size, but could seduce men from their alle-

giance. Less heed was paid to the constitution of armies;
these were composed of the most heterogeneous elements,
contained men of all nationalities; and missile-throwers, chariots and elephants found their uses in bolstering up declining
discipline, tactical resources which Alexander had heartily
despised and never used in action.

The extension of the system of mercenary troops in Greece,
of which the early chapters of this work have treated, was
followed by its necessary consequence. The strength of
the Greeks, of which patriotism was the essence, had disappeared, and the land had sunk to a despicable level of political or military ability. A few exceptions, such as those of
Pyrrhus, king of Epirus, the Achæan and Ætolian Leagues,
and Sparta under Cleomenes, a hundred years after Alexander, only serve to throw into relief the deplorable condition
of the land.

Alexander's magnificent plans in the East had been ship-
wrecked. A salvage of Hellenism remained to testify to the
great conqueror's splendid projects. But soon the old national
tendencies, too strong to be suppressed by an outer coating of
foreign manners, began to struggle to the surface in every
country he had subdued beyond the Euphrates. The descendants of Alexander's generals were with few exceptions
unworthy of their sires or their sires' training; they gradually sank to the level of Oriental despots. The populations
remained the same. The armies grew weak as the monarchs
weakened; and the dependence on foreign accessories sapped
the vigor and self-reliance of the infantry. The average soldier degenerated into a swash-buckler, a bully in peace, a
coward in war.

So far as the territorial limits of Alexander's empire are
concerned, these were within three generations narrowed to a
small part of their original extent. The Parthians under the

Arsacidæ conquered all the lands between the Indus and Euphrates, thus making a barrier to the further encroachments of civilization. India and the southern satrapies fell away from their allegiance not long after Alexander's death. There only remained the provinces immediately adjoining the eastern Mediterranean.

But despite the gradual and certain weakening of the inner strength of the armies, the art of war itself as taught by Alexander did not at once disappear. It lasted as long as his immediate successors lived. These lieutenants of his had received too good an education in practical war to forget their trade off-hand. During the rest of the century, or until these men themselves had disappeared from the scene, we can trace a strict following out of the principles laid down by their great master. The phalanxes grew larger. The diphalangiarchias of eight thousand hoplites and tetraphalangiarchias of sixteen thousand hoplites, or with cavalry and light troops some fifteen thousand and thirty thousand strong, were not uncommon. The marshaling of the line of battle, the marches, tactical formations and evolutions remained substantially the same; and Alexander's favorite attack in oblique order, as best shown at the Hydaspes, was not infrequently employed. Generals understood how to accommodate the phalanx to the various accidents of the ground, and to make use of its strength and supplement its weakness according to the existing conditions. The various battles down to Ipsus by no means show lack of ability. In outpost and scouting duty, and the use of light cavalry and light foot, an advance may even be said to have been made. The strongest symptom of decadence — as above said — was the beginning of reliance on missile-throwing machines, not for their proper uses at rivers and defiles, as Alexander had taught, but in battle; and the employment of such useless devices as elephants and chariots.

In strategic manœuvres, these generals followed the precepts they had learned. They protected their flanks and rear; they marched directly upon their objective; they sought in battle a solution of their campaigns. Down to Ipsus, the Greeks and Macedonians generally fought bravely, if headed by a general who commanded their confidence. But the marches of the armies were accompanied by devastation and cruelties worthy only of the Orient. On the whole, these lieutenants and successors of Alexander proved themselves as apt scholars of the great master as they were faithless to the kingdom he had created for his posterity.

Of all the branches of the art, fortification and sieges grew most. In mechanics, the construction of siege devices, and ship-building, there were marked advances. Demetrius Poliorcetes, aided by the Greek Epimachus, made the siege of Rhodes one of the distinct events of that age. The constructions and machines at this siege were in size beyond anything so far known. Most celebrated is the remarkable tower built for Demetrius by Epimachus, which he named Helepolis. Each side was of fifty cubits (seventy-five feet); the height was one hundred cubits. The three sides towards the enemy were iron-plated. It rested on huge wheels, and had nine stories, connected by ladders. The windows were protected by movable blinds, through which the engines could fire. The roof story was plated, and here archers and missile-throwers were stationed. It took thirty-four hundred men to move the huge structure, which was done from within and the rear. The wonder of Demetrius' work in attack is only equaled by the skill of the defense. This was so fertile in expedients, so able and bold and persistent, that Demetrius finally deemed it wise to make terms.

After the battle of Ipsus (301 B. C.) tactics became Asiaticised, and the lessons of Alexander were gradually forgotten.

From now on, with a few brilliant exceptions, the decadence of the art of war in Greece was quick and certain. Not until Hannibal, whose Greek education gave him access to the record of Alexander's deeds, and whose splendid intellect enabled him to digest them, could rescue the art from oblivion and teach the Romans how to make war, was anything like the method or skill of Alexander to be seen. From the end of the fourth century B. C., the art of war disappears in Greece, to reappear in Italy under the great Carthaginian.

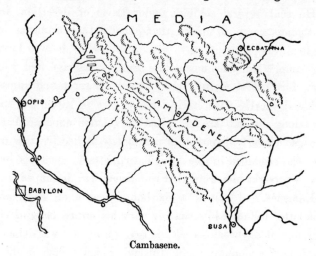

Cambasene.

An example of the campaigning of Alexander's successors is afforded by some of the manœuvres of Antigonus and Eumenes in Asia. Towards the close of 318 B. C., when the season was at hand for both to seek winter-quarters, their armies lay encamped not far apart, and separated only by a mountain torrent and some ravines. The exact locality is not known. The entire region had been so devastated that the troops were suffering for both food and forage. Eumenes had ascertained by spies whom he kept actively at work that Antigonus was proposing to break up the succeeding night for the province of Cambasene (or Corbiane), lying midway between Susa and Ecbatana, which the war had not yet drained of its riches, and whose well-watered upland character fitted it peculiarly for scattering troops in winter-quarters ; for its watercourses, mountain ridges and defiles made the defense of a large section easy. Eumenes had intended later to move to Cambasene himself, and in order to head Antigonus off from his purpose, he made use of the following stratagem.

He sent several soldiers, under guise of desertion, into Antigonus' camp, to inform that general that Eumenes had made all his preparations to attack him while he was breaking camp. Eumenes meanwhile sent his baggage and pack-train forward at nightfall by a hidden circuit, and himself followed shortly after, having taken care to ration his men for a long march. He left a line of videttes opposite Antigonus, so cleverly disposed as completely to deceive this officer, who remained in line anticipating attack, until his light troops brought him word that the enemy had decamped.

Eumenes had gained a six hours' march on Antigonus. The latter followed him sharply with his entire body of cavalry, and at daybreak struck his rear-guard as it was debouching from the mountain defile through which it had made its way that night. Antigonus was unable to attack seriously, but deployed his cavalry force along the foothills, and handled it with such effectiveness and skill that Eumenes was convinced that he had the enemy's whole army to contend with, and was constrained to stop and form line. So well did Antigonus mask his weakness that his infantry gained time to come up, and both armies faced each other in full force. Each wished to fight for the possession of the road to Cambasene. An all day's battle was engaged with alternating success. The left wing of each was beaten. Night put an end to the fray; Antigonus held the battlefield, but had lost more heavily than Eumenes. This latter fact so disheartened his soldiery that he did not dare renew the struggle. He withdrew into Media for the winter. Eumenes had gained Cambasene, and there took up his winter-quarters.

He had given orders to his troops not to spread over too large a territory. But the men, heedless of orders, and far from being well under control, dispersed into hamlets so far apart as to rob the army of all power of speedy concentration in case of attack. Of this fact Antigonus became aware through the reports of his spies. He determined to fall unexpectedly on the enemy, and beat him in detail. From his own winter-quarters there led two roads to Cambasene, one long, through a thickly-settled district and well fitted to sustain an army on the march; the other by a shorter cut, through a sparsely-peopled and poor mountain country, devoid of water, and difficult to traverse. Antigonus chose the latter route because he would be less apt to be discovered, and because it debouched from the mountains directly upon the centre of Eumenes' scattered cantonments. He distributed ten days' rations to his men and forage to the cavalry, collected many water-skins to carry a water supply, and spread a report that he was about to march to Armenia. This was a very probable thing indeed, for Antigonus' army had been weakened, while that of Eumenes had grown in strength, and he had every reason to avoid his enemy, while Armenia offered him a good chance to recruit.

To further sustain the rumor spread, Antigonus set out on the road to Armenia; but he soon filed to the left and into the road leading through the mountains towards Eumenes' winter-quarters. The weather was cold. Antigonus marched at night, and allowed camp-fires to be lighted only during the day. Thus he made five marches towards Eumenes. But the

severity of the weather was such that he could no longer prevent the men from kindling fires at some part of the long
winter night. Eumenes was not careless. He had been on
the watch. Fully aware of the danger he ran from the dispersion of his troops, he sent out a large number of patrols
and spies, who soon brought him in word that numerous
camp-fires had been seen in the mountain region to the north.
This gave him ample warning of Antigonus' approach.

Eumenes' lieutenants advised him to speedily withdraw to
another part of Cambasene. But Eumenes assured them
that he could stop Antigonus' advance long enough to allow
the troops to concentrate — three or four days in any event.
He hurriedly gathered the nearest bodies of troops, and stationed them along the mountain across the path on which
Antigonus was approaching, and ordered other bodies up on
the right and left to occupy the most salient parts of the
foothills at considerable intervals, as if they had come from
different directions. To all these bodies he gave orders to
light numerous fires close together, as would be usual in a
camp, and keep these fires very bright in the first watch
(6–9 P. M.) — this being the time when the soldiers were
wont to rub their bodies with oil before the fires, as well as
cook their meals — then less so in the second watch (9–12
P. M.), and to let them gradually go out after midnight. He
thus counterfeited the presence of large bodies of troops.

Antigonus was duly informed of the existence of these
camp-fires, and was persuaded that Eumenes had concentrated.
Unwilling to encounter Eumenes' better army, unless by a
surprise, he gave up his attempt, and headed in the direction
by which he could reach a territory which would afford him
rest and shelter and food before seeking battle with the enemy. Eumenes gained abundant time to concentrate, and
went into an intrenched camp in a favorable location. Twice,

by clever stratagems, he had thus deceived Antigonus, and gained his end.

One of the last acts in the drama of Greece was among its most brilliant, — the victory by Philopœmen at Mantinæa, third battle of the name, B. C. 206. This great man, "the last of the Greeks," was strategos of the Achæan League. He was a fine type of the intelligent, diligent soldier. Livy says of him : " Philopœmen was possessed of an admirable degree of skill and experience in conducting a march and choosing his station; having made these points his principal study, not only in times of war, but likewise during peace. Whenever he was making a journey to any place, and came to a defile where the passage was difficult, it was his practice, first, to examine the nature of the ground on every side. When journeying alone, he meditated within himself; if he had company, he asked them, ' If an enemy should appear in that place, what course ought he to adopt, if they should attack him in front; what, if on this flank, or on that; what, if on the rear ; for he might happen to meet them while his men were formed with a regular front, or when they were in the loose order of march, fit only for the road.' He would proceed to examine, either in his own mind or by asking questions, ' What ground he himself would choose; what number of soldiers, or what kind of arms (which was a very material point) he ought to employ ; where he should deposit the baggage, where the soldiers' necessaries, where the un-armed multitude; with what number and what kind of troops he should guard them ; and whether it would be better to prosecute his march as intended, or to return back by the way he came ; what spot, also, he should choose for his camp; how large a space he should inclose within the lines ; where he could be conveniently supplied with water ; where a suffi-ciency of forage and wood could be had ; which would be his

safest road on decamping next day; and in what form the
army should march?' In such studies and inquiries he had,
from his early years, so frequently exercised his thoughts,
that, on anything of the kind occurring, no expedient that
could be devised was new to him."

Philopœmen had spent seven years in improving the condition of the army, and had raised it far above the low ebb of
the Greek discipline of the day. When Machanidas, tyrant

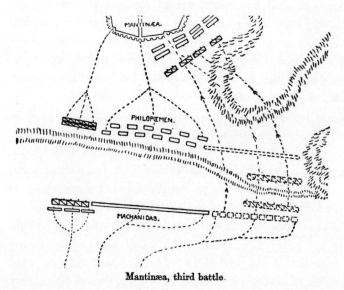

Mantinæa, third battle.

of Sparta, had declared war against the League, Philopœmen
moved to Mantinæa, and there took up a position. Machanidas concentrated at Tegea, south of Mantinæa, from which
place Epaminondas had broken up in 362 B. C. to march to
the second and most celebrated battle of this name.

When ready, Machanidas headed in three columns towards
Mantinæa. He had a large number of missile-throwing
engines following the army. Philopœmen moved out to meet
him, proposing to fight on his own chosen ground, which he

had carefully reconnoitred. The plain south of Mantinæa is inclosed by hills on east and west. Philopœmen drew up in rear of a ravine which crossed the plain from hill to hill, and which, wet in winter, dry in summer, and flush with the surface, was not visible from a distance. This ravine he proposed to use as a sort of field-work. It was much like the railroad-cutting at Manassas. His light infantry was on the left, and leaned on the hills, in its front the cavalry, mounted peltasts, allies and mercenaries. His phalanx was in the centre, placed checkerwise by mores, a new formation originated by Philopœmen. The cataphracti were on the right, and intended to be held as a reserve. Philopœmen made a stirring address to his men. " This day will decide," said he, " whether you will be freemen or slaves! "

Soon appeared Machanidas' three columns, the centre one apparently obliquing towards Philopœmen's right. The latter guessed that Machanidas was proposing to attack in oblique order, left reinforced, kept a close outlook, but altered nothing in his formation; but Machanidas obliqued to the right, and took up, at a distance, a parallel order of battle. Philopœmen then looked for a front attack by the Spartan phalanx; but instead of this the intervals of the phalanx opened, and the ballistas and catapults passed through, and ranged themselves before the line. Here is an instance of what had grown to be usual — the opening of a battle by the fire of artillery. Philopœmen met this threat by throwing out a skirmish line of light horse and foot in front of his phalanx in order to pick off with their arrows and sling-stones the men who served the engines. By active work the machines were silenced.

Machanidas, seeing that the light horse was all on Philopœmen's left, while the heavy horse was held in reserve upon the right, ordered his light troops from the rear of his cav-

alry on the right to march by the rear of the line over to the
left where they might sustain his own horse. Perceiving
this manœuvre, by which the enemy's right was weakened,
Philopœmen ordered his mounted peltasts, backed by the
allies and mercenaries, to move across the ravine at a place
where he had prepared the slopes, and attack Machanidas'
mercenary cavalry there stationed. The rest of both lines
remained *in situ*. But the attack was not lucky. Machanidas' horse beat the lighter cavalry of Philopœmen, which
retired in disorder, carrying the allies with it. Machanidas,
personally in command of his horse on this wing, followed
hard upon. Philopœmen's force fled towards Mantinæa, Machanidas upon its heels.

Philopœmen's line was at first disheartened by this defeat;
but he himself saw that Machanidas had made a huge mistake in personally leaving the field. His own confidence re-
inspired his troops. He ordered his first phalangial line to
move by the flank to the left, and occupy the ground from
which the mounted peltasts, allies and mercenaries had been
driven, and advanced his second line into their place. This
manœuvre was executed with precision. Philopœmen had
cut off Machanidas from return as well as outflanked the
Spartan right. Such of the mounted peltasts, allies and
mercenaries as had not been scattered, and could be got together, he formed in one body, and placed in reserve in rear
of his left, upon the hill slope.

Philopœmen was now about to advance on the enemy, when
he saw the Spartan phalanx moving forward to cross the
ravine. He decided to await their onset. Just as they
reached the bottom of the ravine, and were scrambling up
the rugged slope, he countercharged upon them, thrust them
back, and from the height of the bank threw them into such
confusion as utterly to demoralize them. He then followed

them across the ravine with part of his force, leaving a
strong body at the prepared crossing to meet Machanidas on
his return. The latter, seeking to rejoin his own army, and
surprised that his success had not won better effects, had
ployed his cavalry into a dense column, and prepared to cut
his way through; but at the last moment, perceiving their iso-
lation, his mercenaries forsook him, and dispersed in all directions, each man seeking his own safety. Machanidas, left
alone, endeavored to escape down the ravine, but was killed
by Philopœmen. This general had won a complete victory by
cool-headed tactics, and manœuvres conceived and executed
in the heat of action.

This battle is both a fair sample of the methods of that
era and a fine exemplification of how an able commander
may make use of the accidents of the ground to gain success,
as well as by clear-headed method and personal bearing arrest
the demoralization apt to follow upon an initial failure.

But, despite that she still produced able men, Greece was
no longer herself. She had degenerated from the proud
height she occupied at the time of the Persian wars. Her
preëminence had departed with her spirit of patriotism, her
eye single to the public good, and her simple virtues, never
to return. The same hardy love of country which had given
her greatness birth, was now to be sought in the city on the
Tiber, whose legions were destined to march over the length
and breadth of the earth, as had the phalanx of Alexander.

With Greece fell Macedon. It was but a hundred and forty
years from the time Philip, backed by an army of forty thousand men, had made himself Hegemōn of Hellas, that another
Philip, defeated at Cynocephalæ, was degraded to the payment of a thousand talents of tribute, to an army and navy
of five thousand men and five ships, and forbidden to make war
outside the narrow original boundaries prescribed as his king-

dom. To this condition had the proud nation sunk, whose soldiers, trained by the greater Philip, and led by Alexander in campaigns such as the world has not since seen and never can see again, had increased the skirts of Macedon to cover a territory beyond what Greece had deemed the limits of the earth. A generation later Macedon was broken up.

Alexander.
(From Statue in the Chiaram Collection.)

APPENDIX A.

SOME ANCIENT MARCHES.

By whom Made.	Where Made.	Date. B. C.	Kind of Troops.	Distance. Miles.	Number of Days' March.	Distance per day. Miles.	Remarks.
Spartans.	Sparta to Marathon.	490	Infantry.	150	3 days.	50	
Ten Thousand Greeks.	Myriandrus to Thapsacus.	401	"	230	12 days.	19	
"	Retreat.	400	"	4,000	215 days.	18½	
Macedonians.	Drill Marches.	c. 350		—	—	30	Mountain road.
"	Pelium to Thebes.	335	All arms.	300	14 days.	21½	
"	Pella to Sestos.	334	"	350	20 days.	17½	
"	Phoenicia to Thapsacus.	331	Cavalry.	200+	11 days.	19+	
"	Pursuit at Arbela.	"	"	70	1 night and day.	70	
"	Uxians to Persian Gates.	"	All arms.	113	5 days.	22½	Bad mountain road.
"	Persian Gates to Araxes.	330	Cavalry.	40	1 night.	40	
"	Ecbatana to Rhagae.	"	All arms.	229+	11 days.	20	Hot sandy road, part desert.
"	Persian Gates to Araxes.	"	Cavalry.	400	11 days.	36½	"
"	Pursuit of Darius.	"	Cavalry.	175	4 days.	44	"
"	"	"		47	1 night.	47	Desert.
"	Hecatompylos to Aria.	"	All arms.	500+	20 days.	25	Desert.
"	To Artacoana.	"	"	75+	2 days.	37½	
"	Capture of Bessus.	329	"	150	4 days.	37½	Ptolemy's march.
"	Jaxartes to Maracanda.	"	"	170	3½ days.	48½	
"	Desert of Sandar.	325	"	57	1 day.	57	Desert.

APPENDIX B.

LOSSES IN SOME ANCIENT BATTLES.

WHERE known, the losses of all noted battles are given. The wounded are mostly estimated at the usual ancient rate of ten wounded to one killed, which is low. Twelve to one would be nearer.

Battle.	Date. B. C	Number Engaged.	Nation.	Killed.	Per Cent.	Usual Per Cent.[1]	Killed and Wounded.	Per Cent.	Usual Per Cent.[2]
Marathon.	490	11,000	Greeks.	192	1¾	5	2,100	19⅛	13
Platæa.	479	110,000	"	1,360	1¼	4	15,000	13½	13
Chæronæa.	338	50,000	"	2,000	4	4	18,000	36	13
Thebes.	335	33,000	Maced's.	500	1¾	4	5,500	17	13
Granicus.	334	3,000	Mac. Cav.	85	3	2	935	31	16
Issus.	333	30,000	Maced's.	450	1½	4½	5,000	16½	13
Arbela.	331	47,000	"	500	1	4	5,500	12	13
Jaxartes.	329	6,000	"	160	2¾	7	1,160	19⅛	20
Hydaspes.	326	14,000	"	930	6¾	5	10,200	73	13

[1] In a very stubbornly contested battle. [2] As in our own Civil War.

APPENDIX C.

MARCHES OF ALEXANDER.

SOME of the distances are taken from Colonel Chesney ; some are from Kiepert's maps. Exact accuracy has not been aimed at, as the old roads and the location of many places are not known.

Routes in Greece.   **Miles.**

Pella to Corinth 240

Corinth to Pella 240

Pella to Danube 350

Peuce to Pelium 300

Pelium to Thebes 300

Thebes to Pella 180

Pella to Hellespont 300   1,910

Routes in Asia Minor.

Hellespont to Granicus 50

Granicus to Sardis 180

	Miles.	
Sardis to Smyrna and back	100	
Sardis to Ephesus	50	
Ephesus to Miletus	60	
Miletus to Halicarnassus	60	
Halicarnassus to Telmessus	160	
Telmessus to Phaselis	160	
Phaselis to Side	85	
Side to Termessus	85	
Termessus to Sagalassus	70	
Sagalassus to Celænæ	60	
Celænæ to Gordium	170	
Gordium to Ancyra	80	
Ancyra to Tarsus	320	
Tarsus to Rugged Cilicia and back . .	160	
Tarsus to Myriandrus	100	
Myriandrus to Issus	25	1,955

Routes in Phœnicia.

Issus to Tyre	300	
To Sidon and Libanus Campaign . .	100	
Tyre to Jerusalem	120	
Jerusalem to Gaza	60	
Gaza to Pelusium	140	720

Routes in Egypt.

Pelusium to Memphis	120	
Memphis to Alexandria	150	
Around Lake Maræotis	120	
Alexandria to Parætonium	140	
Parætonium to Temple of Jupiter Ammon .	170	
Temple of Jupiter Ammon to Memphis .	340	1,040

Route: Egypt to Persepolis.

Memphis to Gaza	260	
Gaza to Tyre	135	
Tyre to Thapsacus	380	
Thapsacus to Bezabde	290	
Bezabde to Arbela	125	

	Miles.	
Arbela to Opis	180	
Opis to Babylon	90	
Babylon to Susa	230	
Susa to Uxian City	130	
Uxian City to Kal-eh-Sefid	190	
Kal-eh-Sefid to Persepolis	85	2,095

Routes in Media and the Caspian Region.

Persepolis to Ecbatana	480	
Ecbatana to Caspian Gates	285	
Caspian Gates to Hecatompylos . . .	215	
Hecatompylos to Zadracarta	115	
Mardian Campaign	600	1,695

Routes from Caspian to Caucasus.

Zadracarta to Susia	550	
Susia to Artacoana	130	
Artacoana to Prophthasia	200	
Prophthasia to Alexandria Arachotia . .	450	
Alexandria Arachotia to Nicea . . .	200	
Nicea to Alexandria ad Caucasum . .	35	1,565

Routes in Bactria and Sogdiana.

Alexandria ad Caucasum to Drapsaca . .	110	
Drapsaca to Zariaspa	220	
Zariaspa to Nautaca	205	
Nautaca to Maracanda	120	
Maracanda to Jaxartes	170	
Scythian and Seven Cities Campaigns .	100	
Jaxartes to Maracanda	170	
Polytimetus Campaign	150	
Maracanda to Zariaspa	325	
Five Column Campaign	450	
Final Campaign in Sogdiana	200	
Xenippa Campaign	150	
Rock of Sisimithres and return . . .	250	
To Sogdian Rock and Rock of Chorienes .	700	
To Zariaspa	200	
To Alexandria ad Caucasum . . .	330	3,900

Routes in Cophen Country.   Miles.

Alexandria to Nicea	35
Nicea to Ora	400
Ora to Astes' Fort	100
Astes' Fort to Aornus	75
Aornus to Dyrta	180
Dyrta to Indus	40
Indus to bridge	175 1,005

Routes in Five Rivers Country.

Indus to Taxila	50
Taxila to Hydaspes	100
Hydaspes manœuvre	30
Hydaspes to Glaucians	170
Glaucians to Acesines Crossing	70
Acesines to Hydraotis and beyond	60
To Pimprama and Sangala	100
To Sopeithes' and Phegeus' Kingdoms	250
To Hyphasis	60
To Nicæa	180 1,070

Routes on Indus.

Nicæa to confluence of Indus and Acesines	250
Mallian Campaign	210
Campaign and discoveries on Lower Indus	800 1,260

Route back to Susa.

Indus to Arabis	85
Arabis to Paura	450
Paura to Pasargadæ	400
Pasargadæ to Susa	420 1,355

Final Routes.

Susa to sea	220
Sea to Opis	450
Opis to Ecbatana	330
Cossæan Campaign, forty days, and to Susa	400
Susa to Babylon	230
Babylon to sea	350
Back to Babylon	350 2,330
Total distance marched	21,900 miles.

APPENDIX D.

GENEALOGY OF ALEXANDER. (From Reineccius.)

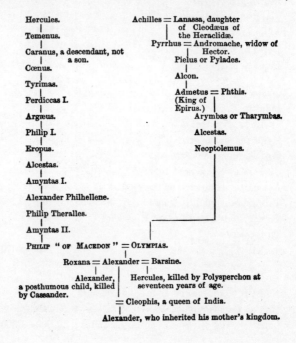

Hercules.
|
Temenus.
|
Caranus, a descendant, not
    a son.
|
Cœnus.
|
Tyrimas.
|
Perdiccas I.
|
Argæus.
|
Philip I.
|
Eropus.
|
Alcestas.
|
Amyntas I.
|
Alexander Philhellene.
|
Philip Theralles.
|
Amyntas II.
|
Philip " of Macedon " = Olympias.

Achilles = Lanassa, daughter
    of Cleodæus of
    the Heraclidæ.
Pyrrhus = Andromache, widow of
    Hector.
Pielus or Pylades.
|
Alcon.
|
Admetus = Phthis.
(King of
Epirus.)
    Arymbas or Tharymbas.
|
    Alcestas.
|
    Neoptolemus.

Roxana = Alexander = Barsine.
|
Alexander,   Hercules, killed by Polysperchon at
a posthumous child, killed   seventeen years of age.
by Cassander.
= Cleophis, a queen of India.
|
Alexander, who inherited his mother's kingdom.

INDEX.

⸻

LIST OF DATES.